THE GROUND BREAKER

Praise for *The Groundbreaker*

"Kanwal Rekhi's life is a testament to the power of the entrepreneurial spirit. From a Silicon Valley pioneer to a champion of India's tech revolution, he has played a unique role in both American and Indian innovation. *The Groundbreaker* tells that story with honesty, passion, and great insights."

—**Nandan M. Nilekani**, co-founder and chairman,
Infosys Technologies Limited

"In *The Groundbreaker*, Kanwal Rekhi shares a life rich with lessons in resilience, innovation, and the enduring importance of values. For over forty years, I have known Kanwal as a man of both vision and integrity, and this book reflects that. It is a powerful reminder that true success lies not just in personal achievement, but in the positive impact we have on the world around us."

—**N.R. Narayana Murthy**, co-founder,
Infosys Technologies Limited

"I've known Kanwal since our days at Novell, and he's always stood out for making bold calls long before they became conventional wisdom. Immigrants like him have shaped the DNA of Silicon Valley, and this book provides a firsthand account of how that transformation took place."

—**Eric Schmidt**, co-founder of Schmidt Futures;
former CEO, Google

"Kanwal Rekhi's groundbreaking, ceiling-defining story—from post-Partition India to being a Silicon Valley pioneer—is a powerful reminder of what's possible: resilience, entrepreneurship, and leadership forged through the immigrant journey. It spans a remarkable personal and professional arc, and a legacy of mentorship that has shaped both his homeland and his adopted country."

—**Laxman Narasimhan**, former CEO, Starbucks; former CEO, PepsiCo, Latin America, Europe and Africa

"*The Groundbreaker* recounts a compelling narrative of innovation, discipline, and resilience. Kanwal Rekhi tells an honest story, detailing both his successes and his failures. Through anecdotes and good humour, Rekhi illustrates his unconventional path, showing how the American Dream is accessible to those who dare to try—and fail—and try again."

—**Raja Krishnamoorthi**, member of Congress

"Kanwal Rekhi's *Groundbreaker* is more than a memoir; it's a powerful testament to the impact one individual can have on the entrepreneurial ecosystem. I've been fortunate to benefit from Kanwal's guidance throughout my journey, from the early days of Kaboodle to the growth of Poshmark. This book captures the essence of his wisdom, strategic thinking and unwavering commitment to helping entrepreneurs build and thrive."

—**Manish Chandra**, founder and CEO, Poshmark

"I couldn't put *The Groundbreaker* down—finished it in one sitting and found myself returning to it again and again. Each reading offers fresh insights. The book is packed with lessons—almost every page teaches you something. What struck me most is the author's clear, honest communication style—something I've personally witnessed as a powerful force for solving tough problems.

"The entrepreneurial journey captured in this book runs parallel to India's rise as a global technology leader. It reflects the essence of what I call the Maverick Effect: daring to think differently, collaborating deeply and building ecosystems that uplift an entire industry. I'm also deeply inspired by the author's commitment to mentoring others and nurturing global entrepreneurship through TiE. A remarkable story, honestly told."

—**Harish Mehta**, author, *The Maverick Effect*; co-founder, NASSCOM

"Kanwal is a pioneer, a change agent and an incredible trailblazer. He always challenged the status quo and achieved many firsts, redefining 'entrepreneurship' in the process. *The Groundbreaker* chronicles his inspiring journey from his humble beginnings to his enormous success, proving that with tenacity and hard work, you realize your full potential no matter where you start."

—**Jayshree Ullal**, CEO and chair, Arista Networks

"In *The Groundbreaker*, Kanwal Rekhi emerges as an innovator and leader who blazed an entrepreneurial trail, proving that ideas are a dime a dozen—what truly matters is execution. This inspiring narrative showcases an Indian American entrepreneur who not only scaled the American Dream through entrepreneurship but also profoundly impacted both worlds, bridging continents with his vision and relentless drive."

—**Uday Desai**, founding director, IIT Hyderabad

"Kanwal Rekhi narrates an inspiring story of impactful transformation—of his personal growth, of seeing and seizing opportunities to transform industries, and of evangelizing a culture of entrepreneurship. The book is truly a must-read for people interested in the US–India relationship, for entrepreneurs, and more generally for young people who wish to aspire and achieve."

—**Arun M. Kumar**, corporate leader, diplomat, investor, author

THE GROUND BREAKER

Risks, Rewards and Lessons from a Legendary Entrepreneur

KANWAL REKHI

HARPER
BUSINESS

An Imprint of HarperCollins *Publishers*

First published in India by Harper Business 2026
An imprint of HarperCollins *Publishers*
HarperCollins *Publishers* India, Cyber City,
Building 10-A, Gurugram, Haryana – 122002, India
www.harpercollins.co.in

2 4 6 8 10 9 7 5 3 1

P-ISBN: 978-93-7307-827-4
E-ISBN: 978-93-7307-459-7

Typeset in 11.5/16 Minion Pro
by HarperCollins *Publishers* India Pvt. Ltd

Printed and bound at
Replika Press Pvt. Ltd.

MIX
Paper | Supporting responsible forestry
FSC™ C016779
FSC
www.fsc.org

This book is produced from independently certified FSC® paper to ensure responsible forest management.

HarperCollins *Publishers*, Macken House, 39/40 Mayor Street Upper,
Dublin 1, D01 C9W8, Ireland

For my mother, Raj Kaur Rekhi, and
my wife, Ann Holt Rekhi (née Ann Douglas Holt)—
the two women who believed in me from the beginning
and gave me the confidence to go after my dreams

The detailed notes pertaining to this book are available on the HarperCollins website. Scan this QR code to access the same.

Contents

Foreword

I FIRST MET KANWAL DURING a pivotal moment in my career. I had decided to run for Congress, driven by a desire to bring a new voice to Silicon Valley, a voice that understood the intricacies of technology and its potential to uplift communities across America. I was young and ambitious, but my first attempt ended in defeat.

It was in the aftermath of that loss that Kanwal reached out. I had already come to view him as a mentor, but at that moment he didn't offer platitudes or hollow words of encouragement. Instead, he delivered a dose of the tough love that has become his trademark. "You've only lost when *you* have given up." That advice was a turning point. It was Kanwal's unwavering belief that reignited my resolve. I ran for the House again, and this time, I won.

In the ensuing years, I have come to realize I am not the only one who has benefitted from his frank wisdom. *The Groundbreaker* embodies the best of his principles and advice. It is more than a memoir; it's a masterclass in resilience. It's the story of a man who dared to dream, who overcame obstacles, who broke glass ceilings and built a remarkable career in the heart of innovation. But it's also the story of a mentor, a guide, and a force for positive change. Kanwal holds a deep commitment to empowering others, understanding that success isn't a solitary pursuit; it's a collective endeavor. The greatest satisfaction comes not with one's own gain, but with fostering the environment where all boats can rise.

As someone who represents Silicon Valley, I see firsthand the profound impact of Indian Americans on our technology and innovation sectors. Rekhi's journey is remarkable not just on its own, but because it mirrors India's own transformation from a developing nation to a global economic powerhouse, driven by the ingenuity and ambition of its people. As the son of Indian immigrants who worked hard to provide opportunity for their children, I am struck by how much his story embodies the spirit of the America I believe in: a place where anyone with big dreams and true grit can come and succeed, and in the process create a more prosperous world for all of us.

Reading *The Groundbreaker* feels like you are in a private mentoring session with Rekhi. In recounting his incredible journey, he reveals universal principles that apply to any field, from finding your purpose, to following your dream, to getting back up after you've been knocked down. Kanwal's reflections on leadership and decision-making especially resonated with me. Risk isn't something to fear but is instead a necessary feature of progress. His emphasis on first principles thinking, on cutting through the noise and getting to the root of a problem, is just as crucial in governance as it is in entrepreneurship.

Reading these pages reminded me of why I got into politics to begin with. True leadership isn't about personal ambition, but about serving a greater purpose. He reminds us that excellence is a lifelong pursuit, and that the greatest reward lies in applying our talents to make a difference in the world.

The Groundbreaker is a must-read for anyone who believes in the American Dream. You'll discover the story of a visionary, a pioneer, and a friend. You'll learn from his triumphs and his challenges. You'll be inspired by his unwavering belief in the human spirit. And you'll come to understand why Kanwal Rekhi is not just a successful entrepreneur, but a true groundbreaker in every sense of the word.

Ro Khanna

Member of Congress

Introduction

IN TODAY'S UNITED STATES OF America, it's almost expected to see Indian Americans at the helm of global giants like Microsoft, Google, PepsiCo, FedEx, Adobe, MasterCard, and Starbucks. The joke making the rounds is that being Indian is practically a prerequisite for becoming a CEO. The fact is that beyond corporate boardrooms, Indian Americans have also carved out significant influence in the corridors of power, holding key roles in the United States government, including state legislatures, the House of Representatives, and at one time the vice presidency of the United States.

But when I arrived in the United States (US) in 1967, it was a different world. America was in the thick of a space race with the Soviet Union following the launch of Sputnik. Its space program was in full stride, and the late President Kennedy's promise to land a man on the moon before the decade's end was about to be fulfilled. As a nation full of inspiring inventiveness, America was at the top of its game, and it beckoned to young scientists and engineers like me.

India, on the other hand, was grappling with profound challenges. Just months earlier, it had survived a near-famine, sustained only by massive shipments of US wheat under the PL 480 program. The global perception of India and Indians was abysmally low. Despite its dependence on US aid, India stood as one of the most anti-American voices at the United Nations, driven largely by opposition to the escalating Vietnam War.

In June 1967, the Arab-Israeli War led to the devaluation of the Indian rupee by a third, nearly derailing my plans to study in the US. But I remained determined. That August, on my 22nd birthday, I landed in New York, filled with hope and ambition. Back then, America welcomed Indian students like me, though often with a condescending skepticism about the quality of our education.

Yet, we proved ourselves. Many of us, largely IIT graduates, excelled as graduate students and pursued PhDs. Some ventured into the burgeoning computer industry, where we quickly earned a reputation for being smart, driven and competitive.

At first, our contributions were largely technical. It was difficult to imagine Indian professionals as managers, let alone CEOs of major American companies like IBM or Microsoft. But by the early 1980s, Indian Americans began stepping out of their STEM (Science, Technology, Engineering and Mathematics) comfort zones, moving into fields like sales, marketing and finance. A few, including myself, took the ultimate leap—becoming entrepreneurs.

Meanwhile, India was undergoing its own transformation. The Green and White Revolutions of the 1960s and '70s made the country self-sufficient in food production. By the late 1980s, a fledgling IT industry began to take root. Economic liberalization in 1991 unleashed India's potential, setting it on a path of sustained growth. As of 2024, India stands as the world's fifth-largest economy and is poised to become the third-largest in the coming years.

Indian Americans, too, have come a long way. Though we make up just 1.6 percent of the US population, we now account for about 10 percent of university professors, CEOs, and doctors.[1] Our community's success is built upon our embrace of the traditional American values of family, education, and hard work, along with our own immigrant mindset of finding a home where we can have a better life. The added benefit is that our success helped transform India itself. I am fortunate that it has all taken place within my lifetime.

This incredible journey of mine—from a hesitant young student with speech defects to a successful engineer, Silicon Valley's first Indian American entrepreneur, confident CEO, and, as president of TiE (The Indus Entrepreneurs), a mentor to countless entrepreneurs who followed their own dream—is a study of the rise of both Indian Americans and modern India.

It reflects how America influenced us, how we influenced America, and how we brought our experiences back to India. Entrepreneurs have been the drivers of such advances on both continents. We are society's change agents, dreamers and risk-takers. The world has problems. Entrepreneurs have solutions. We go out into the wilderness and come back saying, "I found something." We are the engines of progress.

For those of us with this personality type, it is not a choice—it is who we are. It's who I am and how I found my path in life. I was born into a lower middle class family in India and grew up without running water or electricity. I got mediocre grades in school. I was laid off from my first three jobs. At the 50th reunion of my class at IIT Bombay, all of my classmates had heard of me, but none remembered me. I was ordinary and unremarkable. So what happened? How did I change?

With this book, I hope to share the insights and lessons I have gathered over the years. While luck certainly played its role, as it does in everyone's journey, I would now love to expand on my life's valuable teaching moments.

As India approaches the 100th anniversary of its Independence in 2047, it is destined to emerge as a powerful, developed nation while maintaining its democratic foundations and close relationship to the United States. I believe this is the epic story of our time—a story of two cultures merging to create something extraordinary.

This book is a small and very personal attempt to capture that transformation—of two nations, their people, and a shared dream of excellence.

PART 1

FIRST PRINCIPLES

CHAPTER

1 The Roots of Resilience

March 1985. 12.30 p.m.

THE BOARD MEETING WAS SHORT—JUST thirty minutes. When it ended, I walked out with a new title: CEO. I had co-founded the computer networking company Excelan three years earlier. But this wasn't a celebration. It was a battlefield promotion. The company was in trouble and bleeding. We were losing the fight.

I shut my office door behind me and looked at the painting on the wall—a bull elephant charging through a dense jungle, forging a path where none existed. That was my job now. Break through. Find a way forward.

Truth be told, this was the way it should have been from the start. The company had been my idea. I had sketched the business plan on a napkin over pizza with two colleagues, both fellow Indian immigrants. One of them, smooth and polished, had taken the CEO role. I lacked the confidence back then. Now, the board had decided—he was out, and I was in.

The crisis had come to a head a month earlier. A serious revenue recognition issue had surfaced. The CEO walked out and never returned. For several weeks, we drifted leaderless. Finally, I told the board we couldn't continue this way. They agreed. That morning, they had made it official. It was done with a sobering bluntness.

The company was failing. We had eight months of cash left. I was to be the interim CEO while they searched for what they called a "proper" CEO. I knew what that meant. They wanted someone Wall Street-friendly. A White knight. Not an Indian engineer with dark skin, a thick accent, and a childhood speech impediment. Not a guy who dressed in white shirts and dark slacks, and carried a pocket protector.

The board didn't believe I could save the company. I was told to keep the ship afloat until they hired someone. I knew they were not going to find another CEO unless they invested $5 million in the company, and they made it clear that no new investment would be forthcoming. They were essentially writing off the company.

Returning to my office that day, I knew what this was supposed to be—a slow march to failure. But as I sat at my desk, the shock of it all gave way to something unexpected—relief. I had been in this spot before. Numerous times in my life. But every time I had been written off or laid off or just left on my own, I had defied the odds. So I knew that holding the line wasn't an option. If I played it safe, we'd be dead in a few months.

No. That wasn't in my DNA. I had to act. I didn't know how I knew what to do, but I did. It was instinct. It was survival. It was everything I had learned in my life up to that point. I was ready for the transformation, from employee to boss, from follower to leader. I knew the challenges, the obstacles, and the mess I had to overcome. To this day, I have no idea what made me think I could do it. I just knew I had to do it. I had no choice but to lead.

I took a deep breath, stood up, and walked to my office door. I threw it open and stepped into the bullpen.

"Vish! Jim! Tim! Everyone! In my office. Now."

They needed to hear what I already knew—if we didn't move fast, we'd all be out of a job. It was time to fight.

Resilience Is in My Roots

I often say tenacity and resilience must be in my DNA.

My story began on August 29, 1945, in Sukho, a small Sikh village in the Rawalpindi district of what is now Pakistan. Back then, Sikh, Hindu and Muslim communities coexisted in relative peace. But fate had other plans.

In 1947, the British left after nearly a century of rule, and with their departure came the partition of India and Pakistan. As a solution to the communal divides, the subcontinent was carved into two nations, Hindus on one side, Muslims on the other. Nearly twenty million people were forced to leave their homes. Chaos erupted. Families were uprooted, lives were lost, and over a million people perished in the violence and dislocation. My family was among those swept up in this historic upheaval.

My father—we called him Darji—was a remarkable man. At just thirty-three years, he had already served in World War II, fighting in Africa. With the British gone, he earned his officer's commission in the newly independent Indian Army. When Partition hit, Darji took it upon himself to move our entire extended family to safety in India. This was no small feat. It wasn't just his wife—pregnant with their fourth child at the time—and three children he had to worry about; he also had three brothers, four sisters, his bedridden father, and his mother in tow.

My earliest memory is from that time of migration. I got separated from my family and spent most of the day lost at a gurdwara. Strangely, I didn't feel any fear. I remained calm, certain that I would be found. And sure enough, my father eventually came and got me. His courage and leadership in that difficult time have always inspired me. He did what he had to do, and to the best of his ability. I've always said anything worth doing is worth doing well. I'm sure that came from him.

After six-and-a-half years of moving from one military posting to another, we finally settled in Kanpur in 1954. Kanpur was a classic British cantonment town, but Partition had transformed it. Refugees had poured in from Punjab, Sindh and Bengal, doubling its population almost overnight. It became one of the largest Sikh cities outside Punjab, but like much of India at the time, it was poor and underdeveloped.

Life in Kanpur was far from comfortable. My parents had eight children by then, along with my grandmother and my bedridden grandfather to care for. We lived in a cramped, lower-middle-class household. Space was tight, conveniences were few, and power outages were frequent. I shared a room with three others, and we would roll up our bedding each morning to make room for other activities during the day. My mother cooked on a coal-fired stove, handwashed our clothes, and drew water from a well.

Despite the hardships, there were small joys. Our one luxury was a tube-based radio. Every night, we'd gather around it to listen to music and programs. Sunday evenings were special—the top forty Hindi and Bollywood songs would play, and I never missed it. That old radio was more than an appliance; it was a portal to a world beyond our struggles, a reminder that there was more to life than the daily grind.

Those years in Kanpur taught me to adapt, to find joy in the little things, and to keep pushing forward no matter how tough life got. Resilience isn't just something you're born with—it's something you build, one challenge at a time.

My Mother—The Backbone of Our Family

My mother had a hard life taking care of everyone.

My mother, whom we lovingly called Baji, was the backbone of our family. Her life was a relentless cycle of care and responsibility, with no breaks or shortcuts. From sunrise to well past sunset, she worked tirelessly—serving breakfast, preparing lunch, doing laundry, and fixing dinner. When my father was away on military postings, Baji seamlessly stepped into the role of head of the household, managing everything and everyone.

One of her biggest challenges was caring for my grandfather, who had become completely bedridden after a second stroke left him a quadriplegic. She enlisted me to help in his care, and at a young age, I learned what it meant to shoulder responsibility. It wasn't easy work—physically or emotionally—but my mother taught me to approach it without complaints or tears. You did what needed to be done, no matter how tough it was.

Baji believed in me early on, appreciating a quick-wit, diligence, a sense of responsibility. By the time I was nine or ten, my aptitude for numbers was apparent. Without any formal teaching, I had a knack for math and a natural analytical mind. When I was twelve, my mother entrusted me with a critical task—managing the household budget.

Our large family lived on a tight allowance of 200 rupees a month, which my father sent home. It was my job to stretch that money as far as it could go. I prioritized staples—wheat, sugar, oil—before buying fruits, vegetables and meat. I even managed to save five rupees each month as an emergency fund. Inevitably, we'd need to dip into it for unexpected expenses.

Entertainment was a rare luxury. Every few months, someone in the family would get their turn to see a movie. You got to go to the theater once every five or six months if you were lucky. It was a hard life, but under my mother's leadership, we all got fed, had clean clothes, and stayed in school.

Her quiet strength and resourcefulness shaped me in profound ways. She taught me discipline and the value of responsibility. Managing that budget wasn't just about math—it was about understanding priorities, making sacrifices, and finding solutions in the face of scarcity. Those lessons have stayed with me, guiding me through life's challenges and opportunities.

The Price of a Watermelon

One hot summer day, my Mama (my maternal uncle) visited us in Kanpur. All of a sudden he wanted to go to the mandi (the farmer's market) to buy a watermelon. He also wanted to teach me how to bargain.

"Come on, let me show you a few things," he said. "Let me teach you how to haggle and negotiate … how the world works."

The two of us walked to the mandi. In that environment, walking two or three miles was nothing. No one in our area drove; that was an unimaginable luxury. My uncle and I talked the whole way. He was someone who had lost his way after the Partition. He never got married and was something of a misfit. But he was gentle and good-natured. That day, he wanted a watermelon. He described its sugary virtues the whole walk to the mandi.

This mandi was where the farmers brought their crops and sold them to brokers who in turn sold them to the small village shops. It was like a wholesale market. Produce and other food items were generally bought in bulk and prices were somewhat fluid, depending on your ability to bargain. The watermelon season was in full bloom and this mandi had gazillions of them. Every stall was stacked sky-high. We walked around and around until my uncle zeroed in on the one melon he liked best.

"How much?" he asked the shopkeeper.

"Five rupees."

Mama winked at me and offered four rupees for the melon.

"No, five," the shopkeeper said.

The two of them went back and forth for several minutes. Four-five. Four-five. Finally, Mama gave up, turned me around, and guided me onward.

"The mandi is full of them," he said. "We don't have to buy that particular melon anyway."

We stopped at a few more stands. Mama did not like any of the other watermelons from the thousands on display. He decided to go back to the first stand and buy the one he had originally liked. The shopkeeper greeted us with a smirk. My uncle picked up the melon he wanted.

"All right, I'll pay five rupees," he said.

The shopkeeper shook his head. "No, it's six rupees now."

Six-five. Six-five. Six-five. They went back and forth again. Again my uncle stopped. He put his hand up like a policeman. Once again we turned around and walked off in another direction. The mandi was full of watermelons, he said, and we didn't have to buy them from this guy.

We did another loop around the mandi but now Mama was fixated on that one watermelon. It was not the melon as much as it was winning this exercise in humiliation. He wanted to go back. When we got there, the price was seven rupees. Tired and exasperated, Mama gave up. He paid the seven rupees to get the one he liked. On the way home, he paid me one rupee to not tell anyone that he paid seven rupees for a five-rupee watermelon. With the rupee he gave me, the total was actually eight. But I did not say a word.

I learned a lesson—just not the one he wanted to teach me: don't let your emotions get in the way of a deal.

My Father Wrote Me Off

My father was a man of strength, discipline and duty—a soldier who had fought in World War II, provided for his family, and embodied the ideals of responsibility. Yet, this same man, my Darji, wrote me off early in life. It stung deeply at the time, but in hindsight, it turned out to be a hidden blessing.

To my father, success was measured in military terms. My two older brothers were his pride and joy, both attending prestigious military academies and becoming army officers. In India, a career in the armed forces meant security, status and a pension—everything my father considered the pinnacle of achievement. Having worked his way up the ranks from an NCO (non-commissioned officer), he reveled in their accomplishments. He loved boasting about them.

I, on the other hand, was a disappointment in his eyes. Shy and physically weak, I had stooped shoulders and a speech defect. I struggled to stay awake while doing homework, often nodding off, only to be jolted awake by a sharp slap from my father. Years later, I'd learn that my inability to stay awake was due to a sleep disorder that continued to affect me through adulthood, but at the time, he simply saw laziness. I was clearly not "army material," and to my father, this meant I didn't have much of a future.

For years, his rejection hurt. It left scars that took time to heal. But as I grew older, I began to see the unintended gift in his dismissal. Unlike my brothers, I wasn't pushed into a preordained path. My father didn't guide me or try to mold me into something I wasn't. I was left to chart my own course, and every time I was overlooked, underestimated or forgotten, I found a way to thrive.

By the time I was thirteen, I had started attending Guru Nanak High School, where I discovered my love for math and the sciences. I excelled in these subjects, and for the first time, I felt a sense of purpose. Most of my education was in Hindi, but I taught myself to read English. The local Neighborhood Welfare Center became my second home, a modest library where I devoured history books, Perry Mason mysteries, and American magazines.

The wait for the latest issue of *LIFE* magazine could stretch to two or three hours, but it was always worth it. Those glossy pages transported me to a world I could only dream of—gleaming cars, cutting-edge airplanes, luxurious homes, and daring astronauts racing the Soviets into space. The photographs were more than just images; they were glimpses of possibility, a window into a future of which I wanted to be a part.

My intellectual curiosity never impressed my father, but it fueled a quiet confidence in me. In my mind, I wasn't just competing with my brothers—I was surpassing them. My father valued a traditional sense of masculinity: strength, discipline, and a uniform. But the world was changing. The knowledge economy was emerging, and I could see that intelligence and creativity would be the new currency of success. My father couldn't imagine that shift, but I could.

Being written off by my father freed me from his expectations and allowed me to discover my own potential. It was a painful lesson, but one that ultimately went a long way in making me who I am. I can't say this is true for everyone, but sometimes, being underestimated is a great advantage.

The Cold War Heats Up

The United States and the Soviet Union were battling for the hearts and minds of Indians.

I was a devoted listener to the Voice of America and BBC radio. I was riveted by talk of A-bombs, the Suez Canal, and Sputnik. I listened to reports of Hungary being attacked by the Soviet Union, and I followed the 1960 presidential election in the United States. I was inspired when I heard President Kennedy declare that the space race was on and that one day the US would land a man on the moon.

This was the frontline of the Cold War, and it was clear America was not going to lose. Sputnik had caught the country off-guard, rattling its sense of superiority. Then cosmonaut Yuri Gagarin became the first man to journey into space. The Americans countered with John Glenn, the hero of the Mercury program, who orbited the earth three times. A picture of life in the US formed in my head. I saw an exciting, ultra modern place with powerful rockets, fast airplanes, sparkling appliances, and big, fancy automobiles. Its allure was powerful to those of us trying to imagine our future.

A joke went around my school: What's the difference between a poor man and a rich man in America? A poor man has to wash his own car.

One day, an exhibition on life in America opened in our town. Sponsored by the United States Information Agency, it included a short film that showed everything in the US being driven by science and technology. America was the land of progress. It was the future unfolding in real time. It was part of the Cold War propaganda the country created to appeal to young science-oriented minds. *We want you on our side. Uncle Sam has a place for you.* The message resonated with me. America was a distant land. It was a dreamland. My dreamland.

CHAPTER

2

A Journey of Firsts

AS I FINISHED HIGH SCHOOL, I had a secret. Everyone would know soon enough about my intention to study electrical engineering, but for now I kept it to myself.

In 1950, the first IIT (Indian Institute of Technology) opened in Kharagpur and several more followed at the close of that decade, in Bombay, Madras, Kanpur, and Delhi in 1961.

Modeled after M.I.T. in the US, these schools were where India's best and brightest would study to remake India's future. India's Constitution contained an Article that stated it was the duty of every Indian citizen to "develop a scientific temper, humanism, and the spirit of inquiry and reform." India's Prime Minister Jawaharlal Nehru hammered the point in every speech. He was enamored with science. After Independence, he wanted to build a new, modern, self-reliant India, with new roads, an updated electrical grid, and a whole new infrastructure. To accomplish his vision, he needed engineers. To produce engineers, he needed schools, what he called "the new temples of modern India." That's where the IITs came in. Later, I would find fault with many of Nehru's policies—his economics, his trust in the Chinese, his alignment with the Soviet Union—but he was a dreamer who invested in education, and I benefitted as a result.

Admission was based on scoring high on the JEE—the Joint Entrance Exam—which was given once a year in the spring. An ad ran in the local newspapers. Like everything in India, admission to these IITs was extremely competitive. The numbers alone made acceptance a long shot. The five IIT's accepted only 1,000 students total each year; in other words, 200 were admitted to each school. Given the size of India's population, the odds of getting in were slim to none.

I spotted the ad for the JEE in the newspaper and sent in my application. The process was considered complex, but I managed it rather easily. I did not tell anyone, including my parents. I did not want to set myself up for embarrassment since getting in was such a long shot. This was the gift of my father having written me off. No one knew what I was up to, there were no expectations; this was driven solely by my desire to improve myself and my standing.

The exam was to be given in Delhi in May 1963. I took the train there and stayed overnight with relatives. The rigorous test covered physics, math, chemistry, and English. The open seats went to the top scorers. In July, I received a letter congratulating me on gaining admission. I did not score high enough to choose my major; I was assigned to metallurgical engineering. But I was able to select which IIT campus I wanted to attend. That was easy; I chose IIT Bombay. I wanted to get away from home, and I had never been to Bombay.

My mother was instantly happy for me. She gave me a hug and said she was proud. Her only hesitation came when I explained that I had to leave in four weeks. It was so soon. My father, on the other hand, had not heard of the IITs. He reacted with suspicion and a rather stern interrogation of my intentions.

"So you go there and study engineering for four years?" he asked.

"Yes."

"And then you have a job?"

"No."

"Why would you do something like that for four years without getting a job?"

"To learn engineering."

My father thought it was one more dumb thing I had done until he returned to his army base the next day and mentioned to his commanding officer (CO), a young colonel, that his son had done something foolish. But when his CO heard that I was headed to IIT Bombay, he got up and walked around his desk to shake my father's hand. He was genuinely impressed.

"Oh, is it a big deal?" my father said.

"A very big deal," said his boss. "None of the children of the other officers got in."

Apparently I was the only army brat in Kanpur who got in that year. My father looked up to this officer, so when he came home that night I can't say we had a whole new relationship, but he did pat me on the back the way he did my older brothers when he was proud of them and said something like, "Atta boy." It was the first positive feedback I had ever received from him, and for the first time in my life, I felt validated.

Now it was time to see if I could compete.

IIT Bombay

I left Kanpur for Bombay in August 1963.

The trip to Bombay was the first time I had traveled such a vast distance on my own. Eight hundred miles. Thirty-plus hours. On several very crowded, uncomfortable trains. Until I arrived in Vikhroli, a suburb on the outskirts of the city; there I boarded a dedicated IIT bus that took me and other students to IIT's Powai Campus.

My eyes were pressed to the window as we students traveled through the city. Bombay in the early 1960s was modeled after London, with double-decker buses and sophisticated shops. Everywhere I looked were crowds of people. It was New York and Hollywood combined. The school was a bucolic oasis above the urban sprawl, nestled across 600 acres in the hills between two lakes. Classroom buildings and dormitories were in village-like clusters. The setting was beautiful. I had never seen anything like it.

I was grateful to be there—and more than a bit surprised. I found my dorm room; I had my own bed, desk, and lamp. It was unimaginably spacious and luxurious compared to the modest accommodations back home. The shared bathroom was another improvement I had not considered. Bhopi Dhall was my roommate; his family, like mine, were refugees from Pakistan; we became good friends right away. Umesh Malhotra, who was from a well-off family in Kanpur, was in the room next to ours. He became another close friend.

If high school was about figuring out who you were and where you were going next, those first months at IIT were about comparing yourself to everyone else. For me, this meant convincing myself I belonged. I met people from all over India and Asia, as well as Africans and Europeans. Languages were varied, but English was the common denominator, as many of my new classmates came from wealthy families and top boarding schools and were very accomplished, sophisticated young people. Almost everyone spoke fluent English. I could write and read English but I had not spoken a complete sentence till then, so I was pretty quiet. I did not participate in any extracurricular activities like sports or debate.

I knew my math scores had gotten me into IIT, but when I looked at the others, I still wondered how I got in. It did not seem possible.

Bill Gates once said that he would only hire IIT graduates if that were possible. Classes were rigorous and highly competitive. There were no dummies at IIT. Students were the best of the best and extremely ambitious. Professors were incredibly demanding and strict. Being second rate was not acceptable. There was an immediate tiering up of people within the campus. The kids from the private schools and well-heeled families were at the top. The middle and bottom were kids like me who got into IIT but were not at the same level as the prep schoolers—at least that is the way I saw it.

About two months into school, while still adjusting to campus life, I was on my way to lunch one day and started talking to another student headed the same way. This random conversation was one of the many lucky breaks I look back on as having played a crucial role in forging my trajectory in life. The other guy sat down with me and began groaning about his studies. He was miserable.

"What are you taking?" I asked.

"Electrical engineering," he said. "And I hate it."

"What do you want to take instead?" I asked.

"Anything else," he said.

I mentioned that I had been assigned metallurgical engineering but had really wanted electrical engineering, which was 90 percent math as opposed to the emphasis on chemistry that my current major included. This other guy perked up. Metallurgy, huh? We agreed to swap majors if the school approved. Both of us were excited. We proposed the arrangement to our dean. He said it was quite rare for students to switch majors among themselves but he pondered our proposal, saw we were eager and excited, and gave us a thumbs up.

Funda Singh

When I went home the first summer, I got an internship at the local power company. I was interested in power generation, distribution, transmission, motors, and alternators—the things involved in enabling cities to have power plants, electrical grids, and power lines feeding homes. Many of these things were just emerging, still in their embryonic stages of development. On some level, I might have been trying to solve the problem of the frequent blackouts that had plagued my youth in Kanpur.

Back at school for my sophomore year, Bhopi and I compared notes about our summers and the year ahead of us. It was fun to talk with someone who shared and could knowledgeably discuss the things that interested me. Transistors were around the corner. Computers were coming, too. We knew the world was not just changing but would also soon be completely different.

We were at the right place at the right time. Sometimes we marveled at this stroke of destiny. Both of us were skinny guys not yet out of our teens. I wore a turban and had a head full of hair, what Bhopi called "a complete Sikh." He was also Sikh but without the long hair and turban. He and I aligned ourselves with a few other students from the northern part of India. We all bonded over our dislike of the food on campus; we missed the different flavors of the north and eventually carved out a wing for ourselves in the dorm where we had more influence over the food.

We spent many nights playing cards, including the nights before exams. Three card Indian poker, teen patti, was our game. I earned a reputation as a card shark. There were five or six of us who were regulars at the table. I usually won. I would be quite ruthless because when the others ran out of money, we played for the coupons we used to pay for our food, and Bhopi recalls mornings after all-night sessions when they had to ask me for coupons so they could eat.

One could also argue this was merely a reflection of the school's competitive environment and an important part of the training we received. Everybody wanted to beat the other guy. This is a hard concept to accept. It's also the real world.

The curriculum in each class was built around first principles thinking, an approach to problem-solving in which everything is reduced to its fundamental truths and using these truths to rebuild. The process is credited to the Greek philosopher-teacher Aristotle who believed this was the best way to analyze and understand the world around him. As with all engineering disciplines, you learn to see things as systems and systems within systems, and whether you are studying physics or power systems, you solve problems by breaking things down to their basics. You remove layers of complexity. I need to build a canal. Why? I need to bring water to point B from point A. What do I need to accomplish that? And so on. Business is the same. Nobody is buying my stuff. Why aren't they buying it? Is it priced too high? Don't they need it? What do they need?

Much of this came naturally to me. I remember sitting in the library when I was twelve or thirteen and being amazed by how well the British had done in India. They took over in 1800 with only 7,000 troops. How, I wondered, were they able to take control of a country the size of India with such a small army? I kept asking myself questions until I had reduced the situation to various basics and got my first lesson in leverage.

Perhaps it had to do with the many household responsibilities I managed for my mother as a child, managing our monthly budget and solving the problems that inevitably cropped up. It's impossible to say. But my ability to deconstruct problems and find solutions sharpened at IIT. I had a reputation among my classmates for always asking the professors the same question, sometimes relentlessly: What are the first principles? What are the fundamentals here? It earned me the nickname Funda Singh.

My Brother's Death

Late in my sophomore year, my eldest brother, Kanwar Kulbir Singh Rekhi, found a lump in his neck and was diagnosed with lymphoma. The army transferred him to Bombay, which had the country's only cancer hospital. I was able to visit him frequently and provide the comfort of family.

Until then the two of us were never close. Growing up, he was clearly my father's favorite and I was envious of the attention my father gave him. These feelings lessened as I got older, and when I was accepted into IIT, my brother, knowing the difficulty and prestige of getting in, as well as the prestige of a degree, was proud of me. In a way, our mutual respect brought us closer. By the time he started cancer treatments, I was beginning to see everyone has their own trajectory, their own luck. All you need is one lucky or unlucky break and you are in a totally different place.

I don't mean to sound callous. This is just first principles reality. At the time of his diagnosis, cancer of almost any kind was a death sentence. But for the first six months his health seemed relatively stable and he was in good spirits. Between treatments, he worked his shifts on the base. During treatments, he was hospitalized. We saw each other often and grew closer than at any time during our childhood. The bonds of family were like a rope; the tug that drew us together grew stronger as he became weaker.

The last six months of his life fell during my junior year. He was in the hospital full time. I visited him twice a week. Each leg of the trip to the hospital from campus took two to three hours depending on the traffic. Classes finished at 2 p.m. I didn't get back to the dorm until 10 or 11 p.m. I fell behind in my studies and worried about flunking out. If your grades dropped past a certain point, you had to leave and there was no return. You failed. Everyone, not just me, felt the pressure to perform.

One day I walked into my brother's hospital room and saw he was in very bad shape. The cancer, no longer responding to treatment, was causing him severe pain. He repeatedly told me that he was proud of my achievements and more was ahead of me. No more needed to be said between us. He had given everything to his career. He never married or wanted much outside his life as an officer. However, now he wanted relief. He begged me to get him poison of some kind so he could put himself out of misery.

I had no idea how to do that. Nor did I want to. Then, seemingly miraculously, he got better. His pain disappeared and he grew more coherent. His improvement did not last more than a day or two. When I returned later that week, the doctor took me aside and told me that my brother had a week at most and probably less. It was time, he said, to tell my parents to come. I sent a telegram.

When the end came, I was alone with my brother. It was the second time I had been with someone when they died, my grandfather being the first. My father arrived at the hospital later that day, a couple of hours after my brother passed. He did not show any emotions. He focused instead on the funeral arrangements. I did not cry either, and once again, I saw something of myself in my father. He was a problem solver. He channeled his emotions into work. He removed his emotions from decisions he had to make. He took care of business.

I was the same way and have remained so to this day. Bite your tongue and do whatever needs to be done.

Uncle Sam Wants You

In 1965, President Lyndon B. Johnson signed the Hart-Celler Act (also known as the Immigration and Nationality Act of 1965) into law, prioritizing qualifications-based immigration over race and origin-based immigration. This was major legislation, a major change of intent. The US was fighting a Cold War. More than just military might, it needed brainpower.

When the law was passed, I still had two more years before graduation. But what propitious timing! America was looking at its future at the same time I was considering mine, and Uncle Sam could not have been any clearer. *Come, the door is open.*

The invitation resonated across our IIT campus. News like that travels far and fast. Bhopi and I often heard the mailman inform older students that their packet had come. We would turn to each other and ask, "What the hell does that mean, 'your packet has come'?" By the time we were seniors, we knew those packets were admission documents for students pursuing graduate degrees at colleges and universities in America.

I knew I had to continue my education. The fact that I enjoyed learning aside, it was obvious to me that I still did not know what I needed to know. This was not a knock on my four years at IIT. No, the opposite was true. Because of my training and my ability to see systems and analyze the world as if it were a chessboard, I knew technology was rapidly changing. I was interested in computers, but we did not even have a computer on the IIT campus. And there were no jobs in India.

Nehru saw the need for engineers to build modern India, but he did not let private industry happen. He thought the government should run and control everything, not the private sector. The economy stagnated; it did not create jobs. Entrepreneurism and innovation did not exist. Rich kids went back into their family's business. Middle class kids went into management or sales but rarely anything related to technology. Maybe one could find an opening at the local power distribution plant, but those jobs were few and far between. I also knew that these options were not for me.

People like me who wanted to work with modern technology had to go—and by that I mean we had to go to America.

America was desperate for engineers at the time. The Soviet Union had launched Sputnik, the world's first space satellite, on October 4, 1958—nearly ten years earlier—yet the reverberations of that seismic jolt to the American psyche and sense of security were still being felt in major ways. America was racing to fulfill the late President Kennedy's dream of putting a man on the moon. Its Apollo space program, the successor to the Mercury and Gemini programs, was in full swing.

At the same time, the US was also losing hundreds of thousands of young men to the war effort in Vietnam. In 1966, nearly 400,000 young American men were drafted into the military, according to global data platform Statista. The Hart-Celler Act was an open invitation to graduates from engineering schools in China and India, especially at the IITs. America had always favored White European immigrants over Asians and Africans, but now they wanted us and we were ready. Between 1950 and 1959, a total of 1,850 Indians immigrated to the US. In 1965, 600 Indians immigrated to the US. That number increased to

2,000 the following year. And it would grow even larger in 1967, the year I was set to graduate from IIT.[1]

There was a red, white, and blue promise of jobs and opportunity, and I was swept up in it. Midway through my senior year, I applied to several graduate schools in the US, including Michigan Tech. There was a red, white, and blue wave promising jobs and opportunity, and I was swept up in it. I had heard about Michigan Tech from one of my IIT professors. It was inexpensive compared to the brand name schools on the East Coast ($800 a year versus $3,000 a year for M.I.T.). My friends Bhopi and Umesh also applied to schools, and when we compared where we had been accepted, we found that the three of us had each received a packet from Michigan Tech.

We didn't know exactly where Michigan Tech was—only that it was in America, and that was enough. That name, that place, shimmered on the horizon like a promise, a doorway to everything we had dreamed of. This was it—the biggest decision of our lives, the kind that split time into a before and an after.

With nervous hands and pounding hearts, we filed for student visas, secured our passports, and traced flight paths on maps, imagining the journey ahead. It felt less like travel and more like a launch—like stepping into the cockpit of a rocket bound for an unknown world. We had spent years preparing, building our knowledge like fuel, readying ourselves for the moment of ignition. Each passing day was another tick on the countdown clock, drawing us closer to a future that was both thrilling and terrifying.

Destiny was calling. And we were ready.

CHAPTER

3

Welcome to America

MY FATHER AGREED TO LOAN me 20,000 rupees, the equivalent of about $4,000. That would pay for my airfare to the US plus tuition and expenses for the first twelve months if I did not get the promised financial aid.[1] Then, in June, the Arab-Israeli War erupted, further weakening the already severely devalued rupee. Overnight, it took ₹7.5 to buy a dollar instead of ₹5. Everything became 50 percent more expensive. My funds were now worth less than $3,000—not enough to last a full year in America. I gritted my teeth. The gambler in me was willing to roll the dice.

"I'm still going to go and I'll see what happens," I told my parents.

"We are proud of you," my mother said as we hugged and I said my goodbyes to my family, knowing it would be at least two or three years before I saw them again if not longer. It turned out to be six.

My father shook my hand. "Good luck, son."

I went over the family's finances with my brother Upi. He had been managing everything since the time I left for IIT. He assured me he had things under control. I said goodbye to the rest of my siblings. In a way, I was doing the same to Kanpur. The old was being replaced by the new. During high school and more recently the four years I spent at IIT, I found myself. Now I was going to discover who I wanted to be.

I left for the US on my 22nd birthday, August 29, 1967. Three of us planned to make the trip together—me and my IIT friends Bhopi and Umesh. The three amigos. The three engineering nerds. Only four years ago we had met by chance; now we were supporting each other on this grand adventure of graduate school in America. We spoke about how much we had to learn, how much we wanted to learn, and the jobs we might get. Our excitement calmed each other's nerves. Then, at the last minute, Bhopi's parents would not let him go. He promised to work things out and get to Michigan by the next quarter, which he did.

In the meantime, Umesh and I took a train from Kanpur to Delhi, then caught an Air France flight that stopped in Tehran, Tel Aviv, Rome, London, Paris, and Montreal, before arriving in New York, where we stayed overnight with Umesh's cousin. From there we flew to Detroit, which we were happy to leave as the city was on edge from recent race riots. A ten-hour bus ride finally delivered us to Houghton, Michigan, the home of Michigan Tech, in the middle of a freezing cold night.

The Road to Michigan

It was dark outside, pitch black, and I was exhausted. I had given up tracking the time. It was late at night, and that was enough information for the moment.

The bus had sped along the highway, an endless straightaway. The countryside passed by but it was just shadows and outlines to me as I looked out the window. It was almost straight north through the state, on into the state's upper peninsula. I had noted the small towns and farms and lakes that we passed until the sun went down and it was impossible to see anything. I dozed, I talked to Umesh. I tried to picture the adventure ahead of me. School would be two years. Then I would get a job. And then …

It was impossible to say. I could not see out the window let alone into the future. The only thing I knew for sure was that failure was not an option. This was a long, expensive journey. There was no going back.

Finally, the bus slowed and came to a stop on the side of the road. I looked at my watch. It was almost 3 a.m. Several of us, including Umesh and I, ambled off the bus. The driver unloaded our luggage; each of us had one suitcase. I looked around and saw nothing. There was no building, no depot, no homes, no anything. We were on the side of the road. We could see our breath, that's how cold it was. Shivering, I turned to Umesh and gave him a look that asked, "Where are we?"

Within a few moments, though, several people approached holding flashlights in one hand and blankets in another. A man in a heavy coat, who looked to be in his mid- to late-thirties, said my name.

"Kanwal Rekhi?"

I stepped toward him. "Yes. That's me."

He saw I was cold. He wrapped the blanket he was holding around my shoulders.

"I am your local host. Welcome to America."

On my first night in Houghton, I slept soundly in a dorm on the Michigan Tech campus. My local host, the guy who greeted me with a blanket at the bus stop, showed up while I was eating breakfast. I had only a vague recollection of him but I was still happy to see him, and happier still that he recognized me.

"Let me take you downtown so you can buy a winter jacket," he said.

I had a lot to get used to. Things seemed backward. People drove on the wrong side of the street. The light switches flicked backwards. The phone was like from the future. And the food, it was bland. And it was cold, very cold. The contrast between Bombay, where the temperature regularly topped 100°F, and Houghton, where the highs when we got there were in the 40s if we were lucky, made it seem even colder.

"It's not like home," I had said to Umesh.

My local host said my name.

"Kanwal. Is that right?"

I was still not confident speaking English, so I was not about to explain that my real name was Kanwalnain Singh Rekhi or that growing up I had gone by the nickname Guttu, or that outside my home I was known as KN—after the well-known character actor K.N. Singh. Umesh still called me KN.

"Yes," I said.

Over the next few months my name was mangled into Cannonball, Cornball, Cromwell, and Conwell. If I'd had a more assertive personality, I might have lost patience correcting people. It happened from unfamiliarity, not maliciousness, I assumed. Only a few dozen Indian students attended Michigan Tech and they represented the entire local Indian population, so the name Kanwal was something of a novelty in these parts. My job was to fit in, not to correct people.

Houghton was a quintessential small, Midwestern town. The population was less than 7,000. The cool weather that greeted us upon arrival was merely a warning. The first snow came within a month, in October, and it never left the ground until May the following year. It was one of the snowiest years on record. Several times the mercury dropped to -20°F. The wind chill made it feel like -50°F. Thank goodness for my new winter coat and gloves!

Within two or three weeks, Umesh and I and the few others that arrived with us were fitting in, which has been the way of Indian immigrants in America. The British did at least one thing that was beneficial during their rule of India—they taught us English, which, in a country where there are 121 languages spoken and nearly 20,000 dialects, gave us the ability to communicate almost anywhere in the world. But not everyone was happy to hear from us. There was a presumption by many that Indians came with an inferior education. *You're from that Third World country? You won't be able to keep up.* One of my professors, in fact, kept me after class to warn me the work was going to be very hard.

"Don't get discouraged," he said.

After he gave a surprise test a couple of days later, he called me into his office. I had aced the test. He did not believe I was capable of doing that well and accused me of cheating.

"We don't do that in this country," he said.

I told him that I didn't cheat. The opposite was true, I explained. I found the test to be easy.

He still didn't believe me.

The next time he gave a test, he stood directly behind me the entire time. When I scored even better on this test than the previous one, the professor summoned me to his office again and said, "If you're cheating, you're very good at it." Rather than get upset by his insult, I enjoyed knowing I had done well on the test. It was not my problem if the professor did not believe his own eyes.

Racism and stereotypes were part of life in the US. It was one of the reasons Bhopi's parents had held him back. Jokes about Blacks, Polish people, Irish people, Jews, and women were widely told as if there were nothing objectionable or hurtful in their telling. People used the N-word with ignorant nonchalance. I was referred to dismissively as a CJ—a camel jockey. Other times it was a friendly, "Hey CJ!" I went with the flow, undeterred, unscathed, quietly asserting myself, focused only on what I needed to do to succeed.

My Indian classmates and I learned to keep our heads down, accept the indignities, and focus on our studies. One test score was not going to change anyone's mind, but we were the top students and sailed through our classes easily. We were playing the long game. Welcome to America, indeed.

I learned not to blame other people for my mistakes or their ignorance. I exempted my professor for not thinking I was smart. I understood that he was blinded by his own racism. He had very little experience with Indian students and probably less knowledge of India itself, and that's what a stereotype is, a one-dimensional picture with very little real information to it.

As a kid whose father expected very little from him, I could have used those slights as an excuse for failing or becoming an angry person. But why get mad? That's the way the world was back then. There was no point in blaming him or anyone else when I was responsible for the decisions I made. I was used to being underestimated. It fueled me to work harder. He did not tell me to study. He did not tell me to go to IIT or pursue a master's degree at Michigan Tech. Anger would only hurt me in the end. Success or failure was on me. It was one of those insights that served me well not just in school but also throughout my career, and I emphasize it to those I mentor. When you blame others for your failures, you are looking for excuses everywhere except the place it matters—you. If you play the blame game, you will never improve. Experience has taught me that I need to take responsibility, say it is my own damn fault. I encourage everyone to do the same.

This is a life lesson in general. For entrepreneurs, it should be a commandment. You need to be able to say, "I did not see my vice president of engineering falling behind. I did not see the reasons I was losing customers." When you use that language you begin to change. The monkey has to be on your back. Then the burden to come up with answers and make better decisions is on you.

As American as You Want to Be

Bhopi did not recognize me when I picked him up at the airport in December.

I had anticipated that reaction. When he last saw me, I had a beard and a moustache and long hair tucked under my turban. Now all that was gone. The turban was gone, my hair was short and Americanized by a Houghton barber, and my face was clean-shaven.

I had decided to make this change a month or so earlier. Indians were far from an established brand in the US and so whenever I met people outside my circle of fellow Indians, they only wanted to talk to me about my accent (Where are you from?) and my turban (Why do you wear it? What does it mean? Do you have to wear it all the time? What's under it?). One day someone asked if a company like IBM approved of employees wearing turbans. That gave me pause. Would my traditional appearance be an impediment when I went for job interviews?

"I need to remove it from the conversation," I had told Umesh.

"What about your family?" he asked.

"They will not know until I see them or they see a photograph of me, and I don't know when that will be—only that it won't be soon."

Umesh watched as I walked into the bathroom. With a pair of scissors in one hand, I took off my turban and gripped the swirl of thick black hair in my other hand, and cut it off. I asked Umesh to even up the parts I could not see and later visited a barber to give me an American style. I shaved for the first time in my life, too, and found myself staring at the new me. It was the same as the old me. I was still Sikh. I just did not have to wear my sect on my sleeve.

I explained all this to Bhopi. "I am just being practical," I said.

We leaned into practicality. There were not a lot of Indians at Michigan Tech, but the few of us who were had organized an Indian student association to give each other support, encouragement and a sense of home—with monthly dinners at which we cooked Indian food and played Bollywood soundtracks. But we also sampled American staples like spaghetti and fried chicken and enjoyed the popular TV shows *Bonanza, Mission Impossible*, *Star Trek*, and *Rowan and Martin's Laugh-In*.

We knew that to truly thrive in America, we had to embrace being American, without sacrificing our Indian identities. But there was one part of this new life that was as unavoidable as it was alluring—something even the sharpest minds, poets, and philosophers had struggled with for centuries: romance.

Before Umesh and I had left India for Michigan Tech, one of our IIT friends had given me a cheap silver bracelet and asked me to mail it to an American girl with whom he was pen pals. They had been matched up through a Parker Pen promotion at the 1964 New York World's Fair. I fulfilled his request, as promised. What I purposely did not mention, at least for a couple of months, was that this girl had sent me a thank-you note and from there we had begun exchanging letters with each other.

It was just a few letters at first, but Ann and I—her full name was Ann Douglas Holt—quickly formed a connection. Having someone to exchange thoughts and feelings with, even if only through letters, helped ease the loneliness of being far from home and building a new life in America.

Ann was from Connecticut, the eldest of three in a family that struggled with divorce, alcoholism, abuse, and neglect. It's hard for people today, with instant communication at their fingertips, to understand what a pen pal meant back then. But there was something powerful about it. The wait between letters was filled with anticipation, and writing became a way to process life. The distance and the certainty that we would never meet made it easier to be honest—about our dreams, frustrations, and vulnerabilities.

Neither of us knew how deeply we would impact each other's lives. But that's how life works—unexpected connections shape us in ways we can't predict. As Indian poet Rabindranath Tagore once wrote, "Love is an endless mystery, for it has nothing else to explain it."

CHAPTER

4

Logic, Labor, and Liftoff

I HAD NEVER SEEN A computer in person until I got to Michigan Tech. Even then I only saw it from a distance. The school had an old IBM 1620 and a relatively new IBM 360 in the computer center but kept them locked behind glass doors. You worked out your problems on paper, punched them on cards, and submitted your job to "experts" who would run the program. The results were handed back to you.

Because of the cold and snow, I spent all my free time in the computer center, teaching myself programming. I eschewed the social activities on Friday and Saturday nights, choosing instead my regular seat in the computer center. It was one of the smartest decisions I made. I had the place to myself! When I submitted jobs during the week, it would often take three, four or even five hours to get the results back, depending on how many other people had turned in work. But on weekend nights, I got the results back in a minute or two.

My coursework included classes in computer hardware and logic design. What I did not or could not learn in the classroom I found in books on my own. I read everything I could find about computers, from how they were built to how they were programmed. I have been like this my whole life. Anytime I want to learn something new I immerse myself in the subject matter. I taught myself FORTRAN, an early programming language for doing computations, and by the end of the first quarter I was an expert FORTRAN programmer.

I also had an aptitude for logic design and was able to debug programs very quickly. Computers are built on everything being true or false. If A is true and B is true, then A and B is also true. If A is true and B is false, then A and B is false. But A *or* B is true. This is fundamental logic design. It is built around "and, not, and or." By 1979, this kind of work was done on chips and building your own logic would become a lost art, but it was crucial to know this when I was in school, and by the end of my first year I was on my way to becoming a very good logic designer.

Hot Times, Summer in the City

I ended up in Chicago in the summer of 1968 with only $10 in my pocket.

I had been at Michigan Tech for nine months, much of it snowbound and freezing. Now it was summer, hot and humid. But more than the weather had changed. When I arrived, America was at the top of its game. It had recaptured the initiative in space, the economy was booming, and US military officials assured the public that the war in Vietnam was heading in a winning direction. America had also rescued India from a famine with a massive shipment of wheat. Brand USA seemed invincible—that is, until the calendar changed.

In January 1968, the North Vietnamese launched a major surprise attack on US forces known as the TET Offensive. It shook the US to the core and knocked LBJ out of contention for a second term. In April, Martin Luther King Jr, the central figure of the Civil Rights Movement, was assassinated. Then Robert "Bobby" Kennedy, JFK's dynamic younger brother, was shot after he won the California primary. The Prague Spring of Czechoslovakia turned into fiery summer when

Russian tanks rolled, increasing Cold War tensions. It set the stage for an explosive Democratic National Convention in the Windy City.

The dorms at Michigan Tech had closed for the summer. Umesh went to his brother's in New York, and Bhopi got a job at Parke-Davis pharmaceuticals in Kalamazoo. He was being paid $4 an hour, almost three times the minimum wage! When I was unable to get a job through the placement office, I had to figure out a plan for the next three months. One option was staying with one of the local families in Houghton that took in foreign students over the summer and holiday breaks for a small fee. But even that small fee was too much for me. I needed a job. That's when I decided to go to Chicago.

I arrived in Chicago just as tensions between protestors and the police were about to erupt in violence. I had taken the bus there from Houghton, bringing with me a small suitcase, a few books, and $10. Once again, I was completely on my own, a stranger in a strange land, and yet, as before, I was no more than appropriately concerned, which was offset by a sense that things would work out if I were diligent. I checked into the YMCA hostel, which cost $4 a night, then I immediately walked back outside to look for a job. I figured I could afford two nights if I did not find work right away—two nights if I did not spend any money on food.

People had told me that summer jobs were plentiful in Chicago. Just look for "Help Wanted" signs in the storefront windows, they said.

It was late afternoon when I hit the pavement in search of a job. I walked only a few minutes before I spotted a Help Wanted sign in a restaurant window. So it is true, I thought. I went in and inquired about the job. The manager was hiring for a dishwasher. He asked if I was ready to start right away.

"Yes," I replied, and I had my first job in America.

I was sent back to the kitchen, given an apron, and told to start washing dishes. There was no discussion about salary or anything else. Later that night, at the end of six hours, I was paid $10 in cash and given a hot meal. I was exhausted but I felt great. With $16 in my pocket and a full belly, I was going to survive in Chicago.

After only a few days at the restaurant, the manager promoted me to busboy from dishwasher. He saw I was capable, hard-working, and educated. Since the restaurant work hours were at night, I got a daytime job as an elevator operator at the Hotel Allerton on Michigan Avenue. The hotel was sold out and shorthanded, and I was quickly transferred to room service, which garnered me a small fortune from tips delivering ice and food to the Kentucky delegation staying there for the convention.

Politics dominated all life in the city for much of that summer. Much of it was ugly. By the time of the convention in August, the city seemed like a tinderbox ready to blow. Chicago's Mayor Richard Daley was famously intolerant of the protestors. I remember a joke going around at the time: People in every city are mad at their mayor once in a while but in Chicago, we're mad at our mayor Daley.

Toward the end of summer, I landed work on the night shift on an assembly line at a steel factory. This was no-brainer stuff, but my conscientiousness was rewarded with a raise from $1.25 to $2 an hour. I returned to Michigan Tech with $2,000 in my pocket to help fund my studies, twenty extra pounds around my waist from all the good food I had eaten, and a bit more confidence in my step. Chicago had been a trial by fire for me as a person, but once I knew I was going to make it, I was able to appreciate the excitement of the big city, the political debate, Hubert Humphrey's nomination, and his upcoming campaign against Richard Nixon.

It was a great introduction to America!

Impressions

During my second and final year at Michigan Tech, I saw the impressions of us—Bhopi, Umesh, myself, and the other Indians on campus—had changed.

Bhopi, the top electrical engineering graduate student, became a teaching assistant to the head of the department. I tutored undergraduates in math. Both situations would have been unlikely a year earlier. Then our good grades aroused suspicions of cheating. Now we were assets, star students.

One day I was in the lab, helping a student with a calculus assignment. I presumed the guy was a football player from both his girth and the way he towered over me. He was extremely respectful, though. Every time I answered one of his questions, he said, "Thank you, sir." Or he said, "I don't understand, sir." Everything was "sir." Finally, I began to feel uncomfortable and stopped him.

"You don't have to call me sir."

He objected. "I'm just getting ready."

"Ready for what?"

"For when you Indians take over."

Job Offers

Would I be able to find a job? That question dominated my thoughts as my master's program neared its end.

I shared my concerns with Ann, my pen pal, the only person I felt comfortable enough to confide in. I told her about my visits to the placement office, the recruitment seminars, and my uncertainty about the future. My friend Bhopi had already graduated, secured a job at Texas Instruments in Dallas, and even bought a Mustang to celebrate his new life. "He's more Americanized than me," I joked. But deep down, I wasn't so sure of my own fate. My education should have been enough to give me confidence, but doubt lingered.

Ann, though, had unwavering faith in me; maybe because writing gave me time to organize my thoughts in my letters to her, or maybe because Ann saw me differently than others did. She wasn't just a friend—she genuinely wanted me to succeed. When I admitted my self-doubt, she dismissed it with encouragement. "You're too smart for people to ignore you," she wrote. Coming from her—a young, attractive blonde woman (we had exchanged photos by then)—it meant more than I could express.

Ann, too, was going through her own transformation. She had joined the Air Force and was training as a nurse, following in her brother Mark's footsteps—he had joined the Navy a year earlier as a corpsman. Their home life had been unstable, marked by fighting, divorce, and their parents struggling with their own demons. The military was their escape, a chance to build something for themselves.

I admired her for it. I had grown up around the military—my father and brothers had served. I knew it was a man's world, and for a woman to succeed in it, she had to be tough, determined, and exceptional. Ann was all of those things. And somehow, she liked me. Despite our vastly different backgrounds, we had more in common than I ever expected.

Buoyed by Ann's encouragement and by necessity, I applied for jobs all over the country, and by the holidays, I had about a dozen interviews lined up, including companies such as RCA (Radio Corporation of America) in Indianapolis, Indiana, Collins Radio in Des Moines, Iowa, and Bell Labs in Holmdel, New Jersey. I was disappointed that none involved computers. After a few more interviews, I received two job offers. One was from IBM in Kingston, New York. IBM was the holy grail for new engineers like me. The company owned about 80% of the computer market and likely accounted for the largest percentage of the computer and engineering jobs in the US.[1]

A job at IBM had the security of the option to join the military back in India. It was a job for life. And exciting work. IBM was building computers for NASA's Apollo program, their System 360 mainframe computer dominated the market, and their labs were legendary. IBM was also located in New York's Hudson Valley, one of the most beautiful spots on the East Coast. But the job did not involve computer design, which was the type of work I desired.

My other offer was from Electronic Associates Inc. (EAI), designing computers in their minicomputer space. The company was located in Long Branch, New Jersey, in Monmouth County. I would start as a hardware engineer at an annual salary of $11,250, which was like making $150,000 today. It sounded ideal, and I was on the verge of accepting when a professor of mine spotted me in the lab one afternoon and presented me with another option: getting my PhD.

"I've already spoken about you to a colleague who runs the program at the University of Wisconsin," he said. "They'll hold a place for you."

"I want to work for a few years before thinking about a PhD," I said.

The professor's expression changed to disappointment. "If you do that, you will never get your PhD."

"Well, I have a good job offer in computers."

"I think you should get your PhD and then get a job."

"Okay, let me ask you something: If I do get a PhD, what job can I do?"

"You can become a professor. You can become a researcher. You can do anything you like."

"How much does a professor with a PhD make?"

"Almost $10,000."

"I have a job offer for eleven-two-five with my master's. Why would I spend three or four years pursuing a PhD to make less money afterward?"

My professor could not convince me otherwise. I accepted the offer from EAI. The letter from IBM sat in my desk drawer, ignored. I should have sent a response, politely declining their offer. Graduation was in May, though I didn't officially receive my diploma until July because the professor who had to sign off on my thesis had started his vacation early and didn't come back to Houghton until mid-summer.

During my last two weeks on campus, I was glued to the television, watching Apollo 11's historic journey to the moon. When Neil

Armstrong took that "one small step for man, one giant leap for mankind," it felt like a victory for all of us. A new door had been opened for humanity. Science fiction had become a reality.

As someone about to start a career in the space and defense industry, I felt a connection to the moment—science, ambition, and achievement all coming together. Then, a month from my 24th birthday, I put my meager belongings in a suitcase and took my own giant leap—a job in New Jersey.

PART 2

SURVIVE, THEN THRIVE

CHAPTER 5

Building a Future, One Yes at a Time

I ARRIVED IN LONG BRANCH, New Jersey the same weekend several hundred thousand people around my age were attending a rock and roll concert 150 miles away in Woodstock, New York. Like the other events I had witnessed since arriving in the US, from the convention in Chicago to Martin Luther King Jr's assassination to putting a man on the moon, this three-day music festival added to my impression of America as a country of multitudes—and also, as evidenced by 500,000 young people gathering to celebrate peace and love, as a country unafraid to dream big.

My luggage was lost on the flight to New Jersey. I arrived at my hotel with nothing. I showed up for my first day on the job unshaven and without clean clothes. The company gave me an advance on my first paycheck to buy clothes and toiletries. I rented a small apartment in Asbury Park, which would become famous as the home of rock star Bruce Springsteen. As it happened, the whole area of Monmouth County was the reputed home base for the mafia. I had no reason to doubt it.

The headline news as I settled into my new surroundings was about the unfortunate death of a local judge. The guy's garage door wouldn't open and he died of carbon monoxide poisoning from his car. A few days later, the local police captain died when his brakes failed, causing his car to sail over a cliff and into the ocean. Both of these poor souls had been summoned to testify in a trial against the mafia in Trenton. I myself was briefly and quite mistakenly drawn into this family business.

I had been on the job for a month at most. Several coworkers invited me to meet them for a drink after work. We met at a little Italian restaurant near the EAI office. I happened to be wearing a white shirt, a tie, and the double-breasted blue jacket I had purchased when my luggage was lost. In the dimly lit restaurant, with my dark skin, I could easily have been mistaken for a young Italian man, at least from afar and as long as you did not hear my accent—and that is what happened.

At some point, the bartender casually wiped down the bar and worked his way to where I was perched with my coworkers. He looked directly at me.

"Drinks are free for you guys," he said.

"Free for us?" I asked.

"That's right."

"Thank you."

"And if you want dinner, it's also taken care of," he added.

The bartender saw I was confused. With a slight, barely perceptible turn of his head, he gestured toward a corner booth behind me.

"The old man," he said. "He likes you."

I peeked behind me and saw—in the corner booth facing the restaurant and bar—an old man in a suit sitting with two other younger, larger men. They were eating dinner. The old man nodded at me. The next day at the office, I told several of my coworkers what had happened at the bar. They filled in the blanks. The old man owned the restaurant. He was the local mafia boss. My coworkers said he probably thought I was a clean-cut Italian boy who had broken from tradition and become an engineer.

"He was giving you the thumbs up," one of my colleagues said.

"What if he finds out I'm not?" I asked.

"Careful starting your car in the morning," he joked.

I never went back to that restaurant. But looking back, it is interesting to note that Italian Americans had organized within communities and supported each other in businesses after immigrating to the US. Indians would organize a decade or two later as "the tech mafia"—minus the cement shoes.

After joining work, I bought a new Ford Maverick automobile. I loved it. Outside of school, it was my first real investment in my life in the US. Work at EAI was good. My boss, Ron Heacock, took a liking to me. We became lunch buddies, and he invited me to play in the weekly Thursday night poker game he hosted at his house, though he joked about having made a mistake after I won big my first time in the game. The truth was, he had seen I was a fast learner.

I helped design the CPU (central processing unit) and learned almost all the aspects of how to design, build, and test, though we never manufactured any of our minicomputers. We got as far as testing the design and setting up the manufacturing line when, after I had been on the job for only seven months, the market changed. At the time, IBM owned the market for mainframes, which took up entire rooms and cost millions of dollars; minicomputers were about the size of a filing cabinet and a tenth of the cost of IBM's Goliath. Maybe a dozen companies were making minicomputers, including EAI.

Then Boston-based Digital Equipment Corporation (DEC) released a new version of their popular minicomputer, the PDP-11. The floor tilted in their direction. Everybody was buying from Digital; by the end of winter, they emerged as the winner in the minicomputer market. I was having the time of my life, enjoying my work and the nice salary that came with it, yet the market was sending signs that my job could be in jeopardy. Wanting to hedge my bets, I sent out my resume to a few places.

It was a smart move. In February, my boss left the company for a new job in Florida. Soon after, EAI pulled out of the minicomputer business altogether, sensing it couldn't compete with DEC. Then these changes caught up with me. On a chilly Friday in early March, only eight months into my job, I was laid off.

The next night, I totaled my car. I had fallen asleep at the wheel while driving back from a day in New York City. I was always falling asleep, as I had since childhood. It was sleep apnea, which would not be diagnosed for many years. I was lucky I was not killed or seriously injured in the crash. In fact, I was not hurt at all. If the mafia was out to get me, as I joked, they missed.

But having just lost my job, I did feel like the wheels had come off more than my car.

A New Job

The job search did not start out well.

The postal workers went on strike for the first time in the history of the US Postal Service. The air traffic controllers union was also threatening a strike or slowdown. I was unable to send out new resumes, and I was uncertain whether those I had put in the mail were going to reach their intended destinations. Not hearing back from potential employers put my nerves on edge. I reapplied to IBM, figuring they had offered me a job before, why not again?

They wasted no time responding with a terse letter explaining that since I had never responded to their offer (their letter was still among the papers in my desk drawer), I was ineligible for a job at IBM for life. *For life?* I stared at that letter in disbelief. IBM was almost 80 percent of the industry at the time, as I mentioned before. My friends who worked at IBM chided me for having blown them off. With only 20 percent of the market available to me, I feared my chances of finding a job had just crashed.

After a slow start, the phone finally started to ring. I set up interviews with three companies: DEC in Boston, Systems Engineering Laboratories (SEL) in Fort Lauderdale, and Scientific Data Systems (SDS) in Los Angeles. The day before I was scheduled to fly to Boston for my interview with DEC, it snowed all day and night. Something like three feet of snow came down overnight. It was the biggest blizzard of the winter. When I woke up in the morning, I learned all the flights to Boston from New Jersey were canceled, including mine. Streets were also closed and the snowplows had already been garaged in anticipation of spring. The situation looked bleak. But I wasn't going to miss my job interview, storm or no storm. I quickly redid my plans and took a Greyhound bus to Boston, only to arrive at DEC and find it was closed due to the storm. No one had thought to notify me.

I had no choice but to stay overnight in Boston. The next day, planes were flying again. I boarded a flight to Fort Lauderdale for my next interview with SEL, though because of the problems with the flight controllers, the plane sat on the runway for more than five hours before taking off. I did not arrive in Florida until the middle of the night. When I finally got off the plane, I was hit by a blast of warm, tropical air. It was 89 degrees. In the middle of the night? After the frigid cold of Boston, I asked myself, "Why am I up north in the cold and snow when there are places like this?"

My former boss Ron Heacock had gone to SEL and was among those who interviewed me for the hardware engineer position. They didn't offer me a job on the spot, but the implication was they would. Ron thought highly of me and my work. Next, I flew to Los Angeles and met with people at a computer company near the airport. They wanted to hire me, but I waited to hear from SEL, and by the time I got back to New Jersey, I had an offer with a better salary than I had been making.

I took the job with SEL.

A New Partnership

After three years of exchanging letters, Ann and I decided to shake things up. It was time to meet.

This was the moment of truth. A pen pal relationship could either deepen into something more meaningful or collapse under the weight of reality. We had built a connection on words alone—raw, honest, and unfiltered. There was nothing we didn't know about each other yet meeting in person was a different game altogether.

At first, meeting had never crossed our minds. The anonymity of writing letters gave us freedom, a space to be vulnerable without fear. Over time, this turned into unwavering support. We were both fiercely independent, but we had our struggles. When I was laid off, she was there with words that lifted me. When she faced setbacks, I did my best to return the favor. Through our letters, we became each other's safe harbor.

Then came the moment that changed everything—we exchanged pictures. Suddenly, there was more than just words. There was a face, an expression, a presence—and an Air Force uniform. I found myself reading Ann's letters differently, my heart now fully in it. The anticipation of her next letter became electric.

Ann was stationed in Texas but would visit home in Connecticut from time to time. She suggested meeting up. She could drive to me, or I could go to her. Distance didn't faze me—I had driven to New York, Boston and D.C. without a second thought. Gas was cheap, and Bollywood music made the miles disappear. But life kept getting in the way. No matter how much we planned, we could never make it work.

Then, in late March, I received a letter that had been forwarded from my old New Jersey address to my new home in Florida. She was heading to Connecticut for Easter and wanted to see me. I wrote back: "*Guess what? I lost my job and moved to Fort Lauderdale ... Florida!*"

Her response came fast: "*I'd much rather visit you in warm Florida than chilly New Jersey.*"

Oh boy. Excitement and nerves hit me at once. This was a shift—uncharted territory. It wasn't about proving anything; it was about taking that next step. She felt it too.

To sort out the details, I called her for the first time. Hearing her voice made me smile. I had worried about my accent, my speech impediment. Would it be a problem? It wasn't.

We talked about logistics. Where would she stay? The answer was simple. My apartment.

"I'll take the sofa," I said. "You can have the bedroom."

Before I knew it, we were together in my Chevy Impala and I was driving her around Fort Lauderdale. I had only been at SEL for a few weeks and barely knew my way around the city. It did not matter. I only wanted to look at Ann. From the moment I picked her up at the Miami airport and saw her in her blue Air Force uniform, I could not take my eyes off of her. For the next four days of her visit, we went to the movies, walked along the beach, and packed in as much fun as possible.

I did not want our time together to end. Before Ann left, I took her to the beach for one last stroll on the sand. As we listened to the waves, I gave in to my emotions, took her hand and asked if she would like to be Mrs Rekhi. My proposal caught her off guard, as might be expected following such a whirlwind romance, and she told me that she needed time to think it over during the remainder of her Easter break. At least she did not say no. The problem was, over the next few weeks, she did not say yes, either. Frustrated and anxious, I sent her a letter that put the proposal in the yes-no-or language of logic design.

"If I don't marry you, I'm going to go back to India and have an arranged marriage," I said. "My parents will take care of it."

"No, no, no," she wrote back. "I don't want you to do that."

"Does that mean you say yes?" I asked in my next letter to her.

Upon receipt of my response, Ann had enough. She was tired of the slow pace of this marriage proposal. She had made up her mind and did not want me to suffer any more confusion, so she picked up the phone and called me.

"To answer your question," she said, "Yes, I want to marry you."

Birds of a Feather

Sometimes, a single "yes" can change the trajectory of a life.

When Ann said yes, it wasn't just the start of our marriage; it was the beginning of a transformation for me. I learned that success in business and just about anything else isn't only about ideas or strategies. It's about people. I've always believed that when I invest in a startup, I'm not just investing in a product or a pitch. I'm betting on the team—the people who will carry that idea forward.

Ann's investment in me wasn't about money or time. She gave me something infinitely more valuable—her belief. She saw potential in a skinny, shy engineer who spoke too quickly and often stumbled over his words. She gave me her heart, as well as her partnership for the rest of our lives, and in doing so, she became the first person in my life who truly believed in me for who I was. It was an immeasurable boost of confidence that helped me become who I am today.

Years later, Ann admitted she didn't always follow the technical jargon I threw around, but she said she liked my humor and saw promise in my master's degree in electrical engineering. Thanks to The Beatles and Ravi Shankar, she was intrigued by India, so that helped, too. But that combination of practicality and optimism was quintessential Ann. She grounded me while lifting me higher. With her in my life, I stopped caring about proving my father wrong or meeting anyone else's expectations. For the first time, I wanted success for a different reason—to build a life for Ann and the family we dreamed of having together.

In my father's worldview, a man's worth was measured by how well he cared for the women in his life. That sentiment, though outdated in today's terms, shaped how I saw responsibility and success. Ann completed a part of me I didn't even know was missing.

By the time Ann visited again in June, I was settling into my new job. I proudly introduced her to my boss, Ron, and my friend Jeff, both of whom were instrumental in my early days as a young professional. Later, Ann and I went shopping for an engagement ring. It felt like everything was coming together.

But not everyone shared our excitement. This was barely three years after *Loving v. Virginia* had legalized interracial marriage in the US, and my father, already reeling from my decision to cut my hair and abandon my turban, couldn't quite accept the idea of me marrying a foreigner. It was a lot for him to process.

I wondered how Ann had processed it. Obviously we had spoken countless times about the way we felt about each other. We had also talked about the way The Beatles had helped to make India cool. I guess that worked in my favor even though I was no maharishi.

Still, one day, as Ann and I chatted on the phone, I couldn't help but ask, "You know there aren't too many interracial marriages. Why did you say yes?"

She laughed—a warm, confident laugh I had come to love. "Not too many people with a master's in electrical engineering are asking me to marry them!"

That was Ann—practical, funny, and unflinchingly honest. We may have come from different worlds, but we were two birds of a feather, flying in the same direction.

Looking back, I realize Ann's yes wasn't just about us; it was a vote of confidence in who I was and who I could become. It's a lesson I carry to this day in every decision I make—whether in love or in business. Success starts with belief, and sometimes, all it takes is one person willing to take that leap with you.

A Rocky Start

I did not anticipate any of the bumps Ann and I encountered as we marched forward into our new life together.

Ann wanted to have a church wedding but most weren't open to outsiders. Our local Catholic church said I would have to convert, something I was not willing to do. The nearby evangelical church agreed under the condition we raise our children in their church. I was against that, too. When we walked into the neighborhood Episcopalian church, though, the priest took one look at me and said, "Oh, I know you."

I recognized Father Whitehead, too. We used to play in a doubles game on the tennis courts at the park near my apartment. When I asked if he would marry us, he agreed without any hesitation. Ann was delighted as she had been raised Episcopalian. We set a date for the following March, which was only six months away. At first, all proceeded smoothly. Even with Ann still stationed in Texas, we had honed our long distance relationship into a routine. It was when I checked the mail later that summer that our plans seemed like they might stall. I was drafted. How was that possible given that I wasn't an American citizen yet?

I had procured my green card back in Michigan. That process included registering with the Selective Service. Even though the Vietnam War was winding down, 50,000 people a month were still being called into service, and suddenly I was one of them. I had never been physically strong, and though my family had a long history in the military, I was loath to follow in those footsteps. But I failed the physical, unintentionally, and was not selected for service.

Then came another glitch. I got laid off from my job. SEL was a major supplier of computers to NASA, and by 1970, NASA, having landed several crews on the moon, was winding down the space program. Nixon's "Vietnamization" of the war was bringing hundreds of thousands of men back home from overseas. Unemployment and inflation were up, the dollar was down, the government had frozen wages and prices, SEL lost its major contracts, and I was out of work.

Ann was a tremendous support. This was the second job I had lost due to issues beyond my control and I took it as a serious blow. Ann never wavered about our upcoming wedding, and I am sure the confidence she had in me was one of the reasons my latest stint of unemployment did not last long. RCA Computer Systems, in West Palm Beach, liked what they saw on my resume and heard in my interview, and they hired me as a circuit designer.

The job was forty miles from Fort Lauderdale. That did not even register as a problem. I happily commuted for several months so we didn't have to change the location of our wedding. Our small ceremony took place on March 26, 1971, with my two IIT buddies, Bhopi and Umesh, in attendance along with Ann's mother and sister. Travel was too expensive for those on my side, though my mother sent her blessings. Ann's brother was on a ship off the coast of Vietnam, and her stepfather didn't approve of me.

My friend from work, Jeff Katz, hosted a reception at his house with deli platters and spiked punch. His wife was an Orthodox Jew, so everything was kosher. I felt like we were covering most of the bases. Ann and I honeymooned in Key West. The original seven-mile bridge connecting the Keys to the mainland was still open to automobiles then, and after stopping for dinner in Key Largo—that is where Ann and I both fell in love with key lime pie, a favorite to this day—and resuming the drive, I recognized that I wasn't merely crossing another bridge in my life, I was setting off on this journey with Ann by my side. We were doing it together.

CHAPTER 6

From Setbacks to Silicon Valley

IT WAS THE SUMMER OF 1971, and I was doing well at my job at RCA Computer Systems. The hours were long, but I received lots of praise in a short time. RCA was an enormous company, having expanded from its roots in electronics, radio, and television to include rental cars, publishing, frozen food, carpets, and computers, among other things. On Wall Street, RCA was said to stand for Rugs, Chickens & Automobiles.

We were building the Spectra 70 series of IBM 360 compatible mainframes—enormous computers that went for millions of dollars. Our marketing slogan was "10 percent better for 10 percent less". I was involved in logic design, exactly what I wanted to be doing, and my bosses were impressed with my work and the speed at which I did it. Meanwhile, Ann received her discharge from the Air Force and we moved into a nice beachfront cottage in Palm Beach Shores.

However, just as our idyllic life began to take shape, IBM came out with a new mainframe, the 370 series. It was bigger and faster than its predecessor and 40 percent cheaper. Overnight our sales took a nosedive. I went home after work and turned on the NBC Nightly News. I heard a report that stopped time for me. RCA was pulling out of the computer business. What? I had not heard anything about such a dramatic shift. At the office the next morning, everyone was as confused as I was.

It took about six weeks for word of our fate to officially wind its way through the bureaucratic labyrinth of the giant corporation, and it was what all of us feared—we were being laid off. I tried to put on a stoic face but the reality was too much. It felt like the ceiling had crashed down on my shoulders. This was my third time being laid off in two and a half years. My friends from Michigan Tech were still securely employed in the jobs they took after leaving school. What was I doing wrong?

That was a hard but necessary question. Of course, it was not just me being laid off; RCA was closing its entire computer division, thousands of people were affected. Yet I had to look deep into myself and the decisions I had made to figure out why this had happened again and again. After much thought and soul-searching, I concluded that I did not understand any of the three businesses that had hired me. Yes, the jobs were good, and I was good at them. But I had not done any diligence about the companies. I had not investigated their business, their position in the market, or the executives in charge. In interviews, I had not asked my share of questions: *How was the company doing? Was it competitive? What were its successes? What were its challenges? What were its prospects for the future?*

I had been so focused on them judging me that I had neglected to do my homework about them. And look what happened.

I vowed I would not be laid off again. How could I be certain? I couldn't but I could reduce the odds dramatically by doing my due diligence. The first step was taking responsibility for all three layoffs. Rather than point a finger, I said it was my fault for not being more aware of or informed about the health and management of the company where I worked. Was this radical thinking as some might believe? Most people would think getting laid off is unfair or that something bad happened to them that was beyond their control. I blamed myself for not seeing it coming, not doing my research.

I sent out my resume, and RCA was very good about offering resources to help its employees find new jobs, in addition to providing two months of salary; but having been burned three times, I was leery of longevity in any new job. I concluded that a job is an economic arrangement. Companies will keep you as long as you are doing a good job and the company is doing well and not a day longer. Similarly, you should not feel loyal or attached to a job after it is no longer fun or satisfying. Just as in any relationship, it's only healthy if it is mutually beneficial.

Go West

In 1971, the US economy was no better than it had been seven months earlier, only now the freeze in prices, wages, and the slowdown in production had a name: stagflation. The economy in Florida was depressed. While I looked for work in my field, I took on odd jobs, whatever I could find, including part-time work in a fast-food restaurant. Two hours here, two hours there. Every dollar mattered.

In November, I had two job offers in California, one with the Los Angeles-based company I had met with before and the other one, Singer-Link, which was up north. I interviewed at Singer-Link's headquarters in Sunnyvale, about thirty-five miles south of San Francisco, and I liked the area, and more specifically Santa Clara Valley, soon to be better known as Silicon Valley. The emerging semiconductor industry was already carving out a place among the apricot orchards and farmland. Things were happening here.

Ann and I got to Sunnyvale in December, following a long, leisurely drive across the country that included a stop at the newly opened Disney World in Orlando and an overnight stay with my friend Bhopi in Dallas. Ann and I lived at the local Motel 6 while we got acclimated to the area. This was back when a room went for $6 a night. Then we rented a nice apartment. A small Indian community was starting to build nearby.

Singer-Link was a defense contractor. Given that my previous employer, SEL, had done work for NASA, I had some residual trepidation about job security. But from the due diligence I did, I saw no signs of imminent danger. They had a brand new government contract. They made flight simulators for the Air Force and Navy. The flight simulators were used to train Air Force and Navy pilots and navigators. The simulators were very large, specialized computers in which we implemented complex algorithms in hardware to process data that produced images that a pilot would see out the windows and on his radar screen.

These machines, like the world itself, were changing to digital from analog. Advances in technology were pushing things forward. I was the first digital engineer Singer-Link hired. It was a lucky break. I had the freedom to learn, experiment, and try new things without anyone looking over my shoulder. On my first day, my boss explained the new project that awaited me—a radar simulator for a new Navy plane, the E-2C. It was a twin-engine turboprop with a large radar dome on its top, a slow-flying eye-in-the-sky.

"Our simulator will show the pilot what the radar sees out of the window," he said as he pushed a thick notebook toward me. "Here's the physics of it. It also explains the way we did it in analog. Go figure out how to do this digitally."

Consider the assignment: A plane was flying over land. The radar sent a beam out over a certain radius. It swept around a specific area, say 200 miles, and put an image on the pilot's radar screen. My job was to simulate this, to compute what a beam of energy sees when it hits the ground and comes back, and to put that on the simulator's radar screen. I realized it was a bit of faith on my boss's part to hand this off to me, the new digital engineer, but my knowledge of both hardware and software gave me an edge, and it didn't take me long to figure out how to approach the problem, create an algorithm, compute the data and turn it into an image on the simulator.

To figure out whether the hardware would work, I built models in software, studied the results, and if they checked out, I built the boards—often a couple of hundred boards. I became very skilled at doing massive designs and keeping track of everything involved and was soon regarded as the company's expert in radar simulation. I applied for several patents and was granted two of them. An Air Force general sent a note, calling my work vital and praising me as a real asset to the military.

The initial project and those that followed were hard and complex, requiring deep thinking, which was my favorite part of the job—sitting at my drafting table, paper and pencils in front of me, working out solutions. I had always thrived when left on my own. I was learning and doing things that let me discover my gifts for getting to the heart of a problem and solving the puzzle with an unusually high degree of accuracy. No matter what was assigned to me, I got it done and looked for more work. The work kept me stimulated.

Home

I stopped worrying about losing my job, but I still kept my resume up-to-date and started taking morning continuing education classes at Santa Clara and Stanford Universities.

These "early bird" courses kept me up to date on the latest advances in my field and filled in gaps outside my area of expertise, like business, law, and marketing. I took these classes for years. There was always something new I wanted to learn, some aspect of myself I wanted to improve. Fearing my shyness might hold me back, I took the Dale Carnegie course *How to Win Friends and Influence People.* I stood onstage in front of people and said silly things. I can't say it changed my personality, but gradually my self-consciousness in front of groups of people disappeared.

Ann was my biggest cheerleader, as always. One day, she wanted to know why I never called my parents in India.

"We can afford the long distance charges," she said.

"It isn't the expense," I said. "Believe it or not, we do not have a phone in Kanpur."

"In all of Kanpur?" she asked.

"No, at our home. We do not have a phone there. We do not have a lot of things we take for granted here."

Ann wanted to see for herself. It had been five years since I left home and two years since I got married, and my family had not met Ann yet, so we planned a trip to India, and in November 1973 we traveled to Kanpur. It had been ten years since I had lived in Kanpur, and I realized how much I had changed when I saw how much my hometown had not changed. Kanpur had no hotels or restaurants; our house did not have a proper toilet before I left for IIT; my parents had one installed before Ann and I showed up.

By this time, my family had made peace with my marriage. My father fell in love with Ann the moment we walked through the front door. He heard us call each other by our nicknames—she called me Brownie, I called her Whitey—and thought it was hysterical. My mother also adored Ann, but she didn't speak English, so the two of them mostly nodded and smiled at each other if my sister or I were not around to translate. Both my parents appreciated the $200 I was sending them every month.

Ann and I took brief side trips to Kashmir, Agra, Khajuraho, and Delhi. Security was everywhere, remnants of the Bangladesh war in 1971. I was hassled by guards in the Delhi airport as a potential spy for pulling out a pair of binoculars. When I went to the ticket counter there, I was told seats were sold out for days. Ann walked up to the same ticket counter and was given seats immediately. This was 1973, almost twenty-six years after Independence, and still White people were treated differently.

In Delhi, we splurged on a very expensive hotel suite only to receive a last-minute order to vacate our room because they needed it for VIPs who had reserved the entire floor. Suddenly I was calling relatives in town whom I hadn't seen since my IIT days to ask if Ann and I could spend the night.

Despite all the rough edges we encountered on the trip, one thing worked out better than I had hoped. While in Delhi, I arranged for my old IIT friend who had been Ann's original pen pal to meet us at a restaurant. I had never asked about their correspondence but recalling that he had asked me to mail that silver bracelet to her when I got to the US made me wonder if they'd had a serious connection. Then he showed up and I wondered no more. After greeting me, he turned to Ann and said, "Hi Cathy."

She laughed. "I'm Ann."

He stuck out his hand. "Hi Ann."

The six-week trip felt like an eternity. I had not taken a week off—let alone six weeks. My bosses at Singer-Link were worried that I would not return. They sent me a telegram saying the company would pick up the expenses of my trip and give me a 20 percent raise when I came back. That let me see the way companies will take care of their star performers. Businesses are fluid and flexible. They have policies on the way people are supposed to be treated. In reality, though, they find ways to let their star performers know they are valued.

The Choices One Makes

Six months later, life was settling back to normal.

I got my raise and Ann and I bought our first house in San Jose's North Valley. We were in a new development, but there were still enough farms in the area that early on some mornings I heard roosters crowing as they greeted the new day. India was not on my mind very often. But I was playing poker with friends one Thursday night when a telegram arrived from Kanpur. My father had died in a motorcycle accident. No other details were provided. Just that he had died.

I returned to the poker table. I did not want to tell my friends and ruin their night. I told Ann only after they left. Despite wearing a stoic mask, I ran through a gamut of emotions, starting with anger. Though I had processed my anger toward the way my father had treated me as a child years ago, my anger this time was directed at his recklessness. Over the years he'd had about a dozen motorcycle accidents, many of them because he would ride and nod off the same way I often fell asleep doing homework, at work, behind the wheel. I am sure he suffered from the same undiagnosed sleep apnea. But he rarely wore a helmet despite all the accidents. Alas, one lives by the choices one makes in life.

I was also angry that I had not been able to bring him to the United States. Seeing America, and New York in particular, was one of his lifelong dreams. I think he would have fallen in love with California. I can picture him riding a motorcycle along the coast. When Ann and I were in India, I had promised to arrange a trip for him. He had worked so hard all his life to provide for his family, but sadly for all of us, he didn't live long enough for me to make his dream come true. At least he had met Ann and seen that I was doing well.

We never got to resolve our differences, but I knew from the way he treated Ann when we were in India that he was proud of me, and I have to believe that he knew I felt the same about him. He was the rock of the family, a role model if only for the way he ferried the entire family to safety after Partition. But his influence on me was more than those heroics. A lot of my drive as a person came from a desire to prove him wrong about me. To show him that I was actually worth something.

I spent a lot of years wishing we'd had closure. The reality is, we often have to find our own closure. I came to understand that the best of me was in no small part due to him. His greatest lesson was a lasting one. *Do your duty without complaining or boasting, and do it well.*

CHAPTER

7
The Seeds of Ambition

I WAS SUSPECTED OF WRONG-DOING by the American government. My actions were well-intentioned on my part. To see firsthand the way radar worked, I flew on an E-2C Hawkeye, a C-130 Hercules, and various other planes out of Wright-Patterson Air Force Base in Dayton, Ohio. I wanted to hop a ride in an F-111 Aardvark and experience flight in this fabled attack plane, but there was no room in the two-seater for a joyrider like myself. Just a pilot and a weapons officer.

Then I was assigned the task of simulating the radar of an F-111, but I didn't get the full specifications I needed to do my work. Requests for the correct information were repeatedly denied by higher authorities. I tried to look up specs to make sure I put the correct numbers in the algorithm, but the specs for the F-111's terrain-following radar were classified as top secret, and even though I was the system engineer, I didn't have sufficient clearance to access them.

While searching for a workaround, I found an issue of *Air and Space* magazine dedicated to the F-111. In it was a description of its capabilities to the nth degree. Why was such information published when it was classified as secret? I assumed it was a sophisticated, under-the-radar leak letting our allies and enemies know some of our latest military capabilities. I used the information to program the algorithms and led a demo of the simulator for a contingent from the Air Force.

Though impressed, one officer wanted to know how I was able to do the work when I didn't have the specs. I told him about the magazine, thinking my resourcefulness would be admired. It wasn't. It raised concerns of a serious security breach. Air Force security called me in and interrogated me on how I managed to see top secret information. Nothing I said calmed their concerns until I showed them my issue of the magazine as proof that all their top secret information was right there on its pages. Even then, they had questions. My answers and that magazine kept me out of the brig.

More On-the-Job Training

In July 1976, days after the country's bicentennial celebrations, I flew on a B-52 bomber. The training mission was routine; my seat on it was arranged so I could experience the fabled aircraft while updating the simulator.

I flew to Fairchild Air Force Base in Spokane, Washington. Though the B-52 had been in service for nearly twenty-five years, it was still a mainstay of the Air Force and an essential part of the nuclear triad that included nuclear submarines and ICBMs (intercontinental ballistic missiles). It was designed to be a high-altitude, long-range bomber with aerial refueling capability so it could stay airborne for long stretches, around the clock for an indeterminate amount of time if necessary. During the Cold War, two planes were always in the air.

The plane carried two sets of crews. While one flew, the other rested. Inside, there were no creature comforts. I rode in the radar station and sat on what was essentially a wooden stool for the whole mission. It was freezing cold as my perch was the lowest point in the plane. The AC intake was next to my feet and it blew cold air up my legs. Our mission lasted nine hours. We flew all over the western US, refueling at 20,000 feet and making several practice runs over the Nevada firing range.

When it was time to land, the pilot decided to work on his touch-and-go landings and takeoffs. He came in, the wheels touched the ground, and he immediately pulled the wheel back and headed up in the air again. He did this at least a half dozen times. I lost count after pulling out the plastic bag they had given me earlier. I am sure the green pallor of my face told the crew what I thought of the flight.

But this picture did not tell the story. I actually looked forward to these on-the-job training exercises. And sometimes I even surprised people. Like the time the advanced systems division at Wright-Patterson Air Force Base invited me to experience the physiological training pilots were put through to see how they responded to high altitude and loss of pressure. This division managed our work, and I had built up a reputation with them. Their invitation was considered a perk. I did not want to decline.

The test was conducted in a hyperbaric chamber inside which various high altitudes could be simulated. I was in there with other pilots. After the pressure in the chamber was raised to 18,000 feet—most people need supplemental oxygen at 18,000 feet—we were asked to stand, jump up and down, and solve a few math problems. Those who couldn't function were asked to step out. They kept raising the pressure incrementally. At 22,000 feet everyone but me had exited the chamber.

Few people can function without oxygen at 20,000 feet. I had no problem. At 25,000 feet, I was still going strong and would have kept going if the guy in charge hadn't called it off. He had never seen anyone function at this level without oxygen. Many years later I would realize this seemingly superhuman feat was the result of my sleep apnea. I was used to functioning on less oxygen than most. But back then I was merely curious. I suggested we could keep going to see where I topped out. He refused.

"I don't need you to find your limit," he said. "You might just keel over and die without showing any signs."

"Good point," I said.

Make Yourself Indispensable

Singer-Link was famous for falling behind schedule. It seemed to me that nearly all the projects in the defense industry, not just at Singer-Link, fell behind schedule because of unrealistic delivery schedules and workers who weren't motivated due to long-term government contracts that basically guaranteed their jobs for life. The system bogs down or breaks. Projects get into trouble. Incentives and accountability are misaligned. The people bidding on new contracts are the same people who are working on the old projects.

I remedied some of the problems I saw by voluntarily helping people who were having trouble. I set up systems throughout the company that solved problems and kept projects on schedule. Digital designs required processes. How a computer was wired required a process. Converting a paper design into a manufacturable required a process. I did this for a number of teams even though it wasn't my job, and as a result, I became the company's unofficial process designer.

Looking back, I can see that I was unusually self-motivated. My boss knew this and left me alone. I worked late and was the only one to go in and work on Saturdays. That was not the only reason my work was always finished ahead of schedule, but I had a knack for getting the job done well—and right. If it was a six-month project, I finished my design in eight weeks and had it working in about that same time frame, which left me with a month or two to help other teams.

I was stimulated by the variety of work I found. I was also eager to apply the new technologies and methodologies I was learning in my early bird classes at Santa Clara and Stanford. The things others called drudgery were challenges to me. My boss gave me the freedom to roam, but not everyone appreciated my help.

I started using new chips. I set up a system for myself, then gradually different teams adopted my system. A project manager on a logistics team discovered his reports were using a system I had set up. He got upset. He felt I was undermining his authority.

"Not a problem," I said, careful to not let my disdain for him show. "Let me uninstall it."

I did, and very quickly everything ground to a halt. I was not trying to be vindictive. On the contrary, I was following orders—the orders of someone who let emotions and ego get in the way of good decision-making. Two days later, this same project manager pleaded with me to restore my system. I can still hear him say, "Just get it all running again." If you are good at your work and have extra time, don't sit idle or complain about boredom. Take initiative. Find things to do. Look for ways you can add value. Make yourself indispensable.

This should be obvious, but I have had to repeat it countless times. If you have finished your tasks, help someone else. Build relationships, strengthen your position, show your worth. I can't stand hearing, "The work isn't interesting" or "I'm not challenged." If that's how you feel, find something that excites you. Time is too precious to waste—yours and everyone else's.

The Trouble with Reviews

At my end-of-year review with my boss, he scored me Excellent in every category except one. In that, he had written Very Good.

"I thought I was excellent in that category, too," I said. "What did I miss?"

"I don't know," he said.

"How do I improve?" I asked.

"I don't know," he said.

"So why did you not rate me as Excellent?"

He shifted in his chair, started to say something, stopped himself, re-read the review, then reached for a pen, crossed out that rating, and wrote "Excellent."

The lesson? In a world where sales and performance are paramount, you must sell yourself. If you don't stick up for yourself, no one will.

Who Makes More Money?

Soon after, I was promoted to lead engineer. One of the first things I did was hire my old summer intern, Duane Murray, as a full-time hardware design engineer. Unofficially, he was my sidekick. Duane was a very bright electrical engineering student when he began helping me on a project as an intern. I had him write software on our supersized "minicomputers" (they filled an entire room). Then he became my key report.

We were a two-person fire brigade, constantly being brought in to save projects going up in flames. The two of us redesigned, rebuilt, and tested one major project in just six weeks. Normally that same project would have taken two years. We pulled off a miracle thanks to good engineering and eighty-hour work weeks. I felt we were performing at a very high and mostly efficient level. The Singer-Link GM (general manager) from the New York headquarters had a different opinion.

He was new, and he visited our California plant as part of his introduction to the company. During a dinner he hosted for management and senior people like me at a fancy restaurant, he stood up and in an undiplomatic manner said he was not happy with what he saw. He cited a lack of order, systemic checks on the work, and so on. In short, he said the entire operation was out of control.

"There will be changes," he said. "There have to be changes. And some of you may not end up being happy."

I listened behind a self-imposed wall of silence. I thought we were doing much better than in previous years, if not bordering on excellence. I had witnessed the improvements. But I assumed this executive was talking about me. If he was not happy with the work and the processes by which it got done, he must have also had criticisms of my work. I was the lead engineer, after all.

No one ever spoke to me, so I may have been overly sensitive—or not. Following the GM's visit, an engineer from one of my groups was promoted to a management position. He had been slotted beneath me on the organization chart; now he was on the rise. I did not think highly of him and his work could not compare to mine. In a meeting with my boss, I asked if I had been considered for that promotion.

"No, not really," he said.

"Why not?" I asked.

"You're our best engineer," he said. "You're doing a super job for me. I don't want to lose you."

"Who makes more money?" I asked. "A manager or a good engineer?"

"A manager," he said.

"So why would I stay an engineer if a manager makes more money?"

Why Not Me?

One morning, a headline in the paper caught my eye. It felt as if it had been placed there just for me. A former engineer from my team at Singer-Link, David Jackson, was making waves. I hadn't kept in touch, but according to the article, he had struck out on his own, built a computer company from scratch, and was now on the verge of taking it public.

A wave of emotions hit me. First, admiration—David had done well. Then, envy—I measured myself against him, questioning my own trajectory. Finally, the inevitable spark that every entrepreneur knows: *Why not me?* What was holding me back? If David could do it, why couldn't I?

It's the song that nearly every entrepreneur starts to sing. Once that seed of discontent is planted, it doesn't just sit there—it grows, fast.

I had my own frustrations at work. They were as much a part of my daily routine as my morning coffee. The defense industry valued reliability over innovation, meaning we worked with outdated technology—chips and components that were years behind the cutting edge. My friends outside Singer-Link knew it, too. They never said it outright, but I could sense their unspoken question: *Why are you still there? Why aren't you taking advantage of the latest technology?* It wasn't about my skills; they respected those. It was about ambition. The desire to push boundaries, to work with the best and latest. And that nagging thought in the back of my mind—*Am I playing it too safe?*

Exactly. I was still at Singer-Link because I was playing it safe. As head of a family, I had responsibilities. The comfort and stability of our suburban life in San Jose was something Ann had always craved. My dream came true, too: I became an American citizen. In 1976, we welcomed our first child, Raj-Ann, and three years later Ann gave birth to our son, Ben. Only a few months later, we took our children back to India to meet my family. I went for my sister's wedding in 1980 and returned with my brother Upi, beginning a gradual migration of my five brothers, my sister, and my mother to California.

Life was neat, tidy, and secure. But at what cost?

I had a sense that everyone's life was moving along except mine. Startups had taken root in Silicon Valley. Intel, National, and AMD were among the new companies that were shaping the culture there and reshaping the world. New semiconductor companies sprouted with regularity, like Signetics, Intersil, and MMI (Monolithic Memories, Inc.). Gene Amdahl, the architect of the IBM 360 and 370 series, started his own IBM-compatible company, Amdahl. And Steve Jobs and Steve Wozniak were a half dozen years into promoting their Apple PC as "the appliance of the '80s."

The golden age of the computer chip business had also begun, fueling the greatest outbreak of entrepreneurial fever in the area since a shiny nugget was found about 100 miles away at Sutter's Mill in 1848. At one point there were more than 100 chip companies in Silicon Valley. The Valley was about getting smaller, faster, more powerful, and really rich. Some wanted to conquer the world; the true visionaries wanted to change it; and a few mavericks wanted both.

I was totally destabilized as a person when I read about David Jackson and the company he had co-founded, to manufacture a Z80/CPM-based hotbox—an early personal computer. He'd had a vision of doing something better, and different than what existed, something that filled a gap in the marketplace, and he had executed it. I admired the boldness he'd had to leave his job and strike out on his own.

I was never the same after that—in a good way. Inspired, or perhaps challenged, I looked at myself and my career with the same analytical curiosity and honesty that I applied to problem-solving in my work. And when I did, I asked the questions that begin every entrepreneurial journey: Why couldn't I start my own company? Why couldn't I be an entrepreneur, too? Why couldn't I control my own destiny? Why not me?

CHAPTER

8

Networking the Future

YOGI BERRA FAMOUSLY SAID, "THE future ain't what it used to be."

The David Jackson story set me up, but the true moment of discontent came for me when I saw my trusted colleague, Duane Murray, leave Singer-Link for Tandem Computers. Watching him move on to greener pastures did not only leave me frustrated and questioning my own trajectory, it drove home the truth:

I was stuck. While others were moving ahead, I was spinning my wheels. Then my boss invited me to an Amway distributors meeting. "What is that?" I asked. "A chance to earn extra money," he replied.

Amway, a multilevel marketing business selling everything from vitamins to cleaning supplies, was his side hustle. Some of my colleagues were doing the same. Was this my future? Selling products on the side to make ends meet? I was a hardcore engineer, good at what I did. Was this all I had to look forward to if I stayed at Singer-Link?

That was my breaking point. I quit Singer-Link, ready to find something better. But the reality check was brutal. I sent out over a dozen resumes and heard nothing back. In the commercial world, defense contractors like Singer-Link were seen as second-rate. The big names, home to the Valley's best and brightest engineers—Apple, Atari, and Oracle—didn't even give me a glance.

In their eyes, I was tainted before I even applied. Defense work was a dead end in the Valley. It meant you played it safe, followed orders, and never took ownership. No hunger, no drive, no skin in the game. But that wasn't me. I thrived on responsibility, on making things happen. I just needed a chance to prove it.

Eventually, I landed at Biomation, a company just down the street from Singer-Link. It wasn't a great fit, but I needed the paycheck. Then I heard about an opening at Zilog, a semiconductor company founded by Intel veterans. During my interview, I could see my soon-to-be new boss, Doug Schwartz, saying to himself, "He can't be that sharp. He worked for Singer-Link for nine years." The job was a step down, both in title and pay. I went from $75,000 to $45,000. But I knew I had to take the hit to transition into the commercial sector. "One step back, two steps forward," I told myself.

Zilog had enjoyed immediate success with their Z80 microprocessor. It was a big improvement on the Intel 8080 and helped spark the software revolution to come. But Zilog's next product, the 16-bit Z8000, failed to make the mark and the company began a downhill slide from there. Zilog would probably have gone under right then if not for its biggest investor, Exxon, which was pouring money into the company, thinking it would get them into the computer business so they could eventually take on IBM.

Fixing the Unfixable

In the Silicon Valley, engineering was the universal language, and I spoke it fluently.

I joined Zilog's systems division, and on my first day, my new boss, Doug Schwartz, handed me what I am sure seemed like an impossible task: Build a new Z80-based microcomputer, a micro server, and the network connecting them. They already had these products, but there was a catch. None of them worked. The computer, the server, the network—all were dead on arrival.

Doug assigned me a team, but he didn't expect much. Frankly, neither did I. It was clear why Zilog's sales were in freefall. How could you sell machines that didn't even function? My past layoffs haunted me as I wondered if Zilog could survive with problems this fundamental.

I dove in, playing detective for months. The deeper I went, the worse it got. Timing issues, overloaded circuits—classic design flaws. But the real shock came when I tried to understand the design itself. No one had a clear idea of what the machines were supposed to be. Worse, every engineer seemed to have their own version of the truth.

One day, as I walked through the office, I noticed something peculiar: every engineer had a different computer on their desk. It hit me—no wonder nothing worked. There was no consistency, no shared vision.

I decided to focus. I took three non-working machines, applied my fixes, and got them running. When I showed Doug, he was stunned. Instead of building new units, I proposed a different approach: repair the flawed inventory. It was faster, cheaper, and far more efficient.

Doug gave me the green light. Over the next six months, my team and I repaired about fifty of those flaky machines. The sales and customer support teams treated me like a magician. Doug couldn't have been happier. And my salary? Fully restored.

For a moment, it felt like a victory. But the experience revealed something deeper: Zilog's problems weren't just technical—they were cultural. The lack of cohesion, clarity, and leadership was a far bigger issue than faulty circuits. Fixing machines was one thing. Fixing the company? That was a whole different challenge.

The End of the Line at Zilog

Zilog's machines finally worked. But just as we were turning the corner, the leadership bailed. The irony was hard to stomach.

I blamed Exxon, Zilog's largest stakeholder. The Houston oil giant had no business being in tech. Their only directive to Zilog was to build "next-generation computers." As if it were that simple. The result? Chaos. First, the company president left. Then my boss. Then my software partner. Between the first wave of departures and this latest exodus, Zilog was a ship adrift.

The timing couldn't have been worse—or better, depending on one's perspective. It was the summer of 1981, and the world was shifting. Personal computers were popping up everywhere—Tandem, Commodore, Apple. Microprocessors were growing more powerful by the day.

Then came the moment that changed everything: the launch of the IBM PC in August 1981.

Retailing at $1,565, the IBM PC came with 64 kilobytes of RAM, WordStar for word processing, and VisiCalc for spreadsheets. It wasn't the first PC, but it was the one that hit all the right notes. Businesses and consumers alike couldn't get enough. Overnight, the PC revolution was in full swing, and IBM was leading the charge.

At the same time, another groundbreaking announcement hit the industry: DEC, Xerox, and Intel introduced Ethernet protocols. This was the beginning of a new standard—a way for computers to talk to each other over a single wire. The Ethernet solved a fundamental problem: how to transmit data between multiple devices without collisions. It was like defining traffic rules for the information superhighway.

The implications were enormous. The era of mainframe computing was coming to an end, replaced by a distributed paradigm—a world where multiple computers and servers worked together seamlessly. The future was clear to anyone paying attention.

But not to Zilog.

Zilog was in no position to adapt to this new reality. And as long as I stayed there, neither was I. It was time to face the truth—Zilog wasn't going to lead the next wave of innovation. If I wanted to be part of the revolution, I needed to chart my own course.

A New Idea

Somebody was going to have to connect this new world of heterogeneous computing—PCs, workstations, servers, minicomputers, and mainframes. They'd all need to interact seamlessly on a high-speed network. That somebody could be us.

At the time, the Indian community in Silicon Valley was still small—maybe 5,000 people in the entire Bay Area. My closest friends, Umesh and Bhopi, were far away. Umesh had returned to India to take care of family and run a textile business. Bhopi was still at Texas Instruments, working on cutting-edge technology like GPS.

I missed my old friends, but two colleagues at Zilog, Dr Navindra Jain and Dr Inder Mohan Singh, helped fill the gap. Navin was a BITS Pilani gold medalist with a PhD in computer engineering from CMU (Carnegie Mellon University). Inder, an IIT Kharagpur grad with a Yale PhD, had come to Zilog from Amdahl Computers in Sunnyvale. Among the three of us, Inder was the most refined and outgoing. He'd gone to Doon School, the best boarding school in India, and those qualities were front and center.

Despite our different personalities, the three of us shared a common frustration with Zilog's dysfunction and how it was stifling our careers. It made for a solid and respectful workplace friendship. At lunch, we'd dissect the industry, analyzing trends and spotting gaps. We were engineers, trained to find broken systems and fix them. And Zilog was as broken as they came.

One day, over pizza at our usual spot, I decided to pitch my idea.

"This has been brewing in me for a while," I began. "Not just the idea, but the desire. David Jackson left Singer-Link to start his own company. That made me ask myself, 'Why not me? Why not the three of us? Why not now?'"

I laid out the shifting landscape. IBM's PC was shipping, and sales were exploding—from 15,000 units a month to projections of 200,000 within a year. Apple was on track to sell over 300,000 Apple I and II units that year. The PC revolution was underway, and it was clear: every desk would have a computer.

"But these machines need to be networked," I said. "You've got PCs on desks, minicomputers in the back, and massive mainframes somewhere else. Somebody has to provide the networking. That somebody should be us."

I paused for dramatic effect, studying their reactions. Navin and Inder listened intently.

Inder proposed something grand: building a massive computer company—MCZ systems, servers, networks—the works. He envisioned raising $50 million and taking on IBM and others head-on. I shook my head. "Too much risk, too much capital," I said. "David versus too many Goliaths," Navin agreed.

"I think what I have in mind can be done quickly," I said, grabbing a napkin.

I sketched my idea. "We've got PCs, workstations, servers, minicomputers, and mainframes. They all need to interact on a high-speed network. I've studied the Ethernet specs. I can design boards to implement these protocols—faster than Intel, and with off-the-shelf parts."

My design fit on one board instead of two, as Intel had planned, and it was half the size. "This is our competitive edge," I said.

Inder, though still drawn to grander ambitions, grudgingly agreed. Navin, frustrated by Zilog's constant failures, examined my sketch and nodded. He was in.

"This is practical," I said, smoothing the napkin in front of me. "It's a simple, elegant solution to a problem every business will face sooner or later." I tapped my pen on the table, picturing the opportunity. "It may be even bigger than every business. It may be that everyone will need to be networked."

I sipped my soda, letting the vision sink in. "We might not be the only solution in town," I concluded, "but we can be the best and the easiest."

That napkin wasn't just the blueprint for a new venture—it was the foundation of something big. No detailed plan, no guarantees, just a vision demanding bold steps forward. Each move would pull me in deeper, requiring sharper focus, greater risk, and an unstoppable drive.

We agreed to give our notice to Zilog at the end of the year, December 31, 1981. The next day would be a fresh start, a new beginning. The path ahead was no clearer than that, but for the first time in years, the future was mine to shape.

PART 3

THE MAKING OF A CEO

CHAPTER

9

Taking the Leap: From Security to Startup

ANYONE WHO HAS CONSIDERED LEAVING a secure job for the unpredictable and wholly insecure life of an entrepreneur knows what we were going through: The I'm-Not-Crazy Two Step you do with your family—and yourself—explaining why such a move makes sense, and why you think everything will be okay even as you remove the safety net that lets everyone sleep comfortably at night.

I had many long, in-depth conversations with Ann about this venture. We discussed my two partners, and we talked about why I thought it would change our lives for the better. She believed in me and my abilities as an engineer. She knew I was at the top of my field. She trusted me when I told her about Navin and Inder and why each of them would make a good partner.

As for the idea itself, she listened up to a point. She did not need details on why I thought the Ethernet board that 3Com made was dumb or why the boards we would make would be better business because they would work on a variety of computers. She was indifferent to shoptalk about a Unibus, a Q-bus, a VME bus, a Multibus, and an IBM PC bus, as are most people.

Ann's concerns were practical: What was going to happen to us once I no longer had a regular paycheck? We had two children, a mortgage to pay, and groceries to buy. She had grown up in a household that was always short of money and this leap I wanted to make required a level of faith that made her nervous.

I assured Ann that we were going to be fine for at least a year and hopefully longer if things worked out as I imagined. And if not? I had saved enough money to get us through a year. I had taken advantage of low mortgage rates to build a modest real estate portfolio—four small homes that were rented out but could be sold as needed, which I did one by one over the next couple of years. And then I expected to raise money for the business that would eventually produce a new and steady paycheck.

"I think it will only take four to six months to get the business off the ground and money coming in," I told her. "If I am wrong and our finances get tight, I will do whatever is necessary—extra jobs, consulting—to ensure our family is taken care of. I will go back to Singer-Link and get a job if that's what it takes. No one will suffer, I promise."

She trusted me. But there was a single problem that I could not immediately address—it was the battle Ann constantly fought with her past. She grew up in a home ruled by uncertainty and chaos. She expected the worst. What do they say about trust? It's earned in drops and lost in buckets. Ann saw the transformation in me. From the man she knew and married who had always pursued a stable, predictable, secure job to someone who wanted to give all that up. What was going on? Was it something she was doing or not doing in our marriage?

"Am I making you unhappy?" she asked.

I assured Ann that I was very happy being married to her. We had two beautiful children, a beautiful home, a beautiful life. None of this was about her. Any question about my happiness rested inside me, I explained. This is something entrepreneurs will understand immediately. I felt stuck while everyone around me was becoming an entrepreneur, or so it seemed. I could have remained a defense contractor my entire career. But my colleagues in that world were selling Amway products. What would I have to look forward to? I would stagnate.

I explained all of this to Ann multiple times. When I read about David Jackson, I asked myself: "What does my future look like? What am I doing here?" I was forced to step outside my comfort zone. But I did not want her to feel like she had to also step outside her comfort zone. A spouse or partner, along with other family members, are all partners in your endeavor. They assume the same risks, sacrifices, and stress, but in a different way. This is something I knew was right and true insomuch as it affected our marriage, but I came to appreciate and understand this dynamic on an even more practical level as I mentored other entrepreneurs years later.

Ann had held several jobs over the years—as a nurse, a veterinarian's assistant, and most recently at a semiconductor manufacturer. She was smart and capable. But she always had a problem with authority, got fed up with nonsense, and told them so. Not exactly diplomatic. I liked that about her. She had fire. She was not hesitant about telling me what was on her mind, and she expected the same honesty from me. In fact, she could sniff out a lie or a phony better than anyone I knew.

Ann and I made a deal. She would be CEO of our household while I was starting my business. I saw her as a full partner, carrying equal weight and responsibility. She was vital to my success and, more importantly, to *our* success.

D-Day

On Christmas day, Navin and Inder came to our house for a final meeting. Inder brought his wife. Navin was not married. We sat at the dining room table and the three of us finalized our intentions to leave our jobs at Zilog and move forward with this new venture. The plan was to give notice in a few days and then spend the first three months of the new year getting our affairs in order. We would take any trips and tend to whatever might need attention before we launched our company on April 1, 1982.

We decided that Inder, as the most outwardly confident personality among the three of us, would be CEO; Navin would be the VP of software, and I would be VP of engineering. Inder would find investors, Navin would work on the software, and I would build our boards. Each of us would contribute $10,000 at the outset for initial expenses. We would look to raise money and build prototypes. Our plan looked solid and logical. Our roles were well defined and suited to our strengths. It felt good from all sides.

"What will be the definition of success here?" I asked.

"Each of us will make $2 million," Inder said.

"That's not enough," I said.

"How about $5 million," Inder said. "Each of us will make $5 million."

"After taxes," I added to much head nodding and laughter. "But what else will define success? It's not all money."

"We will still be friends," Navin said.

I agreed, but as a rule of thumb, it's not productive to mix business with friendship, a lesson I would learn the hard way later down the line.

"We will still be married," I added. "There is no reason to do this otherwise. Having our business succeed but our marriages fail would be failure."

Support was unanimous. Everyone was excited. There was just one question left—what were we going to call our new company?

Suggestions flew around the table. We landed on the name Excellence in Local Area Networks. Everyone agreed that it described the business accurately but it was a mouthful to say. We needed something shorter, punchier. Excellent LANS was suggested. So was XLANS. Then Ann proposed Excelan. All of us said it a few times. "Excelan." That worked! There were no objections. I opened a bottle of champagne.

Getting Started

On April 1, 1982, Excelan set up an office in a small space between a 7-Eleven and a Chinese market in a San Jose strip mall.

The guy who sublet it to us worked in real estate and used it as his office. He had the same name as a very famous rock and roll musician, only he spelled it differently. We took him on as a fourth partner because he had an MBA and said he would handle our accounting and business needs. He also put in $10,000 like the rest of us and promised to help raise money.

He lasted about two and a half weeks. He and Inder had a falling out almost immediately. He did not want to give up his real estate business to work with three Indians whose new venture he did not understand in the first place. Maybe he would give it up after we were funded, he said. But realistically there was nothing for him to do. I was designing the board, Navin was writing software, and Inder was looking for money. He resigned immediately.

When he left, he took all the furniture with him. The Valley was loaded with stores that sold office furnishings they had acquired from businesses that went belly up. Desks, chairs, shelves, lab equipment … whatever you needed. It was like salvage from those whose good ideas had disappeared into the Devil's Triangle of failed startups. I went shopping and brought back desks and chairs for the three of us. The only piece of furniture I did not get was a lab table, which I needed to build my boards.

I had seen one that was exorbitantly stickered at $250. Shocked, I stopped by the hardware store, picked up lumber and tools, and built my own for about $25. That is what you do when you are starting out and every dollar counts.

Silicon Valley startup culture was set when David Packard, an outgoing marketing guy, teamed up with Bill Hewlett, a quintessential engineering nerd, to start HP in the 1930s. That combination marketing man and engineering guy came to be seen as an ideal team. Marketing guy loudly wonders why somebody hasn't come up with this or that widget. The market for them would be huge! The engineering guy says, "Really? I can design those in no time." Thus is born a startup—and a partnership.

A Word about Partners

Partners should bring complementary skills and temperaments to the party. Optimist/pessimist. Sales/nerd. Dreamer/realist.

Those are some of the combinations that work well. It is much better to have divergent perspectives to develop a three-dimensional view of a problem. Large teams don't work as well; they become unwieldy. Yaar/Dost (friends) teams are not as good as they might seem; it's hard to be objective about friends. You want to have a clear division of labor between the team. Typically Mr Inside makes sure that the trains run on time while Mr Outside makes sure there is traffic to serve.

Business and friendship don't always mix—something that many learn the hard way.

Who Were Our Customers?

This was one of the essential questions we asked ourselves before jumping into this gambit. It was also the question we had to answer for potential investors. Who were our customers? Our idea was good, but who was going to buy it?

In 1982, the marketplace was full of computers—PCs, Unix Supermicros, minicomputers, and mainframes. Everybody was making some kind of computer, and more people were buying them. It was not just corporations that were plugging in, logging on, and going digital. It was also small businesses, moms in the kitchen, and kids in college. Businesses typically purchased machines from a single vendor, and the machines communicated well with those from the same manufacturer. But they couldn't talk with machines outside this ecosystem.

In other words, IBM and the other big guys provided machines that worked within their own system but not with somebody else's machines. They did this purposefully. They wanted to lock you in. But as far as I could see, the market was heterogeneous. People didn't want to be locked in. They wanted choice and flexibility.

This was my other insight. As the IBM PC took off, more and more people had more than one computer—one for work and their personal IBM PC. At the same time, Unix machines and minicomputers were gaining traction in the commercial sector. That made three types of machines that were gaining in popularity, and if my assessment was right, Excelan would be the only company able to connect a personal PC, a computer running Unix on a common network, and a Digital minicomputer.

"So who is our customer?" I asked Navin and Inder.

None of their answers got to the heart of it.

The PC was cheap; everybody was buying them. It was like color televisions in the 1960s and the iPhone in the 2010s and 2020s. You had to own one to be part of the conversation. The PC was like that, too. Once people had PCs, they realized these were very capable machines and they wanted to implement them into everyday work life. Small and medium-sized companies were also buying machines in large numbers. Startups, law firms, insurance companies, accounting businesses, banks. They might get a Unix machine and ten PCs. Or a larger company would run Unix at their headquarters and largest regional outposts and get PCs for all the offices across the country. Once this happened, they needed to network these computers.

"So who is our potential customer?" I asked my partners again, frustrated by their blank expressions. "It's everybody."

Every business is about solving a problem, so you better know how big the problem is and who you are solving it for.

Techies, Not Bosses

As Indians looking for VCs (venture capitalists) to fund our startup, we were doing something completely novel in the Valley. This had not been done before, not by Indians.

We were techies. That was our brand—and it was highly regarded. I thought that our reputation as good techies, along with the strength of our business plan, would be more than enough to attract investors. I was wrong. For months I had to grit my teeth and soldier on as Inder returned empty-handed from meetings with VCs. It was harder than we imagined. Even after we made our first sale—three boards to Plexus Computer for $7,000—the answer was still no.

The VCs would find reasons. We did not have experience running a company. We didn't have any businesspeople on the team. None of us were salespeople. How were we going to market our product? Who was going to buy from us? Those who liked Inder's pitch and recognized the potential of Excelan's solution to the networking issues that were fast becoming commonplace, would request a meeting with the team and then, after sitting down with the three of us, they would come up with a way to say thanks but no thanks.

"Is this the whole team?" they would ask.

I realized their reluctance had nothing to do with our business plan or the intelligence of our boards. It was personal. It was us. We did not have a White guy on the team. The VCs were not accustomed to minorities pitching to them. Despite our advanced degrees, successful track records, and even my high-level security clearance from Singer-Link, they couldn't get past our dark skin and accents.

Indians were not seen as managerial material. We were good workers, not executives, not leaders, and just too risky.

My Mistake

After we made our first sale to Plexus, I needed someone to help build and test the boards while I set up the lab and continued to work on the design. I called my former Singer-Link protégé Duane Murray at Tandem Computers.

"We're doing a startup," I told Duane, and before I could explain the rest or formally offer him a job, he said, "Do you have room for me?"

We never negotiated salary, title, or position. Duane trusted that I would take care of him, and I trusted that he would do a good job. That kind of belief is rare. He hand-wired the first three Ethernet boards we made for Plexus and accepted seventy- to ninety-hour work weeks without complaint. This commitment is a non-negotiable if startups are going to have a chance, and Duane understood and willingly stepped into the fire.

Hiring Duane caused two problems. First, our tiny office did not have room for four people. One of us had to be doing something out of the office for the other three to have enough room to work. We had to move.

The other problem was on me. The 25 percent of the company that originally belonged to our former partner with the famous name was still unclaimed. We gave 10 percent to Duane. Inder took over the remaining 15 percent. It gave him 40 percent ownership and reinforced his position as CEO while Navin and I stayed at 25 percent each. It was one of the worst mistakes of my career.

With friends, you often want to be kind or generous. But friendship can blur your vision and dull talk that should be sharp. In the end, it's what's on paper that is most important.

A Lucky Break

A second order came later that summer.

My old boss Doug Schwartz had also left Zilog and became a consultant for Victory Computers, a startup launched by the former head of sales for Altos. They were building a Unix hotbox. Doug called and asked if we could design an Ethernet board for their machine. "Can you help me get networking on this board?" he asked. Overnight we had a $100,000 contract from them—plus a $50,000 bonus if we completed the work in three months, which we did.

Though Excelan was small and fighting for its life every day, we appeared to have a product the market wanted. Our core module, about three by five inches, could be easily strapped on to any design. For my demos, I built three multibus boards that went into three different computers. You could type on one machine, send that message to A, B, or C, and see the data transferred back and forth. It worked, and everyone to whom I was able to give a demo was impressed.

But I knew it was not a complete solution to networking needs. Those who bought the boards still had to write their own software, and the problem with that was the process was a slow one. Someone would buy two boards from us and it would be eighteen months of writing before they had their "instant" solution. Then they had to sell it, which our future orders were dependent upon, and that took more time.

These were flaws that became apparent only after we began operations. Once I saw them, I began trying to fix them, improve upon them, at least in my head, and I knew that eventually, or ultimately, our solution had to work out of the box. But that was down the line. We were still in phase one. Despite a couple of sales and some cash in the bank, we needed funding, and then we needed both time and money to hire enough people to create the product I had in mind. Everything hinged on finding investors.

As for our competition, 3Com was the major player in our lane, and they were interesting. Their founder, Bob Metcalfe, had invented Ethernet at Xerox PARC, the legendary computer research lab in Palo Alto. Like us, 3Com was focused on networking. They had started about eighteen months before Excelan and had a board for multibus. But I had designed our board with a microprocessor and memory on it; you could write the software on the board then easily plug the hardware *and* software in any machine. The design had a simple, practical elegance.

By comparison, 3Com's board only had Ethernet on it; the software had to be written on the host computer, which meant it had to be written over and over for different computers. It lacked our modularity, easy adaptability and efficiency, and the ability to plug into any computer without much work. But those differences did not add up to the lucky break that saved our neck.

No, the lucky break was a decision made in 3Com's executive suite. After IBM PC sales took off, 3Com announced that it was going to make boards that only networked IBM PCs and IBM PC servers. Instead of networking a heterogenous environment, they focused on the IBM PC. If you only had IBM systems, they were great. If you had two or more computers made by different companies, you had to look for something else—and that left the field wide open for Excelan.

It was our lucky break as long as we could capitalize on it.

It's Time to Bet on Indians

Excelan was six months old and still without funding.

Despite our progress, breaking through the venture capital world was proving tougher than expected. The venture capitalists Inder met with—and the few we pitched to as a team—were reluctant, blinded by their biases. I didn't expect it to be this hard to raise money.

At the same time, I was getting an unfiltered view of the corporate world's cutthroat nature. I was serving on a grand jury that met monthly for a year. Among the cases we reviewed was an FBI sting operation that caught Hitachi, Fujitsu, and NEC Corporation (Nippon Electric Company, Ltd) executives attempting to illegally purchase IBM's trade secrets. Over twenty people were eventually indicted. The business world was not for the faint of heart.

As things got tighter, I turned to an old ally—my former boss at Singer-Link, Roger Dahlberg. Roger respected my ambition and had once mentioned that his wife, Marilyn, worked for John Freidenrich, a founding partner of the prestigious law firm Ware, Fletcher & Freidenrich in Palo Alto. They were major players in Silicon Valley. Roger had told me that when I was ready to pitch a startup idea, John might help. That moment had arrived.

Roger arranged the introduction, and I brought Inder and Navin to the meeting. We pitched to John in his firm's conference room, and I took the lead. I laid out Excelan's vision—networking computers in a heterogeneous environment, the untapped market potential, our early sales traction, and our competitive edge. John listened intently, taking copious notes. By the end, he was impressed.

"We'll invest $25,000 right away," he said, "and provide $20,000 in legal services, deferring fees until you secure funding." Then came a game-changing offer: John would arrange a meeting with Bay Partners, a venture capital firm he had helped start—though he didn't disclose this detail at the time.

The introduction to Bay Partners brought us face-to-face with John Bosch, a seasoned executive with no-nonsense candor. Bosch had a solid pedigree, from Fairchild Semiconductor to co-founding a consulting firm. He began due diligence on Excelan, reaching out to our early customers, Plexus and Victory. His questions were thorough and his style direct—qualities I would come to respect.

When we met in person in December, Bosch shared his reservations without any sugar-coating. "Who's going to buy from you? Will White guys work for you?" It was a stark reminder of the biases we faced. We countered with examples of our team, which now included Dale Way, a White marketing veteran from Zilog, and Duane Murray. Bosch, however, remained skeptical.

"I like your plan," he said. "It's smart. Why don't you hire some businesspeople to help you implement it?"

"We already have sales," I said.

After considering this, he said something unexpected. "Indians haven't been entrepreneurs," he mused, almost to himself. "Why not? They're smart, they're hardworking … Maybe it's time to try."

He made eye contact with each of us—Navin, Inder, and me—before delivering his decision. "We'll put in one million dollars," he said, "and either you or I need to find someone else to match it. For 50 percent of the company."

Bosch stood, but before leaving the room, he made his terms clear. "This offer is non-negotiable. Take it or leave it. I'll give you fifteen minutes to decide."

CHAPTER 10
Crossroads of Crisis

WHAT HAD SEEMED IMPOSSIBLE FOR nearly eight months was now happening with lightning speed.

After accepting the offer, our attention quickly turned to finding another VC willing to invest $1 million. Someone had decided to bet on us and we weren't going to waste one precious moment of this opportunity. Within days, John Bosch arranged for us to have a phone conversation with John Dougery, a business acquaintance who had recently started his own VC company with two others after breaking away from Citi Corp Venture Capital. Dougery had an MBA from Stanford Business School and had launched and sold a startup to Xerox Corp before getting into the venture capital game.

Dougery knew his way around the battlefield. He was also a perfect match for us in the sense that his VC company was new, and when you are new in that arena, you have to go looking for good investments. The best deals go to the established players. So Dougery was motivated to find a good opportunity.

Dougery and one of his partners visited us in our cramped office. At this time when businesses were being launched in bedrooms and garages, Dougery paid no notice to our location in a strip mall; as we showed him our small lab in the area behind our desks, he let us know that he liked what he saw. He was impressed by our experience, skills, and maturity. He liked our focus on doing one thing well—networking. He also agreed with our assessment of the market.

"You are pretty much in the infancy of this area," he said. "There's a wave to ride. And I don't see any substantial incumbents to compete against in this particular area."

Dougery backed his opinion in the most meaningful way—with his money. He invested the other $1 million to match Bosch's investment. It is always easier to go in once a first investor has done all the work. Many years later I asked Dougery if he'd had any reservations about investing in a business run by Indians. It was such a rarity at the time.

He said that while Indians were regarded as topflight engineers, he thought they had been unfairly stereotyped and added, "I am personally not interested in a particular person's skin color or religion or ethnicity. As long as they have a good idea and are driven to succeed, I'm interested."

About a year after making his investment, Dougery was speaking with an old colleague of his who had become a prominent executive recruiter in the Bay Area. The recruiter asked Dougery about his latest investment. Dougery told him about Excelan. His recruiter friend wanted to know about the people running this business. He described us as smart and driven, really good, solid bets. He said we also happened to be Indian.

There was a pause on the other end. "I'd never back an Indian," the recruiter said.

"Why not?" Dougery asked.

"I don't trust 'em," his friend said.

Perceptions would change over time, but that was the harsh reality of Silicon Valley in 1982 and, as I would experience, it was still reality a few years later. But the deal went through at the end of December. We had our funding, finally. Coincidentally, our former real estate agent partner with the famous name notified us that he wanted his office back. We quickly found a new space, an office suite on the top floor in an unfinished office building in an industrial park that was still under construction. It was a step up from the strip mall—or would be soon. We moved over a weekend.

Settling into the new space had its moments. One day there was a bad infestation of ants in the office, the aftermath of a flood outside the building. Navin and I chased each other around the floor, each of us jockeying for position in front of the other. Someone asked what was going on and it highlighted in a comedic manner the differences between a Jain and a Sikh. "I'm killing ants," I said, holding up the bottle of Raid in my hand. Navin was scooping them up in a cardboard box and taking them outside.

"They might feel the same pain as us," he said.

The winter of '82 was one of the coldest in anyone's memory. Our new office space was an unfinished shell of a building that did not have any heat, any walls or any flooring for that matter. My brother and I bought some plastic sheets and stapled them on the rafters and used bricks to hold them on the ground. We found an ad in the paper for carpet remnants. We added a heater and the place became workable, though if you stepped outside the plastic it was freezing. Nobody left their desk. It reminded me of my first winter at Michigan Tech, when the snow was the worst on record in decades and I never left the computer lab.

When the dozen or so people we now had on payroll came to work on the following Monday, I handed each one of them a stuffed penguin. Those employees were forever known as Penguins; and years later, after Excelan went public and made many of them millionaires, they pointed to their penguins as a badge of honor.

The Flaw

By February, the competitive landscape was just as I had pictured. It was the Wild West.

Sun Microsystems was up and running. Unix operating system was coming into its own, and there were about fifty startups building super microcomputers around various powerful micro-processors; standard busses were being announced on a regular basis. IBM and Digital had their own communication protocols. Major corporate players like Boeing and GM (General Motors) and even European countries pushed for a standardized protocol, one language that would let computers talk to each other. Most saw OSI (Open Systems Interconnection) as the nirvana for down the road.

Inder, Navin, and I met often to discuss this situation, knowing every decision we made would shape the future of our company. There was no room for hesitation—Excelan would either lead in this game or struggle to survive. A middle ground didn't exist. It was a point I hammered about repeatedly: computers needed to talk to each other. Ethernet provided physical connection and hardware connectivity, but real interoperability, the final step, rested on the software protocols needed to connect at the application level.

The question was, which one? IBM, SNA, DECnet, OSI, or something else? That was the debate. The industry was at a crossroads, and so were we.

Inder wanted to wait, to see which protocol would emerge as the winner. I pushed back—waiting meant falling behind. I had to sell my boards now, not gamble on what might happen later.

My original concept turned out to be flawed.

We did not offer a *complete* solution. We offered hardware, not software. We sold to OEMs (original equipment manufacturers) and they wrote the software for their machines, which not only took them time, but after completing that job, they needed even more time to sell their computers and that slowed our sales. We were selling raw hardware that end users were unable to use. It was like selling a car chassis without the engine.

We were a cog in the process, only half the solution, not the saving grace. As such, Excelan's business was dependent on middlemen, the OEMs. I took responsibility for not seeing this issue earlier. It was one of those things I could not have known until we got to this point. One day it dawned on me that the reason IBM's PC was so popular was because it arrived with the software, word processing and a spreadsheet, so that it could be used immediately. Excelan could connect machines but did not provide the software so they could talk to each other. The customer still needed an application to enable them to communicate.

Still, we were busy. We had thirty-five OEM customers, but they were not buying enough product from us. We did not have enough focus, we were under-resourced to write software for each of our OEMs, and we did not have the right story for the marketplace. We did not have the complete story, the story we needed. I would sound like a broken record. I knew what needed to be done but I wasn't able to manifest it. Inder and I were constantly at odds about company priorities. Our CFO, Jim Tolonen, a relatively new hire, sensed the tension between us. Inder spent much of his days in his office. I was hands-on with our employees. We were two different poles of energy and ideas.

We were supposed to do $2 million in revenue in 1983 but only did about half a million. I was very disappointed with Inder and felt that he was not holding his end well. I worried we would be in big trouble with the VCs. For some reason, though, they continued to believe and gave us an additional $2 million at 2X the previous valuation.

YAFO

Despite the funding, I feared for Excelan's still young and fragile existence. Inder had the opposite reaction. He felt empowered.

He was not only CEO, but thanks to the additional percentage of stock he got when we hired Duane Murray, he was also Excelan's majority stakeholder. He never gave up his idea of running a full-fledged computer company, and he exerted his influence to lead us into manufacturing an Ethernet monitoring machine, basically a network analyzer. It was called Nutcracker.

It was a trouble-shooting device that sat on the network and monitored the flow of traffic—or the lack of it. *Why is this computer not responding? Why is that computer not sending?* We bought the computer from a company in Southern California and assembled the parts ourselves: an Intel-8086 processor, a 10Mb Winchester drive, and a floppy drive. We put our board inside, and we wrote the software. We spent about $1 million on inventory to build about 100 units, not including the salaries for our engineers.

Nutcracker was available from March 1984. Units were priced at $50,000. Without a seasoned sales force or marketing strategy, though, Nutcrackers sat unsold. A Carnegie-Mellon University evaluation of the product concluded the hardware was "quite unreliable," "there were many unexplained system crashes," and "from a functional point of view, a very serious shortcoming of the Nutcracker is its inability to communicate with any other computers on an Ethernet."

In my opinion, Nutcracker was an example of the mistake so many startups make. They stray from the mission, lose focus, squander resources, and eventually find themselves in trouble, which is what I feared would happen to Excelan. A CEO's job is to make choices, often hard choices and hopefully the right choices. I did not think Inder was being decisive, and while he waited for a specific networking protocol to emerge victorious, he indulged in Nutcracker—what I refer to as a YAFO.

YAFO stands for "yet another friggin' opportunity." YAFOs are distractions that a founder pursues when they are not focused on the opportunity the startup is trying to address. They move the target or they add another one, resulting in, among other things, confusion. Startups are fragile and typically under-resourced. Under the best of circumstances, they are likely to fail. When a founder starts to think of other potential opportunities, they exponentially increase the chances of failure.

YAFOs are what kill startups. YAFOs take away time, focus, energy, and precious resources—and I saw that happening to Excelan. Decisions needed to be made.

TCP/IP

The time had come to eliminate the need for our customers to write their own software. We had to sell a more complete solution, the hardware *and* the software. The question was: What should we choose?

Everyone had their own solution. Many industry groups were adopting ISO protocols. IBM and DEC had their own proprietary networking protocols (SNA and DECnet) that they were selling while also promising a future move to ISO/OSI. Big corporations like Boeing and GM had lined up behind ISO/OSI, and it seemed like most of the networking startups were going with Xerox PARC's XNS.

Confused? Everybody was. There were too many choices but no real solutions.

I landed on TCP/IP. The protocol had been developed by DARPA (Defense Advanced Research Projects Agency) at UCLA. In keeping with the Defense Department's gift for acronyms, it stood for Transmission Control Protocol/Internet Protocol. If the Ethernet was the highway that connected one computer to another, TCP/IP was the vehicle that transported packages of information along this road, making sure there were no stalls or crashes along the way.

TCP/IP did not enjoy much industry support. DARPA had built it for the slow and unreliable phone networks on a battlefield. All the inherent recovery routines in it gave it a bad rap among people who only prioritized speed. Indeed, in the world of the tortoise and the hare, TCP/IP was the slow moving, unfashionable turtle with short, stubby legs and hard shell exterior. But who won the race in the fairy tale?

TCP/IP had two very useful, ready-made applications—FTP (file transfer protocols) and Telenet (virtual terminal protocols) that could be used immediately. I reasoned it would scoot along quite nicely and reliably on the Ethernet, and I was right. I hired two outside consultants, Bill Northlich and Bruce Borden to port TCP/IP to our Ethernet boards and by early spring of 1984, it appeared I had chosen correctly. We were the go-to for TCP/IP.

When I was growing up in India, there was a billboard promoting the popular pain reliever Aspro. It was ubiquitous. It said, "For headache, take Aspro." That made an impression on me. It was simple and direct. It stated the problem and provided the solution. I made a bet on TCP/IP. I did not have any formal training to help me understand the market or marketing, but my background in first principles problem solving let me understand it intuitively. One, identify the problem customers have; and two, let them know you have the solution.

I identified the pain—the machines people were buying couldn't be networked. Our solution? Excelan's board with TCP/IP would solve this problem and work straight out of the box.

A Company Divided

Inder was still enamored with Nutcracker. He did not believe in my solution. He was not marketing TCP/IP. We had a plan to do $10 million and be profitable in 1984. But we fell short again, doing only $5 million and losing $2.5 million. We were a company divided. We had problems, and the board was about to wise up.

I Was Embarrassed

As accounting buttoned up for the year, a revenue recognition problem surfaced. Revenue that was being counted did not actually materialize. The sales were not quite sales.

Apparently, we were sending products, mostly Nutcrackers, to customers based on their promise to pay if it worked; and if it didn't work, they didn't have to pay until we fixed it. In other words, we were shipping products on a contingency and recording sales for which we had not yet received the money. It was not an uncommon practice in the industry. Neither was it illegal.

The board summoned Inder for questioning. It was a delicate moment for Excelan as we had recently closed a new round of financing and the board felt that crucial information had surfaced after the fact. As CEO, Inder was responsible for providing explanations, and ultimately, we had to revise our sales and revenue numbers down. As a result, the board slashed our valuation from $15 million pre-money to $10 million. Inder accepted the decision without protest.

I was irate when he told me. How could he agree to reduce our valuation without discussing it with me? How could he have not pushed back? Did he understand the implication?

The two of us met in January 1985. His position was in jeopardy, he said, and the three of us—Navin, him and me—needed to stick together. All for one and one for all. If we threatened to walk out together, the board would not touch us. Otherwise, all three of us would be let go.

He did not make sense to me. I had no idea why John Bosch and John Dougery would want to fire any of us. As we continued to discuss the situation, the revenue recognition problem came out. It also came out that the board assumed that Navin and I knew of it and approved. I connected the dots and was immediately horrified by the picture it painted of me. I was angry that my character would be questioned. Why would I do anything to jeopardize my reputation? Or Excelan itself?

The company was not only my idea, but I was also living and breathing its ups and downs every day. It was my life.

There Were Conversations

I did not know it at the time, but board members were having conversations.

Jim Tolonen, our CFO, was employee number fifteen or thereabouts. He joined Excelan in the spring of 1983, after the weather began to warm and I stopped handing out penguins. We had a good relationship based on mutual respect. He once asked me how I became so good at math. I told him my grandfather, before he had his second stroke, walked with a cane, and when he heard me coming down the hall, he would shout out a math problem, like 232 divided by twelve. Then he would hit me with his cane until I gave him the answer. The situation at Excelan reminded me of those trips down the hall. I felt like I was being hit again.

Board member John Dougery asked me to meet him for lunch at his firm's office. He was waiting for me in the conference room. It was just the two of us. I sensed tension as soon as I walked in. Once small talk was out of the way, Dougery got straight to the point. He told me about the revenue issues that had come up. Without revealing all his cards, he said the board intended to take action of some sort, but more immediately he wanted to know if I would leave the company if he was no longer part of it.

"Absolutely not," I said.

"What about Navin?" he asked.

"He'll stay, too."

The only one who left was Inder. He went home one day and never returned. His absence was not explained or officially acknowledged to the board or me or anyone else. Jim Tolonen let me know confidentially the board was having conversations about finding a new CEO and what was next for Excelan. I was not privy to these talks, but I knew what they were asking each other. Should they search for a new CEO outside the company? Or was one of the other founders able to fill the role?

From what I heard later on, most were convinced they needed to look elsewhere. But apparently when that last question was posed, Jim immediately mentioned my name. In a small startup, he said, it did not make sense to bring in someone who did not have the trust and respect of the team.

"And Kanwal has it?" someone asked.

"Yes," Jim said.

A Battlefield Promotion

I did not know what was going on with Inder, whether he had been let go, quit, or he had simply decided to sit at home and see what might happen next.

From my perspective, all that mattered was, Inder was missing in action and his disappearance put Excelan in a precarious situation. We spent several weeks without a leader. Decisions had to be made. I endured until I felt the situation was becoming detrimental to the company. I reported it to John Bosch. We were rudderless, I said. Excelan could not hold a steady course much longer without a captain at the helm.

A meeting with the board was hastily arranged. I walked into the conference room and everyone was there—Bosch, Dougery, and Ed Shea, an influential real estate developer who had joined the board. There was a review of the revenue recognition problem that had surfaced and initiated the circumstances we found ourselves in now. Tones were clipped, tempers were on edge, and the money that had been invested in us was mentioned several times.

John Dougery railed against Indians, characterizing them as liars and cheats. He explicitly referred to me, Navin, and Inder as bastards.

"We never should have invested in this company," he said.

I jumped up from my chair and stepped toward Dougery, ready to defend myself, my family, and my people. I was not a physical person, but until you have experienced the sting of such prejudice, you can't possibly know the force with which it hits. I was a forty year old man. I had raised a family, worked hard, become an American citizen, chased the big dream, and lived an upright life. I wasn't going to take that kind of personal attack sitting down. I wanted to hit back.

"You can't talk to me that way," I said in a harsh voice that immediately put the entire room on pause.

I am happy to say that John Dougery and I would go on to become great friends and partners and investors in many startups, but in that moment, emotions took the meeting in a direction it shouldn't have gone. Rarely does the glass ceiling crack without some bruises or bloodshed. Excelan was in serious trouble and the reality of that hit everyone hard. Once tempers cooled, a more productive conversation ensued. Our core business, networking, was doing well. The problem areas were problems. How could we quickly address them?

John Bosch explained the board needed to find a CEO, the implication being that he had been right all along that we didn't have the experience to run a company. However, until they made that hire, I was given the title of interim CEO. It was a battlefield promotion. Not exactly a vote of confidence. It was a desperate act by men hoping not to lose their money, but ready and willing to turn the page if necessary.

There would be no new financing until Excelan had a new CEO. That was the board's decision. We were in a tight spot—no, a chokehold. We had $800,000 in the bank and were burning $150,000 a month. That gave us not quite six months to live, assuming nothing changed. But things had to change. The board's directive to me was blunt: Stop losing money. Don't do anything reckless. Keep the lights on until we find a proper CEO to take charge.

I walked back to my office, shut the door, and let the silence settle for just a moment. It was the eye of the storm, a brief pause before stepping back into battle. It was the temporary calm before a hurricane. The painting of the elephant on the wall behind me told me everything

I needed to do: cut a new path through the jungle. Some wondered what that path should be. I didn't.

I had spent the last year arguing with Inder, pushing for a leaner, sharper focus on interoperability. I had watched opportunity slip through our fingers, frustrated at our inefficiencies and wrongheaded decisions. Without fully realizing it, I had been thinking about this day for a long time. What surprised me was how naturally I stepped into the role. Maybe it was because I had no choice. But leadership is one of those things—you either have it, or you don't.

The board trusted me—but just enough. Others doubted me. None of that mattered. Life gives you a few turning points. This was one of mine. If I hesitated, Excelan would die. I didn't hesitate.

Within no time, I had all my department heads in my office. The air was electric—part fear, part uncertainty, part excitement. They knew something had shifted, and they were right. I laid it out clearly—Inder was gone, I was in charge, and the game was changing. No, it had changed. And when I said "immediate," I meant *right now*.

The moment they walked out of that office, they were stepping into a new world, the same as me. I needed them to understand the stakes—to commit fully or step aside.

Failure wasn't an option.

CHAPTER

11

Making Moves: The Art of Survival

TIME IS THE MOST PRECIOUS resource given to any one of us. Rich or poor, powerful or weak, intelligent or ignorant, we all have twenty-four hours in a day. No one gets a second longer. How much time we have in our life is unpredictable and different for everyone.

The same is true for how we use it. Do you waste time? Do you take advantage of the time you are given? Do you see time as money, as Benjamin Franklin did? Do you agree with the Greek philosopher who said, "Time is the most valuable thing a man can spend"? I was more in agreement with William Shakespeare who said, "Better three hours too soon than a minute too late."

I drove home that night hearing the clock ticking. I broke the news to Ann and my family. Ann gave me a look that said it was about time and let me know she had full confidence in my ability to turn the company around. As always, getting the nod from the family's CEO meant a lot. My children thought it was cool that I was the chief—like an Indian chief. My head was filled with ideas; I spent the night organizing my To Do list. The company was mine. I had a free hand to do what I wanted, what I thought was necessary and vital to Excelan's survival.

The next morning I arrived at the office, early. It was day one of my term as interim CEO, and I began it in a dramatic fashion: I laid off one-third of the employees. Nearly all of them worked on Nutcracker.

People think of layoffs as heartless. But sometimes and in fact many times, they are about survival. Businesses are amoral entities. Survival is an imperative. You do whatever you need to do as long as you are following the laws of the land, the laws of physics, and the laws of economics. I estimated those layoffs would preserve enough cash to last the company eight to twelve more months. Were there going to be more cutbacks? That was the question everyone asked, and I didn't blame them. But I didn't know yet.

"Part of this house is on fire," I said. "I need to let that burn so I can save the other side of the house."

Our Only Hope for Survival

I am not much into airy-fairy strategic thinking or pie-in-the-sky plans. I like clear, recognizable goal posts. My most immediate goal, and the only one that mattered, was to keep the company alive for as long as possible, and I knew our only hope for survival was our bread and butter: TCP/IP technology.

Starting day one, I sharpened the company's focus. It was a hard turn of the wheel. No more hardware; we were going to embrace what was working, our networking software. This was the work Bill Northlich and Bruce Borden had done porting TCP/IP to our Ethernet boards. I decided to only support the networking of IBM PCs (which were selling almost 100,000 a day), UNIX machines (sales were about 10,000 per month), and DEC minicomputers (they were selling about 3,000 per month). This focus would reduce complexity within the company by almost 99 percent.

What do I mean by that? It narrowed our market, but it gave Excelan something it had lacked before—a clear and well-defined story to tell the marketplace. A clear story is for both insiders and outsiders. If the employees believe in the product, they will buy into the work. If the focus is sharp, everybody up and down the line can make good decisions. They see the goal. The sharper the knife, the deeper it cuts. Do one thing right rather than two things half-assed.

If you had a problem networking your computers, Excelan had a solution for you. "For headache, take Aspro." The message could not have been any more simple, clear, or straightforward. *If you have a problem networking your computers, Excelan has a solution for you.* I wrote it on a white board and sent it around in a memo. It became the company's focus for the next ninety days.

Then there was the matter of the Nutcracker. I put our network analyzer on a fire sale to clear out the inventory. We had forty or so unsold boxes. We had been selling them for $50,000 a piece. I cut the price to $25,000 and heavily incentivized the sales staff to move them quickly. Over the next few months it brought in $1 million that had otherwise just been sitting on the shelf. That plus the $800,000 I had plus the salary I was saving from the layoffs bought me even more time to consider my next moves.

The clock was ticking ...

Value Pricing

We had a pricing issue.

Excelan was by and large a technology supplier to OEMs—about three dozen of them by the time I became CEO in March of 1985. These OEMs built super-microcomputers using a variety of microprocessors and busses. Most of them ran a version of UNIX, many of them were packaged as engineering workstations with CAD (computer-aided design) applications bundled in. By the time I became CEO in March of 1985, Excelan had signed more than thirty OEMs. We had everybody but Sun Microsystems as our customer.

These OEMs bundled our TCP/IP and Ethernet boards to network enable their boxes. Unfortunately, none of them generated enough volume for us—nor could they. That was the problem. Our boards were priced at $2,000, discounted to around $800, with a manufacturing cost of about $350. So almost a 60 percent margin, which was good. It was the software pricing where things fell apart.

We sold the open sourced TCP/IP software to the OEMs, which they customized for their machines as a polished, finished product. We charged the OEM a one-time fee of $20,000 and $60 for every copy they sold. But $60 for software for PC, UNIX and minicomputers didn't make sense. They were three different products. Consider: The PC was priced at $2000, and a spreadsheet for a PC cost $400. A UNIX machine was $10,000. The same spreadsheet was priced at $2000. A minicomputer was $100,000, and a spreadsheet that ran on it was $4,000.

We were $60 across the board. Why?

Chevrolets and Cadillacs were the same car under the hood for a long time. But Chevys were half the price. Why? The cars were value priced to the market. Value pricing is a strategy that sets a price based on the customer's perceived value. A diamond may have one price at the mall. Put it in a blue Tiffany box and it's another price.

Once I thought about this, I realized the pricing for our software also had to be redone for the end user market. What would users pay for the software? I looked at the Digital pricelist. I looked at the IBM pricelist. I don't know why I never checked the math before, but once I did, it was a revelation.

I asked our VP of sales how many copies he thought would sell that year. He said maybe 10,000. That meant $600,000 in revenue.

"If you have a blowout year, the best you can imagine, how many will you sell?" I asked.

"Maybe 20,000," he said.

I did the math. That blowout year added up to $1.2 million. I had fifteen engineers on the payroll, each one making a salary of about $100,000 a year.

"My engineers are costing me $1.5 million. I'm still losing money. It doesn't make sense—even in the best of circumstances."

I went back to my office and began looking for a solution. It required breaking down the problem. Every market has three segments—luxury, value, and price sensitivity. At the top, people don't care what they spend. At the bottom, they want the cheapest. The value market looks for something stylish and functional at a good value. Excelan was in the value market.

I set out to discover the highest price I could charge for our software at which our customers would not walk away. In the process, I found an unexpected solution.

The Process

I started every day the same: early, at my desk, writing a memo to myself—a brief, one or two page reflection on the day's priorities.

As my career advanced, these daily memos became a disciplined exercise in thinking through problems; at this early and crucial juncture in my career as an entrepreneur, these daily memos were an essential conversation I had to have about the big decisions I was making and there was no one I could have it with other than myself.

Being CEO of a business is isolating under the best of circumstances. In my position, the isolation was more pronounced. So was the pressure I felt. Every decision I made had the aura of life or death, and I had to make each one on my own. I did not have a mentor, guru, or previous CEO to turn to for counsel. It would have been nice to feel like I had an open door to the board, and who knows, maybe I did. But I feared such discussions with Bosch, Dougery, and the others would only confirm their concerns that I wasn't up to the job.

Hence the daily debate with myself.

Was my understanding of the situation still accurate? Were my assumptions holding up under scrutiny? Was I still on the right path? Was I playing it safe or going for a win? I listed pros and cons. I analyzed the market and the competition. I looked at all sides of an issue or a problem. I relied on my first principles training. I did not have time for maybe. It was either yes or no. You can always find reasons why you shouldn't do something or why you are going to fail. I was always trying to find a reason why I would succeed.

That's how I arrived at the solution that probably saved the company—and it was right in front of me the whole time.

Tweaking the Plan

We were going to sell to everyone.

I called an emergency meeting of all our engineers and salespeople and explained that we were not going to stay in business if we continued to follow our OEM strategy. I announced the change in our business plan. Going forward, we would package our networking solutions directly for end users so we could bypass the OEMs. I was back to one of our original fundamentals: Who were our customers?

"We are going to sell to everyone," I explained, echoing the statement I had made to Inder and Navin about our potential customer base back when we discussed the idea for Excelan over pizza, back when I saw the world was changing and the impending need to be *connected*. "But instead of selling a board and a piece of software to OEMs, we will sell the complete solution, all packaged in a box, including a screwdriver."

I saw a mix of reactions, from confused looks and raised eyebrows to heads nodding in agreement.

"We are also going to include a money back guarantee or we will send a technician to make it work," I continued.

I wanted customers to be able to use our networking product right out of the box. I wanted them to have faith that it would work, that they were getting good value for their money and a product they could trust and manage. And with the promise of sending out a technician or returning the purchase price, I was not only assuming a cost to ensure a sale, but I was also building trust with the customer to ensure a relationship that would result in future sales.

Yes, this was a change in strategy several years into the game, but it was a necessary one—and this kind of pivot is a legitimate tool as long as it helps to sharpen your focus and react to the marketplace. Think of a startup as driving on a mountain road at night. You don't have much visibility as the road bends and turns abruptly. One has to stay on the road by making those sharp turns. Mistakes become apparent. New tech arrives on the scene. The market changes.

A good, solid business plan should have the flexibility to change, too.

Good Business Is Good Math

When we decided to package a complete solution for networking IBM PCs, DEC VAXes, and UNIX machines, we knew we were solving a major pain point for our end users. These customers didn't want to cobble together solutions—they wanted something that worked out of the box. We'd deliver that: everything they needed to connect their systems to Ethernet networks, in one package. Just take it out of the box and start using it.

But there was one critical challenge we still had to tackle: pricing.

I wrestled with the problem, thinking back to a saying from my childhood: *Mehenga roye ek baar, sasta roye baar baar.* Expensive makes you cry once; cheap makes you cry over and over. That wisdom stuck with me. End users weren't looking for the cheapest option—they were looking for value.

Here's how I approached it. DEC was charging $30,000 for DECNet connections, and IBM was charging $45,000 for similar setups. I didn't have their brand power or market clout, but I knew we had the same functionality. The math had to work for us and for the customer. I settled on pricing: $2,500 for PCs, $5,000 for UNIX machines, and $15,000 for minicomputers.

Then came the software. It was priced at $60 at the time—far too low for the value it delivered. I made the call to raise it to $600. My VP of sales thought I'd lost my mind. "Six hundred dollars for a floppy disk?" he exclaimed. But I explained that this wasn't just about a floppy—it was about the complete solution. The software had been priced to sell hardware. Now it was going to be bundled to the hardware. It wasn't an add-on anymore. It was part of the complete solution. It should have a single price.

And guess what? The market validated our decision. Some customers grumbled, sure, but no one dropped us. Why $600? Why not $6,000 or $60,000? Because $600 hit the sweet spot—it was high enough to reflect the software's value, but still felt reasonable to the customer.

This pricing move simplified our business, improved our margins, and—most importantly—made customers happier. They saw value in what we offered.

This taught me a lesson I have repeated countless times. Pricing has nothing to do with cost. It's all about value, and value lives in the eyes of the customer. A good price feels like a deal, even if it's higher than what they paid before.

Mehenga roye ek baar, sasta roye baar baar. Good business is good math. Always.

Marketing

Up until this point, Excelan did not have a sharp focus and consequently it did not have a clear story to tell in the marketplace. We relied on the OEMs to do all the work. But everything was different now. We had a clear story to tell. The entire company was highly energized. I could feel it when I walked through the office. Everyone shared a sense of purpose. We had to tell people what we were doing. Actually, we *wanted* to tell people what we were doing.

We had to make sure people knew we had a solution to their problem. We had to go big with marketing.

I met with Subhash Bal, our VP of marketing and a fellow IIT graduate. I told him that I wanted to launch an aggressive ad campaign. We needed a sharply defined message that would sell the product. "Identify the need, then tell people we have their solution." He said marketing's job is to create awareness, not to sell. I said, "I need to sell. If you won't help me sell, why do I need you?"

Yes, that was a little blunt, but I could be blunt. Subhash knew this about me. He also knew I was on a mission to make Excelan succeed and nothing else mattered, nothing was going to stand in my way, and he fell in line quickly.

On the whiteboard in my office, I wrote the wording that had become my mantra. *We are going to connect your PC to your UNIX machine to your minicomputer. If you have a problem, we have your solution.* I also sketched the illustration I wanted of our products. It was nearly the same drawing I had made three and a half years before on a napkin. It just took us all this time to get back to this place.

The ad was perfect. Clear. Simple. Direct. You could see it, read it, and know not only was it speaking to you, but it was also going to solve your problem.

Because we had less than a handful of salespeople compared to larger companies with several dozen people, I did something novel at the time to reach our end users. The ad copy said that operators were standing by to take orders. You could call us and place an order. Nobody had sold this type of equipment by phone before. It communicated a sense of immediacy. *Got a headache? We got Aspro!* We were ready and waiting to help you.

I budgeted $50,000 per month on advertising. It was one of the riskiest bets I made since the cash burn shortened the runway. The ads began running in industry and trade magazines in June—less than ninety days after I took over as interim CEO and one month before we were ready with the product. I could not afford the product being ready and available without anyone knowing about it. If the new product sat on the shelf, we were doomed. Everything had to be perfectly coordinated and calibrated. The product had to work. The pricing had to be right. The marketing had to reach the right people. Or else.

I will never forget coming into the office the day the ads began to run. I was at the office early. Everybody else showed up soon after. The company-wide buy-in was amazing. All of us were eager for feedback on the marketing, on all the long hours and hard work. And then we got it. The phone started to ring.

CHAPTER

12

Numbers, Power, and Leadership

MARKET FEEDBACK CAN BE INTOXICATING.

There's nothing quite like the buzz of phones ringing with orders, each one a validation of your vision. When I stepped into my first board meeting as interim CEO, I felt great. Over the past four months, we had achieved what most companies would take a year or more to accomplish. I shared with the board the sweeping changes I had made—streamlining operations, cutting costs, and sharpening our focus. The market was responding, and I was riding high on the energy of those early wins. I could even see revenue on the verge of a significant uptick.

"I feel very good about the business and our prospects beyond survival," I began confidently.

Before I could finish, John Bosch, one of the board members, cut me off.

"Yada-yada-yada," he said bluntly. "Spare me the story. Show me the numbers."

His words stopped me cold. I didn't have the numbers yet. It was too soon for concrete projections. I realized this wasn't a rebuke—it was a wake-up call. The board had been burned before, and trust wasn't going to be handed back overnight. Bosch didn't want enthusiasm; he wanted evidence.

Those four words—*Show me the numbers*—were a masterclass in leadership and accountability.

By mid-August, I had the numbers. I sent Bosch a memo outlining our performance:

> **General Overview:**
>
> *The month of July was very satisfactory from the point of view of sales, profits, and gross margins. Net sales of $895K were the best ever. Profits of $47K exceeded expectations, and gross margins stood at a healthy 65.9%.*
>
> **Prospects for the Rest of the Year:**
>
> *Generally optimistic. A slew of new products is being introduced, supported by stepped-up marketing activities. Our sales target of $10.8 million remains achievable.*

Bosch's reply was brief: "Good numbers. Thanks."

That moment crystallized a critical lesson for me. As entrepreneurs, we must run our businesses by numbers, not by feelings or anecdotes. Revenue, gross margins, costs, expenses, headcount, growth rates—these are the vital metrics that tell the real story.

Setting clear numerical goals for yourself and your team is essential. But it doesn't stop there. You must also stay on top of your competitors' numbers and benchmark your performance against them. As your business grows, managing by the numbers becomes the only reliable way to maintain control and drive success.

John Bosch's words never left me. Numbers don't lie. Everything else is just fluff.

The Power Equation

In any deal, you either hold the power, or you don't. Understanding where you stand is key to driving a resolution that works in your favor.

Our old business was still hanging on. About a month into my role, NCR (National Cash Register), one of our biggest OEM customers, reached out, ready to purchase Ethernet boards in volume. Along with Sperry, Siemens, and MASSCOMP, NCR was one of four OEMs driving significant sales for us. Although I had already shifted focus to our new strategy, I couldn't afford to let go of this revenue stream just yet.

Our contract with NCR was detailed. They received a 60 percent discount on hardware and software, agreed to buy boards in lots of 200, and committed to giving us ninety-days' notice for procurement and sixty days for firm orders. To anticipate their demand, I decided to build 200 boards, tying up $60,000 in cash—a risky move for our cash-strapped company. Ninety days passed with no firm order. I felt like I'd made a costly mistake.

Then, at the end of May, NCR placed an expedited order, demanding shipment via FedEx. They ignored our agreed timelines and the clause requiring them to pay expediting and shipping costs. When I reminded their buyer of the terms, he threatened to cancel the order. I had no leverage. We needed the sale to meet our numbers. So, I ate the costs and shipped.

The same story repeated in June. Once again, I pre-built the boards, waited for the order, and scrambled to meet their last-minute demand. They refused to pay the extra costs. By this point, I was irritated and felt exploited. But the reality was clear—I couldn't enforce our contract yet.

Then July came, and our new strategy began to bear fruit. End-user sales were surging, and the phones wouldn't stop ringing. For the third time, I prepped 200 boards for NCR, expecting their usual end-of-month antics. Sure enough, their order came two days before the deadline. But this time, I was ready.

When their buyer demanded expedited shipping without covering the extra costs, I refused. Calmly but firmly, I told him to cancel the order if he couldn't honor our agreement. We no longer needed NCR to hit our numbers. Suddenly, the tables turned. He panicked and pleaded for the shipment. I held my ground, repeating, "Read the contract."

The issue escalated to his boss, who called to "resolve the misunderstanding." I explained that we valued NCR as a customer but needed them to respect the terms of our agreement. After digging into the facts, he apologized and agreed to cover all charges. From that point on, NCR gave us proper notice for orders and even began purchasing our new products. They eventually dropped their in-house networking efforts, recommending Excelan boards directly to their customers—a massive win for us. Our OEM partners saw the value of what we were doing.

Every business relationship has a power dynamic. Recognizing whether you're holding a strong or weak hand is crucial. When NCR's orders were vital to us, I accepted their terms, even if it stung. But once our position improved, I asserted our rights, making sure they understood our value.

In negotiations, timing is everything. A strong hand allows you to enforce boundaries and shape the deal. A weak hand, however, requires patience and adaptability. But knowing the difference—that's where the real power lies.

Duck Theory of Management

As an entrepreneur, I've come to realize the importance of taking charge of everything within your control, starting with yourself. It's not just about managing others; it's about leading by example, maintaining composure, and relentlessly working on self-improvement. This approach has shaped what I call the "Duck Theory of Management."

Picture this: you're by a serene pond, watching a duck glide effortlessly across the water. On the surface, it's calm and collected, exuding grace. But beneath the water, its feet are paddling furiously. That duck was me. I made it a point to project calm and confidence to the world while working relentlessly behind the scenes.

Being an effective leader didn't come naturally to me—I had to work at it. I swapped my classic engineer's uniform—a white shirt, dark slacks, and a pocket protector—for sharp, custom-tailored suits. This wasn't just about appearances; it was about stepping into the role of a CEO with confidence, what I liked to call my CEO plumage.

More importantly, I made it a priority to connect with people. Unlike my predecessor, I didn't stay confined to my office. I walked the floor, offered encouragement, asked questions, and made it clear I trusted my team. This wasn't just friendliness; it was deliberate, inspired by the early management style of Hewlett-Packard. I listened to people, held them accountable, and expected them to hold me accountable in return.

When I pivoted Excelan's strategy, some predicted it would take six months, maybe longer, to implement the changes. But I pushed for three months. Surprisingly, there were no objections or complaints. Instead, the team doubled down, working harder and smarter. Why? Because they understood the mission. Everyone in the organization knew the priorities, and if something wasn't on the list, they didn't waste time asking. They trusted the plan—and they trusted me.

The energy at Excelan felt like that of the championship sports teams I admired—the 49ers and the Golden State Warriors. There was a shared bond, a sense of purpose, and an unshakable belief that we could achieve greatness. That's the magic of trust and clarity. Information is power, and when you share it freely, you empower your team. You build a culture of confidence and camaraderie. Hold it back, and you breed doubt and insecurity.

The Duck Theory of Management is about striking that balance—staying calm under pressure while paddling like hell beneath the surface. It's about being accessible, transparent, and relentlessly focused on leading by example. That's how you inspire a team to rise to the occasion and exceed every expectation.

Owning Your Weaknesses: A Path to Growth

In life, you have two choices when faced with challenges—either recognize your shortcomings and take action to fix them or shift the blame on to others. One choice propels you forward; the other guarantees failure.

At Excelan, Jim Tolonen was often the first person I spoke to each day. Like me, Jim was an early riser. Despite my rapid speech and my accent—which even my wife lovingly teased me about—Jim claimed to have no trouble understanding me. "I've got the right kind of ear," he used to say. But not everyone shared his ability. I'd catch team members leaning over to their neighbors in meetings, whispering, "What did he say?"

As Excelan began turning a corner toward profitability, my role started attracting more attention. Speaking invitations came in, and some board members even asked me to mentor CEOs of other companies they'd invested in. But with this visibility came scrutiny, and my communication issues were becoming a concern.

The board, careful to tread lightly, asked Jim to discuss the issue with me. They needn't have worried. I've always embraced self-improvement. Years earlier, I'd taken the Dale Carnegie course to improve my abilities, attended early morning classes, and had constantly sought ways to sharpen my skills. I was well aware that my communication needed work.

That Dale Carnegie course had taught me that effective communication involves three elements: the source (the person speaking), the receiver (the listener), and the channel (how the message is transmitted). It also taught me that the receiver processes information in different ways. Some people listen, others see, some feel, and others just negotiate their way through. For your message to resonate, it has to address all these dimensions.

While you can't control the audience or the channel entirely, you can control the clarity of your message. So I focused on precision. That was reflected in the ad we ran. Excelan had your solution. "After you call our number, the hard part is over." But now, I needed to turn that focus inward—to the source of the message: me.

When Jim brought the board's concerns to my attention, I replied without hesitation: "I'm ready." Tim Harris, our VP of human resources, connected me with Margaret Price, a local speech therapist. Margaret was old-school, tough as nails, and sharp. She didn't flinch when we offered her $15 an hour—three times the minimum wage back then. Instead, she asked for stock. That was my first clue I was dealing with someone shrewd.

When Tim brought her to my office, I was chatting with Jim. Margaret invited both of them to stay and watch. Without warning, she leaned across my desk, grabbed my tongue, and yanked it out of my mouth. She twisted it left and right, up and down, inspecting it carefully. Then she let go.

"I had to do that," she explained, completely unbothered. "I needed to make sure there are no physical impairments to your speech."

That was just the beginning. For six months, Margaret came to my office daily for at least two hours. She drilled me on diction, taught me how to shape my lips and tongue for every sound, and had me practice in front of a mirror. She identified five sounds I could not pronounce. She made me repeat them correctly 100 times a day. My homework was to read aloud from the *Wall Street Journal*'s opinion section, record myself, and then play it back.

"You'll hear yourself improve," she promised. "Eventually, you won't need the recordings—you'll hear your progress naturally."

Margaret's relentless approach worked. After six months, I transitioned to working with a public speaking coach. Improving my communication became an obsession, part of a broader commitment to always strive for excellence. If you fail to address the weaknesses that are within your power to improve, whether personal or professional, you are doomed, especially as an entrepreneur.

My philosophy has always been to give my best effort in everything I do, whether anyone is watching or not. Self-improvement isn't easy, and it's certainly not comfortable. But the rewards are undeniable. The choice is simple: face your weaknesses and grow or blame others and stagnate. For me, the answer has always been clear.

A Sales Insight

We had to learn to speak the customer's language.

One day, during my usual walk around the office, I paused outside the sales area. Susan, our internal salesperson, was on the phone. She seemed to be struggling, fumbling to answer questions about our product. My first thought was that maybe Susan wasn't the best person for handling incoming calls.

Curious, I asked Duane Murray to sit in on a few calls. "Let me know what's happening here," I told him. "Are these serious leads or just time-wasters kicking the tires?"

A few days later, Duane came back with his assessment. "These calls are legitimate," he said. "They're from technical folks who want specific answers about the product—features we have, features we don't, and what's in the pipeline. But Susan can't answer their questions. It's not her fault; she doesn't have the technical background to address them."

It hit me. Of course! When someone with a technical job calls to order equipment, they want to speak with someone who understands them—someone who can respond confidently to technical questions. It was so obvious, yet we had missed it.

I told Duane, "Starting tomorrow, I want you to listen in on Susan's calls. If she can't answer a question, she should hand the phone over to you. You've got the background to handle these inquiries."

Duane took on the task but quickly realized he couldn't sit in on every call. To address this, he created a comprehensive chart—a cheat sheet of sorts—with answers to all the common technical questions. "If they ask about this feature, here's what to say. If they want to know about future updates, here's the plan."

When I reviewed the chart, something clicked. Our salespeople didn't just need a script; they needed the technical depth to have meaningful conversations with potential customers. That's when I introduced the concept of sales engineers.

I pulled Duane out of engineering and placed him in marketing. Over time, he proved so effective that I promoted him to VP of marketing. Together, we fine-tuned our sales process, ensuring that every sales interaction was between a "nerd" and a "nerd." Suddenly, everyone was speaking the same language.

The results? Transformational. Our conversion rates didn't just improve—they skyrocketed tenfold.

The lesson was clear: if you want to close the sale, you've got to speak the customer's language.

In Purchase Orders We Trust

As CEO, I learned quickly that thick skin and a sense of humor were non-negotiable. Call me any name under the sun, take your shots—none of it mattered, as long as I had a purchase order in hand.

Despite Excelan's steady growth, the industry narrative refused to align with reality. The experts and associations couldn't stop predicting TCP/IP's demise, touting OSI protocols as the inevitable future. Boeing and GM, two of our largest customers, even joined forces to push MAP/TOP, an OSI-based initiative. European giants like Siemens threw their weight behind it too, though ironically, Siemens also relied heavily on our products. They even forbade us from naming them publicly as a customer while they championed MAP/TOP.

By 1985, the noise around OSI had reached fever pitch. At an industry conference, Judy Estrin, a co-founder of our rival, Bridge Communications, declared that I must be "brain dead" for pairing TCP/IP with Ethernet. "Why," she quipped, "would you hitch a horse to a finely tuned automobile?"

"Because it works," I thought.

While OSI remained a lofty promise, TCP/IP was proving its mettle in the trenches. Our customers didn't need perfection—they needed reliability. Wall Street firms like Goldman Sachs, Citibank, and Morgan Stanley emerged as major clients. These weren't just financial institutions; they were data-moving machines, and they recognized TCP/IP as the backbone they needed.

Then came a curveball from GM. Their corporate networking czar summoned me to Detroit. GM was spending $30,000 to $40,000 a month with us—a lifeline for a company our size. Once I was seated in his office, he made it clear just how significant that was before delivering his ultimatum:

"If you want to keep GM as a customer, Excelan needs to drop TCP/IP and prioritize OSI. Publicly."

I held my ground. "I'll be ready when OSI happens," I said.

"That's not enough," he replied. "I need you to help lead the way. You need to make OSI your priority."

"I can't," I said. "TCP/IP is what's keeping us alive."

He leaned in, unfazed. "Then Excelan won't see another dollar from GM. We'll blacklist you."

As I left his office and headed for the airport, the weight of the conversation lingered. But then, a front-page story in the *Wall Street*

Journal caught my eye. It was about a state-of-the-art GM plant in Kalamazoo, filled with cutting-edge robots and software. The plant had hosted New York financial journalists to showcase its technological prowess, but during the tour, one of the robots malfunctioned and spray-painted the visitors.

The image of red-faced GM executives trying to explain away a malfunctioning robot was too good. Still smiling, I called my office from a payphone to fill Duane in on the ultimatum I'd just received.

Halfway through my story, Duane interrupted. "You're not going to believe this—we just got our largest order ever from GM. One of their plants. Came in this afternoon."

The irony was rich. While the corporate czar in Detroit played power games, the plant manager, who had to meet deadlines and deliver results, stuck with what worked. He didn't need a robot painting journalists instead of cars. He needed reliable networks.

That moment taught me a lot about the realities of business. Corporate edicts are fine in boardrooms, but on the ground, pragmatism rules. GM stayed a customer. So did Siemens. In fact, Siemens eventually lifted the gag order on our relationship. The tide had turned—TCP/IP was now the standard, not the underdog.

And so, my motto was born: *In purchase orders we trust.*

Congratulations, But ...

I forgot that my role as CEO of Excelan came with a glaring qualifier—interim. I was a stopgap, not the answer.

That August, I brought in Dan Lynch, a luminary in the world of TCP/IP, to help drive industry adoption of this emerging standard. Dan, a brilliant mathematician and former director of computer facilities at Stanford Research Institute, had played a key role in the early days of TCP/IP. He was now at UCLA, asking the crucial question that would shape our future: *How do we ensure that everyone's TCP/IP implementations can interoperate seamlessly?*

Dan became our evangelist, tirelessly promoting the adoption of TCP/IP for six months. His reputation gave Excelan credibility and visibility that we could never have achieved on our own. When he proposed hosting a conference called Interop to bring the industry together, I immediately offered to fund it. But the response was so overwhelming that he didn't need my financial support. Instead, I became the keynote speaker at the inaugural Interop, urging the industry to embrace TCP/IP with the analogy: *Let's not be like England and America—two nations divided by a common language.*

By the end of 1985, Excelan had transformed. We became the go-to company for networking in heterogeneous environments. The numbers told the story: from $5.2 million in revenue and $2.4 million in losses in 1984, we had grown to $10.1 million in revenue and turned a modest profit of $100,000 in 1985. Almost half of those sales came in the final four months of the year.

The team's perseverance was extraordinary. At our holiday party, champagne flowed as we celebrated the turnaround. Not a single person had left during the tough times; only two had been let go since the layoffs. The camaraderie and belief in our mission were evident in the long hours people routinely put in, their mutual respect for each other, and the sound of clinking champagne glasses. We were the best you can hope for in a company of any size—a team connected by a shared sense of purpose. With plans to open three new sales offices in early 1986, the future looked bright.

Even the board recognized the transformation. At the final meeting of the year, John Dougery remarked that both the company and I had changed profoundly. We had, of course, and his acknowledgement meant a lot. It felt like a validation of everything we had achieved together. And then, the curveball came.

John Bosch took the floor and also recognized the company's turnaround. He turned to me and said thank you with an approving nod. Then he paused and said something about looking ahead. That set the stage for the bombshell: they wanted to start the search for a new CEO. I felt my blood turn cold. I couldn't believe the words I heard him say.

Despite the turnaround, despite my leadership through the storm, I wasn't the person they envisioned to take Excelan public. "We need to put some gift wrapping and a bow on this box," he explained.

In retrospect, I know they did not intend to disrespect or insult me. As investors, they had their eye on the prize: going public. And now that the company was doing well, they saw their opportunity. It was time to prepare. I had stabilized the company and made it profitable, which was greatly appreciated, but I still wasn't good enough—in other words, I wasn't the polished package they believed investors would expect. They wanted to install someone else at the top. I was livid.

PART 4

GOING PUBLIC

CHAPTER

13

Stepping Aside to Move Forward

I THOUGHT THE SEARCH FOR a new CEO might fade away over the holiday break as it had through much of the previous year. It was easy to hide in denial. People got busy and distractions cropped up. But I was wrong.

It was early 1986, and I started the new year as if it were business as usual. I laid out plans for Q1 and Q2, went over marketing plans, and met with my department heads. Then came the interruption. John Bosch let me know the search had started up again in earnest. A headhunter had identified several candidates.

I did not hide my irritation and disappointment. I think it caught him off guard. He assured me that I was key to Excelan's success. He said the board did not want to do anything that would upset me.

I took a deep breath, hoping to stop myself from saying anything impertinent. The irony of this situation was maddening. Basically, I had orchestrated my own ouster. Because I was successful, I had to step aside. It was a bitter pill I was being forced to swallow.

My decisions were not being challenged, as had been the case with Steve Jobs at Apple. Excelan was growing and improving its profitability. We were talking about growth, not survival. We loosened our hiring and increased our marketing spend. A virtuous cycle was setting in. And because of this growth, the board figured the time had come to find a CEO who could dress the company for an IPO. Bosch put it bluntly:

"Do you want to be CEO or rich?"

"Both."

"What if I said you can't be both?"

"Then rich."

Sometimes, power isn't about asserting dominance; it's about knowing when to step back. It reminds me of the story about the lion and the elephant. The lion wakes up every morning, thumps his chest, and roars, , "Who is the King of the Jungle?" Every animal he encounters—rabbits, foxes, even hyenas—responds to his question with an obsequious, "You are, Sire!" Then, one day, he meets an elephant. The lion thumps and roars and asks his question, expecting the usual deference. Instead, the elephant picks him up with his trunk and hurls him into the bushes. Dusting himself off, the lion mutters, "Hey, if you didn't know the answer, you just had to say so. No need to get mad."

The moral is simple: If you assert yourself at the wrong time, you risk losing more than you gain.

Like a good soldier, I participated in the search for my replacement. It wasn't about surrendering as much as it was about making a strategic retreat. Sometimes stepping aside is the only way to win the bigger game.

The Deck Is Shuffled

"Life is like a game of cards," Prime Minister Nehru once said. "The hand you are dealt is determinism. The way you play it is free will."

In April 1986, the board hired a new CEO, C. Richard Moore, also known as Dick Moore, who had been the general manager of Hewlett

Packard's engineering productivity division. HP's co-founder David Packard stood six feet eight inches tall, and he had a history of only promoting tall people to senior management positions. Dick Moore fit the bill. He was six-five, good-looking, charismatic, with degrees from Princeton and Berkeley. If you were going to cast a CEO in a movie, he was your guy.

Dick knew that he was walking into a good situation. I filled him in on the company's roadmap for the year and brought him up to speed. We had a great pipeline of new products. Our offices were next door to each other. Dick did not really do anything major without talking to me. In that sense, he was never a true CEO, calling the shots the way I had with TCP/IP. We appeared to be a team, a traditional Mr Inside and Mr Outside duo. I was the technical guy, and he was the business guy. I did not try to dispel that impression.

I had my direct reports assigned to him. I kept a dotted line. I wanted to make sure that Dick had the respect he was due. He could drive the process in front. He took over running our senior staff meetings. I respectfully stepped in when he stumbled, and spoke up when I saw him pause and glance in my direction for help with questions he didn't know how to answer. I thought about the irony of being someone whose speech impediment had always made me reluctant to speak up, yet now I was the voice people waited for and wanted to hear.

I did my best to make the partnership work. That summer, Dick told me that he sensed a slowdown. He did not have any numbers to support this, he said, when he brought this to my attention. He had a hunch. It was not the most reliable way to run a company. I left for Lake Tahoe on a much needed vacation with my family, the first time off I had taken in years, and when I returned a few weeks later the mood at the company was decidedly downbeat. While I was gone, Dick had instituted a hiring freeze and cut back on the marketing in anticipation of the slowdown. What happened as a result? His slowdown materialized.

I studied the numbers. Our sales had declined at the same time we had cut back on our advertising. Was it a coincidence?

I met with Dick and told him that I sensed growth about to return. A real boom, I said. I overrode him and increased the marketing spend. It was the first time we had a conflict. You don't respond to a hunch. Your numbers have to show where you are going. It is like driving a car. If you apply the brakes, the car slows. If you step on the gas, it will go faster. Within days, the leads flowed in and growth resumed.

Behind the scenes, I continued to call most of the shots. Dick was fine with that arrangement. We ended 1986 with a 120 percent increase in sales totaling $22.3 million and $3.5 million in profit. The numbers would have been higher if not for our brief "slowdown."

Going Public

Taking a company public is still about sales. Instead of your usual customers, you are selling to Wall Street.

Our IPO took over the last quarter of the year. There was much anticipation as Microsoft and Sun Microsystems had very successful public offerings back in March, demonstrating the riches to be had in the industry. Numerous investment bankers wanted to work with us. We chose Alex Brown and L.F. Rothschild to take us public. Dick and I spent months crafting the story that went into Excelan's prospectus. Everything in the company's history had to be disclosed in it. There could be no surprises about the business or the people running it.

A prospectus is a combination marketing-slash-legal document. It typically begins with all the reasons why purchasing this company's stock is risky and likely to result in you losing all your money. Basically, here are fifty reasons why you should stop reading and run in the opposite direction. Once you get past the risk factors, though, the tone changes. The lights come on, the music gets loud, and dollar signs start to shimmer like a chorus line of dancers at Radio City Music Hall. *Have I got a deal for you!*

We did have a good deal. Excelan had an excellent story and the numbers to back it up. Our revenue run rate was around $50 million and we could easily see potential growth hitting $70 million and $100 million. How would that translate in terms of worth as a publicly-traded company? A couple of times the revenue. Several hundred million dollars in market capitalization was a reasonable goal.

We spent the opening month of 1987 practicing our presentation. Dick provided the overview. I handled the tech, the market, demand, and a general Q&A. CFO Jim Tolonen addressed the numbers. The three of us and our bankers took the show on the road the last two weeks of February, meeting with investors in San Francisco, New York City, Chicago, Dallas, London, Frankfort, and Edinburgh. The plan was to sell 10 percent of the company. At the end of our meetings, our bankers asked investors how many shares they would buy at $10 per share. How many would they buy at $13?

You want to sell at the price at which there is twice the demand for the number of shares you want to sell. This ensures buyers when people want to sell.

On the 26th, we flew back on the Concorde from London to New York and then on to San Francisco. The IPO was happening the next morning. Spirits were sky high. Our meetings had gone as well as we could have hoped. Our prospectus estimated shares of Excelan opening anywhere from between $9 to $12 a share, and from all the notes and number crunching everyone had done the past twenty-four hours, I thought $12 a share was the right price for the open. Everyone agreed.

But later that night our chief banker had a change of mind. He feared demand was weak and we needed to open at $8 a share. Dick agreed with him.

"Let's open at $8."

"No," I said. "If demand is weak, let's delay the IPO. We don't need the money. The company has money in the bank. We will do the IPO at some other time."

Our disagreement surprised our banker. He looked caught in the middle.

"How about $9?" he said.

I shook my head. "It's $12 or let's not do it."

Excelan did have money in the bank. We were profitable and had no reason to think we would not continue to be profitable in the future. I did not feel compelled to undervalue the company based on our banker's *feeling*. I dug my heels in. Twelve or nothing.

In the morning, we rang the bell at NASDAQ. It was the ceremonial start to the trading day, though for me, it was more than symbolic. I became the first Indian-American founder to take a venture-backed company public. I also became a millionaire. We listed at $12 a share and opened at $15 before settling around $14 at the end of the day. The IPO was extremely successful. The company was priced at $120 million on the cover of the S1, the IPO filing form.

When I got to the office the next day, Excelan was buzzing with excitement. Many of our employees had been issued shares of stock in the company when they were hired and as part of their end-of-the-year bonuses. They were unable to sell them until after the company went public, but my unwritten rule was that everyone at a certain level should be able to buy a house with the money they made from stock after four years with the company. The IPO made ten employees immediate millionaires. That number would rise to 100 within three years.

Later that same day I went to the local Porsche dealer. I pointed to a candy apple red Porsche 928 S4. "I'll take that one," I said. The salesman asked if I could afford it. I showed him the prospectus, which I had carried with me to avoid any doubt. I pointed to my name, then showed it matched my driver's license. Taking the keys from the salesman thrilled the little boy and the engineer in me. This was the American dream come true, and I roared off the lot (in second gear).

Back at the office, people lined up outside to admire the shiny new sports car. Everyone wanted a ride. It wasn't just about my success—it said that we had all arrived. Over time, others at the company bought their own Porsches. The irony? I drove so slowly that cops kept pulling me over. To them, anyone handling that much horsepower at a crawl had to be under the influence.

A few weeks later, I gave a speech at the latest Interop conference. It was titled, "TCP/IP is Paying for Porsches." And I noted, "On paper, the acronym IPO stands for 'initial public offering.' But in practice, as some of us know, IPO is short for 'instant Porsche ownership.'"

CHAPTER 14

Navigating Success and Setbacks

SUCCESS IS INTOXICATING. IT FUELS confidence, validates choices, and sometimes blinds us to the immutable laws of nature, business, and life. But like gravity, these laws don't vanish just because you're on top. What goes up must come down—unless you plan and execute with foresight.

Excelan's successful IPO was Wall Street's way of applauding our journey: "Well done. Here's a war chest to expand, acquire, and grow." The expectation was clear—you use the capital to push boundaries, not let it idle. But not every CEO understands this outright. Some insist they aren't financial engineers, as if that exempts them from strategic thinking. Dick Moore, our CEO at the time, fell into this category.

Dick was skilled in sales and an earnest leader. I liked him but felt he lacked the mindset of a *wholistic* CEO—someone who sees the entire chessboard and orchestrates moves with purpose. Dick, like many GMs at large corporations, was a product expert, not a strategic visionary. At big companies, GMs often operate under tightly controlled mandates. Their job is to deliver results, but the strategy, budget, and priorities are handed down from above.

Being a CEO is entirely different. You aren't handed a roadmap—you create it. You make the hard calls, align resources, and inspire people to move toward a shared vision. When I became interim CEO, I didn't have the luxury of time or deep pockets to experiment. Failure wasn't an option. Every function—sales, marketing, R&D—had to fire on all cylinders.

By the time of our IPO, we had proven our model. We had been profitable for two years running and had $15–20 million in the bank. The big question was: *What next?* In business, as in chess, you don't win by standing still. You must move your pieces.

I saw an opportunity in the booming sales of Apple computers. They weren't yet networked to our systems, but a startup called Kinetics, located nearby in Walnut Creek, specialized in exactly that. Acquiring them was a no-brainer. After getting Dick and the board's buy-in, I closed the deal for $6 million.

During the closing process, Kinetics' CEO complained to Dick, claiming I had taken advantage of them. Sympathizing, Dick offered to raise the purchase price to $8 million without consulting me. When he brought this back, I refused outright. A deal is a deal. I suggested Dick point to the board as an immovable force to avoid renegotiating.

Kinetics turned out to be a perfect fit. They filled a critical gap in our lineup, allowing us to network Apple's Macintosh II, which was rapidly gaining traction in the corporate world. Their AppleTalk-over-Ethernet technology was a game-changer.

Usually after acquisitions, layoffs and restructuring are common. But I didn't touch Kinetics' team. Why? Because we acquired them for their capabilities, not just their assets. My goal was to amplify what was already working, not disrupt it.

We provided Kinetics with the resources to scale—inventory, marketing, and technical support. The results were spectacular. Their revenue shot up from $1 million to $10 million, which, in turn, boosted Excelan's performance.

Success demands movement, but not reckless moves. It requires strategic thinking, calculated risks, and a clear vision for the future.

When you see an opportunity, act decisively—but respect the fundamentals. Whether in physics, business, or life, gravity is always waiting. The only way to stay ahead is to keep climbing.

Staying Ahead

Just as a company can fall behind, so too can its CEO.

This reality became clear to me as Excelan navigated its transformation. Recognition of our success followed the acquisition of Kinetics. Venture Magazine, in conjunction with the accounting firm of Arthur Young, named me Bay Area Entrepreneur of the Year in 1987. Although the latest quarterly report still bore Dick's name, the award reflected the direction in which I had taken the company—a testament to decisions that had turned vision into bottom-line success in the fast-evolving tech industry.

As Excelan grew, I grew alongside it—a lesson I emphasize to young entrepreneurs at every opportunity. Leadership demands growth—professionally, intellectually, and spiritually—especially in a startup environment. The problems grow in complexity as the company scales, and you must grow faster than the challenges. Fall behind, and trouble is inevitable.

The early transitions are straightforward—moving from an individual contributor to a first-level manager is about direct relationships. You see results firsthand. But becoming a second-level manager, with managers reporting to you, changes the game. Now, others see results before you do. As you climb higher, especially to the CEO role, the delay between decisions and outcomes stretches—sometimes four, six months, or even a year.

This growing abstraction transforms how you lead. You're no longer immersed in the daily realities of the business. Instead, you return to first principles, working through layers of input from your team. Your role becomes strategic—you're playing a chess game against the market.

If I make this move, what will the competition do? What comes three, four moves down the line?

Surrounding yourself with the right people becomes critical. They handle the details while you focus on the big picture. At Excelan, this shift in focus helped me see ahead of the curve. I recognized that what we were building was exactly what Microsoft and Novell would need—before they even realized it themselves.

That foresight, honed through deliberate growth and learning, became a core advantage that I could execute in Excelan's favor. Staying ahead as a leader means mastering this balance—between abstraction and action, between today's realities and tomorrow's opportunities.

The Crash of '87

In the summer of 1987, the Dow Jones Industrial Average hit a record high of 2,700. By October, the music stopped abruptly. On Friday, October 16, the market dropped 500 points. The following Monday, it plunged another 500. Within a week, the Dow was down to just under 1,700.

At Excelan, the impact was swift and brutal. Our stock plummeted from $18 to $6. On paper, our valuation crashed from $180 million to $60 million. I was in Boca Raton, Florida, at the Venture Magazine–Arthur Young celebration of Entrepreneurs of the Year. Despite the palm trees and festive backdrop, the mood was anything but celebratory. Fear and pessimism gripped everyone.

I didn't let myself succumb to it. Crashes like these happen. Perspective is essential to survival in business, and I reminded myself of that. The market wasn't singling me out. I hadn't made a mistake, and Excelan wasn't broken. Yet, that was cold comfort for many of our employees, who came to work scared and looking for answers.

As CEO, Dick should have been the one to rally the team, but that wasn't his strength. So, I stepped up. I told them what I knew to be true:

this crash wasn't about us. Our fundamentals were strong. We were profitable, our sales were growing, and our balance sheet was solid.

This wasn't blind optimism—it was fact. We had built a company that could weather the storm, thanks to the hard work of everyone on our team. Our new WorkPlace product was a testament to that. In partnership with Quarterdeck, we developed a solution that allowed PCs to run multiple applications across windows without dropping connections. Microsoft Windows couldn't deliver this functionality yet.

Others noticed our momentum, too. Novell saw how our product complemented their NetWare system, while the Department of Defense signed a contract with us to build LAN products, leveraging TCP/IP, the very protocol they had funded in its infancy.

By 1988, Excelan had grown to nearly 600 employees. Our building, which had been an empty shell two years earlier, was now full. I jokingly told people I was no longer the sharpest tool in the company—a nod to the exceptional talent we'd hired, including PhDs from MIT and Carnegie Mellon.

Our weekly product planning meetings, which I chaired, became a breeding ground for innovation. Our stock price hadn't yet recovered, but I didn't let that distract us. I reminded my team that stock prices don't keep companies in business—products and customers do.

The crash of '87 taught me a critical lesson: when the market is in turmoil, the fundamentals matter more than ever. We didn't just survive that year—we thrived. And we did so because we stayed focused on what we could control.

The Unexpected Wildcards

One truth about life and business is that variables will always disrupt the status quo. Count on it: tomorrow will not look like today. Interest rates fluctuate, geopolitical tensions escalate, and collective fears drive

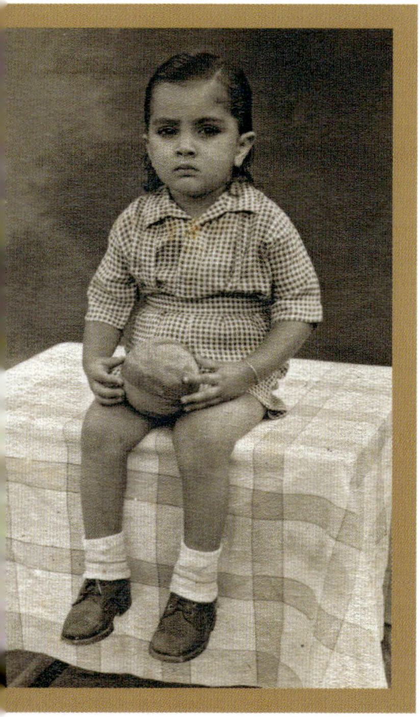

ca 1947/1948, earliest known photo of
I probably was 2 years old.

My high school ID photo in 1960

econd year at IIT in 1964. From left: Bhopi Dhall, SB Singh, me, Tejinder Singh and Inder Pal
a. Bhopi Dhall has been a lifelong friend and was with me at Michigan Tech and attended my wedding
Ann.

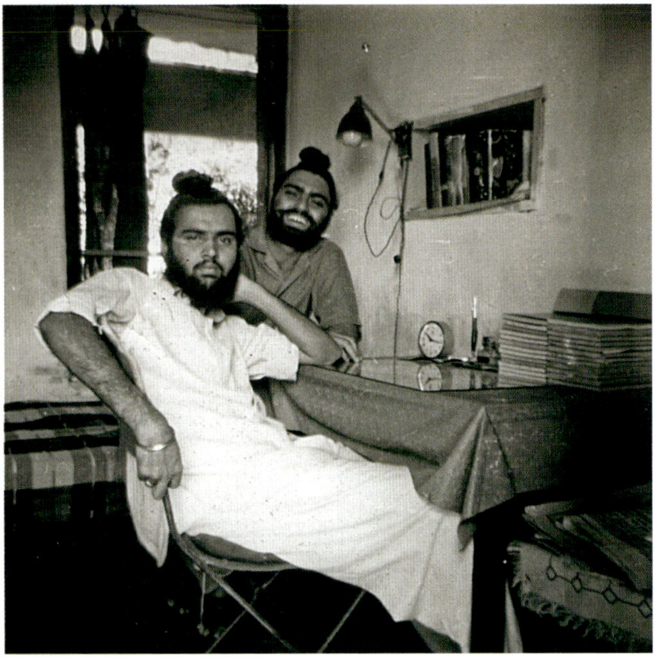

With my friend Tejinder Singh
my IIT dorm room

My first day in New York City i
September of 1967. I am the or
with turban. My late friend Um
Malhotra is in sunglasses. Ume
was with me at Michigan Tech a
was my best man at the weddin
He returned back to India to ta
care of his parents and the fam
business.

Around graduation time at Michigan Tech in 1969

ront of John Hancock tower in Chicago in the summer of 1968. Tower was still under construction
to credit: Umesh Malhotra

Nerdy me in the uniform of engineers in Ft. Lauderdale in 1970

Ann and me at our engagement dinner at Benihana of Tokyo in Ft. Lauderdale.
My friend Jeff Katz and his wife Rudy are in the picture.
Photo credit: Bhopi Dall

n and me after announcing engagement at my boss Ron Heacock's house.
oto credit: Bhopi Dall

wlyweds at our reception after the ceremony.
oto credit: Umesh Malhotra

My mother, father and sister (Baji, Darji and Ruby) with Ann in Kanpur during 1973 visit.
Photo credit: Upi Rekhi

Navin Jain, Kanwal, Inder Mohan Singh and Bob Dhillon on the first day of Excelan. We had just taken over Bob Dhillon's realty office in a strip mall in North San Jose.

d taken to wearing white shirts and tie after I became CEO in 1985.

. Excelan management team at IPO celebration in 1987. From left; Dick Moore, Vish Mishra, n Jain, Kanwal, Jim Tolonen, Subhash Bal and Duane Murray.

With my son Ben and the Red Porsche that I bought on the day of the IPO (hence the cliche....Instant Porsche Ownership). Photo credit: Raj-Ann Rekhi

With Bill Gates, announcing the ill-fated partnership with Microsoft in 1988

With Ray Noorda on the day of merger with Novell in 1989

s With candidate Bill Clinton in 1992

Discussing new telecom policy with then leader of opposition but later PM Manmohan Singh. Saurabh Srivastva is in the background.

Con 1996 group photo. Photo credit: Roy Prasad

Led a delegation of TiE stalwarts to meet PM Vajpayee in 1999. The idea of a new telecom policy for India was mooted at this meeting

Launching TiE in India in Mumbai around 1999. Harish Mehta, US Consul General David Good and Vijay Mukhi are in the background. Photo credit: Ben Rekhi

Leading a TiE delegation to meet President Pranab Mukherjea at At the Rashtrapati Bhavan in Delhi in 2016. Photo credit: Ben Rekhi

Conquering Mt. Tamalpais, the highest in the bay area in 200 It was a goal set in 200 when I decided to get fi Photo credit: Arpit Up

and I endowed Kanwal and Ann Rekhi Hall, computer Science building at Michigan Tech in 2. We earlier had endowed Kanwal Rekhi School nformation Technology at IIT Bombay too.
to credit: Ben Rekhi

With my family in 1998, at the groundbreaking ceremony for Kanwal Rekhi School of Information Technology at IIT Bombay. (*L–R*) Raj-Ann, me, Ann, and Ben

I and Ann celebrating our 50th anniversary in 2021
Photo credit: Mark Holt

Pavan Gill, Ben Rekhi, Kanwal, Raj-Ann, Rumi and Mark Holt in Maui during the Christmas of 2023. Ann was diagnosed with cancer soon after this trip and passed away a year later

You'd think someone would finally straighten out the Ethernet interoperability tangle.

Someone has.

The Someone is Excelan.

You just plug in our high performance front-end processors and high-level protocol software built on the TCP/IP standard.

Immediately, you can talk to the widest range of computers, including VAXs, UNIX micros, PC ATs, PCs and PDP-11s. And if you need a solution for a custom system, we'll put it together for you faster than anyone.

With an Excelan solution, you can get absolutely everything you need, all the way from the transceivers to the application software. Off the shelf.

Total Interoperability?

In a word, yes.

Our EXOS 200 Series front-end processors work with all standard buses — Multibus, VMEbus, Q-Bus, Unibus and PC-Bus. Our EXOS 8000 Series protocol software covers the most popular operating systems —Sys V, Xenix (or any UNIX), VMS, PC/DOS, and RSX-11.

Further, you don't have to compromise your system performance and delivery time just because of your proprietary bus or operating system. Our technology transfer program can put our solution to work for you fast. Just like it already has for many of our customers.

Together, our hardware and software give you total connectivity. So you can transfer files between computers with FTP and remotely log into any system with Telnet from any location withir the network.

The rewards of doing it rig

Our solution does all this because, unlike anyone else, we built from tl ground u That me we can you tl industry's implementa of communication technology current and emerging standard

For example, where we zero in on software issues, the real b tleneck in performance and fle bility, the results were impressi Our commercialized TCP/IP is most robust, field-tested versic there is, with support of all ISC layers, 4.2 BSD functionality, F and Telnet.

*VAX, PDP-11, Q-Bus, Unibus, VMS, and RSX-11 are trademarks of Digital Equipment Corporation UNIX and Sys V are trademarks of AT&T Bell Laboratories Multibus is a trademark of

One of the series of ads we ran in 1985 that put Excelan on the map.

markets in unpredictable directions. Leadership, especially in a public company, requires navigating these uncertainties while maintaining integrity, trust, and stability.

And so it was when suddenly I had to deal with a situation that was as personal as it was professional. Dick, our CEO, was going through a tumultuous divorce. During this time, rumors swirled about his involvement with one of our sales directors. Confronting the issue wasn't easy, but as chairman, it fell to me to get to the bottom of it. Dick denied the rumors outright, and I communicated his assurances to our board, confident that the matter was settled.

But life—and business—rarely unfold that cleanly. Soon after, I received explicit photographs from an anonymous source, proving the affair was not only real but significant. When I pressed Dick again, he admitted everything, explaining it wasn't just an affair—he was in love. They married later that year and stayed together until his passing in 1997.

Love may follow its own rules, as poets say, but running a public company is governed by a different set of expectations. Trust in leadership is non-negotiable. Dick had crossed professional boundaries and lied about it, compromising the company's reputation. The board was understandably concerned about the potential fallout—a scandal would hammer the stock price and invite shareholder lawsuits.

The board's solution? Sell the company. It was a pragmatic but uninspiring decision—a way to quietly bury the problem without addressing its root cause. For me, it was a bitter pill. I had envisioned a different future for Excelan, one where we controlled our destiny. Yet, I wasn't in charge, so I watched as our bankers quickly found a suitor, NET, a hotshot T1 line-switching company in Silicon Valley.

From the start, the deal felt wrong. NET's leadership, fresh out of Harvard Business School, oozed arrogance. During our first meeting, their CEO smugly announced he'd be taking my office. I decided then that if this deal went through, I wouldn't be sticking around. This was not the future I envisioned for Excelan—or myself.

My skepticism deepened when one of their executives made an extraordinary claim: they could predict revenue down to the penny six months in advance. That's not confidence; that's a red flag. Business doesn't work like that—variables make certainty impossible.

I voiced my doubts to our board, particularly to Ed Shea, who now owned 10 percent of Excelan. My concerns about NET's books resonated with Ed, and together, we uncovered a critical oversight: NET hadn't secured full shareholder support on our side. They needed 90 percent approval for the deal to qualify as tax-free. Without Ed and a few others, they were stuck.

Sensing leverage, I demanded a significant premium—$35 million more—arguing that the terms had fundamentally changed. NET balked, but they had two choices: pay the premium or face a staggering tax bill. Neither option appealed to them, and by July, the deal was off.

It didn't take long for my instincts to be validated. NET soon found itself embroiled in litigation over "false and inflated financial records," and their stock plummeted 90 percent. Had we merged, our investors would have been wiped out.

The failed acquisition shifted power back to me. With Ed's support, I stepped into the CEO role and Dick left the company. There was some talk of beginning the CEO search again, but I killed the idea immediately. There would be no more searches for outside leadership—I was done deferring to others. John Bosch, who had guided us through earlier phases of growth, exited the board shortly after. He'd made over 10x his initial investment but lost control of Excelan's direction—and of me.

Excelan emerged from the ordeal stronger, leaner, and with its integrity intact. Business, like life, is full of variables. The key is not avoiding them but navigating through them with clarity and conviction.

Making Moves

I proposed buying 25 percent of Cisco for $10 million.

Excelan was a LAN company (local area networking), connecting machines within a building or a single campus, and Cisco was a WAN company (wide area networking), able to connect offices in New York to offices in California. There was a natural partnership between the two networking companies; Excelan and Cisco could provide a more comprehensive solution.

My board did not agree and vetoed the investment. Cisco went on to become a company worth nearly $500 billion, and Excelan missed a chance to have a piece of that rewrite its destiny. Meanwhile, our LAN WorkPlace product caught fire. For the first time, PC users could work locally and be connected to the corporate network. It was revolutionary—a game-changer for individual productivity.

Our work with Novell grew closer. NetWare, their flagship product, was designed in such a way that it did not allow any other protocols on the wire. It monopolized the network, shutting out other protocols like TCP/IP or AppleTalk. It was like having a thousand-channel cable box but only one channel ever worked. We stepped in and showed them how to coexist with other protocols on the Ethernet—a crucial breakthrough.

Microsoft also came knocking. They had seen our work with Quarterdeck and realized it was superior to their existing Windows software. They asked for help on Windows 3.0. Together, we solved key issues like preserving the "state of network connection" when switching between windows. Before that, Windows was basically a single-window, one-trick pony.

Things went so well that Excelan and Microsoft announced a partnership. I shared the podium at an industry networking exhibition with the Lord Almighty himself, Bill Gates. I thought our two companies were destined for a beautiful marriage. But Bill Gates was not just a tech visionary; he was a shrewd and ruthless businessman. His legendary $75,000 acquisition of Q-DOS, which became the foundation of MS-DOS and launched Microsoft into the stratosphere, was a masterstroke.

I should have been less enamored. The previous year Microsoft had partnered with IBM on OS/2 and then Microsoft ended the year by bringing out Windows 2.0 as a competing product. Ouch. And then it happened to us.

We were helping Microsoft, they were telling us they loved us, and we had a very close, good working relationship. Then, out of nowhere, Microsoft announced a deal with 3Com for a new LAN manager. At a conference in San Francisco. This was just months after Bill and I had posed for pictures together. Shocked, I called one of Bill's minions and said, "Wait a minute. We're your partner." He said, "You're right, you *are* our real partner."

But if that were true, how come Bill was announcing a partnership with 3Com? I felt like a kept woman. "So you're in love with me but you're marrying her?" I decided then and there never to partner with Microsoft again—though it was a promise I ultimately did not keep. Why let enemies get in the way of sales?

We finished a very strong year in 1988 with almost $60 million in revenue and $10 million in profits. The stock market had rebounded, too. And TCP/IP had emerged as a winner in the protocol wars.

Technology moves at breakneck speed. Success demands vision—not just seeing the present but predicting where the future is heading. As Wayne Gretzky famously said, "Skate to where the puck is going to be, not where it has been." I had a pretty good idea where the puck was headed next.

CHAPTER

15

The Power of the Next Move

IN BUSINESS, EMOTIONS MEAN NOTHING. Strategy means everything. It's not about telling me how you feel—it's about showing me your plan and your next move.

Despite their partnership with 3Com, Microsoft signaled that they wanted to still find ways to work more closely with Excelan. That normally means: "Hey, maybe you should move in with us because as a public company we cannot work with someone more closely unless we acquire them."

Was this more gamesmanship from Bill Gates? I never knew. The conversation stopped before it started. But while one door closed, another opened when I received a call from Ray Noorda, the legendary CEO of Novell, late on a Friday morning. Novell was the second biggest software company in the world at the time and Microsoft's biggest competitor.

"I'm in town," he said casually. "Maybe I can stop by and we can have lunch."

The timing wasn't coincidental. I had already been tipped off by a former Excelan employee, now with Novell, that they were eyeing us. Rumor had it they were gathering intelligence, running numbers, and evaluating a potential acquisition. Ray's call was less of a surprise and more of an inevitability.

"Sure," I said, keeping my tone neutral. "Let's do lunch. But it's late—tough to get reservations anywhere decent."

"Not a problem," he replied. "I'll come by."

Twenty minutes later, Ray was shaking hands in my office. My guess? He made the call parked just around the corner.

"Do you like Mexican food?" I asked.

"Love it," he said.

"There's a spot nearby—enchiladas for a buck sixty-five, burritos for two dollars."

Ray's eyes lit up. Frugality was part of his brand. This was the man who, despite heading a $300 million company, famously flew Delta standby on $85 senior fares, hopping city to city like a backpacker. The cheap lunch was more than a meal; it was a nod to his ethos.

Over enchiladas, Ray cut to the chase. "We should find a way to put our companies together," he said.

I reminded him of the complexities: Excelan was a public company. Shareholders had the final say. He didn't blink. "We'll make it worthwhile," he said. Then he leaned in, his plate nearly untouched.

"What do you think it will take?"

"Fifty percent premium above market," I replied without hesitation.

Ray paused, chewing both food and numbers in his head. Finally, he nodded. "We can do 50 percent."

The next morning, I was back at my desk, not celebrating but strategizing. I started with a memo to myself—my way of thinking through big moves. This wasn't just any memo; it was the groundwork for a merger that would reshape the networking landscape.

"Excelan," I wrote, "is an engineering-driven company breaking into mainstream networking by packaging a suite of solutions: Microsoft LAN Manager, Sun's NFS, Apple's AFP, and our own technology. Our strength lies in hardware expertise and the breadth of our offering, but we are still building our distribution.

"Novell, on the other hand, is a marketing powerhouse with a dominant position in PC networking through NetWare. They've resisted hardware, focusing instead on partnerships that extend their reach into other environments. Their distribution network is unmatched."

The combination? A Silicon Valley innovator joining forces with a Provo giant. Together, "it will be a much stronger position vis-à-vis its competition, than either of the companies alone, and could be the dominant supplier of desktop networking solutions."

Hours and then days passed as I dug into the reasons each company would want to merge. What motivated Excelan? While we had grown and innovated every year since 1985, the long-term prospects were uncertain. "There may not be room for a junior 3Com whose successes depend on 3Com's failures. As such, it may be a good time for Excelan to make a deal based on its current strength."

And Novell? The company's strength was marketing and distribution, not technical, and "with Microsoft entering the arena with a very strong product," the stakes were raised considerably. For Novell, the acquisition was a smart strategic move and "a relatively cheap transaction" even with a high premium.

The bottom line: NetWare only helped PC users share files. We could network PCs—both Apple and the IBM variety—to UNIX machines of all types, DEC minicomputers, and IBM mainframes. We were a technology-rich company, they were a distribution-savvy company.

It was clear to me that a new destiny beckoned. This wasn't just a good deal; it was the right deal. The rest was execution. In business, as in chess, it's not the position you're in—it's the moves you make next.

A Done Deal, A New Beginning

"That wasn't what Ray meant."

Really? I had just gotten off the phone with Ray's lawyer from Wilson Sonsini, the kind of heavyweight Valley law firm that doesn't call unless it means business. He was suddenly revising Ray's offer—downward. Way down. A "misunderstanding," he claimed.

"Since you want to sell—"

I cut him off.

"I don't want to sell. Ray wants to buy."

"Yes, Ray is interested, but—"

I interrupted again.

"I'm happy not to sell."

With that, I ended the call. There was no need to waste time. If the terms were changing, the deal was off. To me, it looked like a classic good cop-bad cop routine. That's a weak move when you have no leverage—it only makes you seem unreliable.

Not long after, Ray called to sort things out. I laid it out for Ray. He sounded surprised. Maybe he was, maybe he wasn't.

"I'm going to make this right," he said. "Let me get back to you."

Interesting way to put it.

Word spread quickly, as it always does in the Valley. Microsoft came knocking almost immediately, hesitant but curious. Their pitch was cautious—"If you're merging, why not with us?" They floated an offer, but it was half-hearted and far from competitive. At $12 a share—simply market price—it wasn't even close to Novell's original proposal. The Novell deal offered liquidity and certainty, a straightforward path for everyone involved. But was it on?

Yes, it was. Ray got back to me as promised—and he fixed things as he also promised, by reinstating the original offer, which I accepted *again*.

The headlines broke in late March 1989. By July, the deal was done. Ray continued as Novell's CEO, while I stepped into new shoes—executive vice president, chief technical officer, and a member of the "office of the president." A board seat came with the package, sealing my place in the company's leadership.

Even in the earliest days of my transition into Novell, I noticed Ray wasn't the hands-on CEO I had expected. He had leaned heavily on two senior executives to keep things running, but they had both departed before the merger. That void became my new domain. Suddenly, I wasn't just a technical leader. I was Ray's sounding board, his spokesperson, and, for all intents and purposes, his right hand.

It became clear that Ray hadn't just wanted Excelan—he had wanted me. I stepped into the role of the number two executive at the second-largest software company, gaining a front-row seat to Silicon Valley's meteoric rise during the '90s tech boom. Suddenly, I was no longer asking, "Why not me?"—I was living the answer. I had made it to the top tier, sitting at the same table as industry giants. I would soon cross paths and cut deals with the biggest names in tech. But beyond personal success, I had become something I hadn't fully grasped at the time—a groundbreaker. For the next generation of entrepreneurs who looked and sounded like me, I was proof that their ambitions were possible. "Why not me?" would no longer be a rhetorical question. They would see that it could be done.

But success is never as clean and straightforward as it looks from the outside. The real challenge began after the deal was signed. Like any new partnership, it was a marriage of sorts. The question was no longer about acquisition—it was about whether Ray and I could build something even greater together.

What seemed like an endpoint was actually the beginning of a far more intricate journey.

CHAPTER

16

Mergers, Rivalries, and Bold Moves

EVERY MERGER HAS BUMPS. BLENDING cultures and strategies is not as simple as replacing one sign with another.

I encountered my first problem as I set up my office at Novell's Provo, Utah, headquarters—coffee. There was none. Not in the building. Not outside the building either. There was no coffee or tea anywhere. I asked my assistant how this was possible.

"We're in Utah," she said, looking slightly amused at my ignorance.

This was my first but not my last introduction to this new reality. Provo was 97 percent Mormon. Mormons are instructed not to drink coffee—and hot drinks in general. Hence no coffee or tea. But with all due respect, I was not Mormon. I asked my assistant to find me some coffee and buy a coffee maker.

"Ray may not like it," she said.

I offered a light-hearted grimace. "But I want a cup of coffee."

Soon we had coffee in the office—and then not just in my office but throughout the building. It turned out there were a lot of other grateful coffee drinkers besides me, Ray included. I was the new guy, but because of this little convenience, I started as a hero. Of course, my new routine included more than a hot beverage. On Monday morning, I flew to Utah and returned home on Wednesday evening. I spent Thursday in the Valley. On Friday morning, I went back to Utah and flew home later that night.

Thanks to Novell's corporate jet, and Ray's preference for flying commercial, my commute was relatively easy and stayed that way after Austin and New Jersey were added to my weekly travels.

My Provo office was next to Ray's. We met and talked throughout the day, anytime either one of us had the inclination. It was a private area, a joint office suite. Everybody else had to go through Ray's assistant and set up a time to meet with him. So I was his partner, his peer. We got along very well. He was a great and prolific storyteller; over time, I heard all of his stories. Both of us were news junkies and history buffs. On our joint travels to South America and Europe, we never ran out of conversation. Neither of us was into golf, but we played many sets of tennis together.

In almost every aspect of Novell business, from immediate decisions to long-range planning, he relied on me as a sounding board. He involved me in one of his side businesses mentoring executives at other companies. I felt like I had his trust and respect; he seemed to love and appreciate my judgement. He never told me what to do. I was always the one proposing something. I had a free hand.

Our honeymoon phase would last about three years. It was a remarkably fulfilling window for both of us, I think. One day, there was a meeting with the top people at Intel. I was there with Jim Tolonen and Duane Murray. It was Excelan's A-team only we were part of Novell now. We used their chips to make WorkPlace faster, and they wanted to know how we were getting more speed from their product.

Good old-fashioned gumshoe engineering, that's how. Duane had debugged their chip, found errors, and improved their performance.

Ray loved it. When he wanted to get out of the hardware business but could not articulate why, he turned to me. Until the PC took off, hardware had been part of everyone's business, including Novell's. But as the price of PCs dropped and it became a standard commodity, it was hard justifying doing your own hardware. If you were doing something special, you put it on the PC.

And that is what I told Ray. NetWare had its own hardware, but it should be discontinued; our value-addition was software. That was where I thought our resources should go. I explained it in a memo. *Sales will drop, but margins will improve. We will make up any losses in software.*

This was just math. Say you are buying hardware for $1 and selling it for $1.20. You are only making 20 cents per sale even though you are charging $1.20. When you get out of the hardware business, you are only getting out of 20 cents of business. If you increase software sales by 20 cents, you will be whole very quickly. If you increase the price of software by 50 cents, you're making more money than before.

There are more benefits: You don't need the same amount of inventory. You also don't need as many people. You're cutting costs while making more money.

Something else was going on behind my recommendation. Software was driving the whole industry. If the software changes, all the guys making hardware have to scramble just to stay where they are. They have to design and engineer, buy parts, build, and sell. If they make hardware that is twice as powerful, the software becomes twice as powerful without doing anything. The value only goes up.

"There may be a little pain short term," I told Ray, "but getting out of hardware will be very good for us in the long run." Ray agreed. He had been thinking along these same lines, but his thoughts were based on instinct. He was a seat-of-his-pants thinker, whereas I was logical, and in this instance, our first conversation of real significance, he loved my logic. It confirmed his hunch and his trust in me grew.

The Lotus Position

But there was still much about Ray for me to unravel.

In April 1990, Ray agreed to merge Novell with Lotus. The $1.5 billion dollar deal was announced in April. A straight stock swap, it was expected to be the largest software industry deal at the time. *The New York Times* noted that networking was "the most rapidly growing segment of the computer industry" and framed the deal as "an effort to deliver a competitive blow to the Microsoft Corporation, the leader in personal computer software." Ray seemed to see it that way, too. But later analysis of the deal in *The Times* questioned whether the merger really was "an ideal match."

I never thought it was. Novell was the better, more profitable company, yet we were going to become a subsidiary of Lotus. It made no sense. And Ray? He was uncharacteristically absent—and apparently unreachable—when details needed to be hashed out. As the senior executive in charge, I was asked for directions. *What do we do? How do we make this merger work? Where's Ray?*

Lotus CEO Jim Manzi complained that he couldn't reach Novell's CEO. I had to admit I couldn't reach him either.

"How are we going to do this deal?" he asked.

"I don't know anything about the deal," I said. "Ray hasn't told me anything."

This was not the way deals got done—not serious ones, anyway. Yet the theatrics continued. When Ray resurfaced, he told Manzi to come up with the deal points. "Fill in the blanks," he said. That was another bizarre request. Discussion of the deal among our board added to the surrealism of the situation. Ray listened while company attorney Larry Sonsini praised him as a visionary who had shaped the industry and championed his audacious move to take on Microsoft.

Some of the board members chimed in with their endorsements. Then it was my turn. I held nothing back.

"The merger doesn't make sense to me," I said. "None of the terms make sense to me. None of it does. But if Ray wants to do it, who am I to stand in his way?"

Ultimately the board fell into line like dutiful soldiers. Ray had the support he needed. But not so fast. A twist was still to come. Ray had the final word. This was his company after all. All eyes turned to Ray. He hadn't spoken a word the entire meeting. He scanned the room, letting the tension build, and after a long pause, he finally addressed us.

"Why are we doing this merger?" he asked. "You all seem to think we should do the deal?"

I interrupted. "I don't want to do it."

Then Larry, who had sung the deal's praises moments earlier, changed his tune. "Ray, I don't understand why we are doing it either."

In a stunning reversal, Ray agreed. It was the only time he spoke. And only four weeks after the merger was announced, the deal was dead. Ray told me to call Lotus's CEO. I refused, it wasn't my mess to clean up. Larry delivered the news instead. In hindsight, I don't think Ray ever intended to make a deal. It was about making a statement. Ray wanted to solidify Novell's position as an industry heavyweight while giving Microsoft a scare. Ray knew what he was doing. It was a masterclass in corporate theater. And in that respect, he was very successful.

But something about this gambit nagged at me. Why was Ray wasting time and resources on mind games? It was a red flag, and this fixation ultimately led to Novell's undoing.

Back to the Future: Silicon Valley and India's Awakening

In the early days of Silicon Valley, India wasn't on anyone's radar—not yet. The tech world was exploding, but India was seen as little more than an afterthought, a distant market that didn't warrant serious attention. That changed for me in the most unexpected way.

The merger with Novell catapulted me into a new role as the first Indian director of a billion-dollar company. It was a milestone not just for me but also for the growing Indian-American community in the Bay Area. By then, Indians were making their mark. Over 80 percent of Indian professionals in the Valley had arrived post-1970, with more than half holding advanced degrees. Nearly a quarter of all foreign-born engineers were Indian. We were no longer outsiders. Tech had leveled the playing field, and in the Valley, it wasn't about where you came from—it was about what you could build.

And then Harish Mehta walked into my office in Utah.

Harish was different. A young entrepreneur with the optimism of a dreamer and the persistence of a hustler, he had a message I hadn't expected to hear: India was ready. "The same tech language you speak here is being spoken in India," he told me. He wasn't just making a pitch; he was planting a flag. "India is changing. It's going to be an IT powerhouse. You should sell your software there."

At the time, like most of those in tech, I viewed India as we did Europe—a market we'd get to eventually, but not one to prioritize. Harish was undeterred. He had returned to India after earning his master's in electrical engineering and working in the US, determined to help shape its tech future. He co-founded NASSCOM, a body that would go on to define India's IT sector, and launched his own software company, Onward Technologies. Now, he wanted to partner with Novell.

I wasn't convinced. India didn't seem like the opportunity Harish was making it out to be. I declined his proposal outright. He listened patiently, then leaned in with the quiet confidence of someone who knew he was right. "You don't have to invest a dollar," he said. "Just license me to sell your software in India."

His persistence worked. We created Onward-Novell, a joint venture where Novell held 51 percent and Harish 49 percent. We licensed him our product at a steep discount—65 percent. Harish kept his promise.

Onward-Novell became a runaway success. Novell gained a new revenue stream from a market it had deprioritized, and Harish built the groundwork for India's emerging IT industry.

But for me, this wasn't just about the bottom line. India was always in my heart. Even though my entire family had joined me in the US by then, it was still home in ways that words can't fully capture. Walking back into India through this partnership felt like returning to a place I'd never fully left.

Looking back, Harish was my wake-up call, and his vision was prophetic. He saw what the rest of us couldn't yet: that India wasn't just catching up—it was taking its place on the global tech stage. Sometimes, it takes someone else's conviction to change or broaden your own trajectory. For me, that someone was Harish Mehta, and the journey we started together opened up a new path—for Novell, for me, and, in many ways, for India.

The Synergy of Bold Moves

NetWare 3.1 and 3.11 were done under my direction. Though I faced some resistance within the company as always happens when someone tinkers with the primary revenue source and people question whether it is a smart thing to do, it was a smashing success. The upgrade was released between October 1990 and March 1991 and showed the synergy of our two companies.

Novell was a bright light within the industry. Sales and profits took off and the stock price began a steep climb that continued for a couple of years. Ray and I could not have been closer. We met with Oracle founder Larry Ellison. Oracle had got itself in a financial crunch; Larry wanted to borrow $200 million. Ray, in a gesture of trust, let me lead the conversation, which irked Larry.

"Does he speak for you?" he asked.

Ray nodded. "Yes."

My offer—$200 million at LIBOR (the cost of borrowing among banks) plus a 10 percent warrant coverage at the market price of Oracle stock—upset Larry, who stomped out of the meeting and never spoke to me again. Ray confided that he would have asked for harsher terms—LIBOR plus 2 percent plus warrant coverage, but the lesson was clear: knowing your worth and playing to your strengths matters, even if it ruffles feathers. Larry got his loan elsewhere and obviously did just fine. We moved on, too. For me, the lesson was clear: knowing your worth and playing to your strengths matters, even if it ruffles feathers.

Despite our camaraderie, one aspect of Ray's leadership baffled me—his deep animosity toward Microsoft. His disdain for Bill Gates and his second-in-command, Steve Ballmer, bordered on obsession. Ray often referred to Gates as "Pearly Gates" and Ballmer "the Emballmer," quipping, "You have to pass through the Emballmer to get to the Pearly Gates." It was a peculiar blind spot for an otherwise strategic thinker and only added to my insight in the almost religious war Ray was engaged in.

In February 1991 I went to Ray with a move that I knew would resonate with his competitive instincts. I proposed buying UNIX. It was a bold way to compete with Microsoft, giving us a powerful application server to complement our file server. UNIX's existing challenges—lack of profitability, standardization, and distribution—were problems Novell was uniquely positioned to solve. Our distribution network, engineering capabilities, and customer base made the acquisition a perfect fit.

We would have another powerful product to send through our sales channels to our existing customers and most likely add new customers. And we would inherit a top-notch engineering team. All for stock.

"It's hard to imagine anybody besides Microsoft who is likely to be very unhappy," I told Ray. "A Novell backing of UNIX may put Microsoft's future OS's (NT) at great risk. That alone may justify doing it."

I knew my audience. Ray loved the idea.

"Go out and do it," he said.

I pitched the idea to AT&T, which owned UNIX Systems Laboratories (USL) but was pivoting to hardware through its NCR acquisition. Software was no longer a priority for them. I initially prepared to pay up to $1 billion but sensed an opportunity to negotiate. I offered $250 million. AT&T countered with $300 million, and we had a deal. The agreement was announced in December 1992 and finalized in July 1993.

Post-acquisition, I quickly turned the economics in our favor. USL had $50 million in the bank, effectively reducing our cost to $250 million. I negotiated one-time fees for perpetual UNIX licenses with IBM, Sun, and Hitachi, securing $235 million in total. This move effectively recouped our investment, and we still retained full control over UNIX. It was a masterstroke.

Now Novell was positioned to compete directly with Microsoft's NT on an equal footing. However, unbeknownst to me, it also stirred up internal tensions. What I viewed as a strategic coup began to sow division within the company. Paranoia and animosity surfaced, and over time, these undercurrents would lead to my exclusion from Ray's inner circle.

But separate from that, the story of UNIX's acquisition and integration epitomizes the power of bold, strategic thinking. It was a golden deal by any measure, proving that calculated risks and decisive action can yield big rewards. Yet, it also serves as a reminder of the complexities of leadership—how external victories can sometimes exacerbate internal challenges.

Leadership, as I've learned, isn't just about making great deals. It's also about navigating the human dynamics that come with them.

NeXT

Meanwhile, after Novell's acquisition of UNIX was announced, I received a call from Steve Jobs. He requested a meeting. I didn't know Steve but obviously knew of him, and I had been present at Davies Symphony Hall on September 19, 1990, for the announcement of NeXT computer. There he claimed to have orders for 15,000 of his new computers! That turned out to be a little bit of an exaggeration.

We met for dinner at Gaylord's, his favorite Indian restaurant, in Menlo Park. Steve arrived with an entourage of seven. A connoisseur of Indian food, he said that he had called ahead and pre-ordered dishes for the table, assuring me that I would approve of his selections . Why waste time looking at menus? Within minutes, busy waiters filled the table with tandoori chicken, fish curry, aloo gobi, and other dishes. Small talk ceased and Steve got straight to business. Whatever Novell was up to with UNIX, it was the dumbest thing he had ever heard. Yes, he was that blunt.

And even more intense. He wanted us to take his software and compete against Microsoft Windows for desktop dominance. He didn't propose this as much as he declared it as necessary as breath, as obvious as the color of the sky. It must be done. Except Novell software didn't make sense on Steve's machine. And when I told him that and explained why—because his was a desktop machine designed to compete with Microsoft and we were server providers—he flew into a somewhat restrained rage. We were in a restaurant, after all.

I could only imagine the man's wrath in a conference room. He called our strategy dumb and insinuated that I was no better. Then, suddenly, dinner was over. Steve got up and walked out, his entourage trailing behind. I was left alone at the table, staring at eight mostly untouched plates of Indian food—and the bill for the whole lot.

Understanding Ray's Obsession

Sometimes, you only understand a person when you see their battles up close.

My perspective on Ray's fixation became clearer during a critical period when I was deep into securing the UNIX deal for Novell. Around the same time, Ray orchestrated the acquisition of Digital Research, the makers of DR-DOS. His intent? To challenge Microsoft head-on. Windows 3.1 had just come out, bundled with Word, Excel, MS-DOS, and LAN Manager. It didn't matter that some of those products weren't as good as ours—Microsoft knew the power of the bundle.

The deal for Digital Research came in at $80 million, done as a flat stock transaction. "Here's $80 million worth of Novell stock," was the offer. Straightforward, but poorly timed. Novell's stock doubled in value shortly after the announcement, effectively making the acquisition cost $160 million. Digital Research's team walked away ecstatic; I wasn't as thrilled. But Ray? He didn't flinch. As *The New York Times* put it, "Novell was adding weapons for the contest with Microsoft." They were right—this wasn't just business competition. For Ray, it was personal. It was war.

That's when I began to see a side of Ray I hadn't fully grasped before. There were two powerhouse software companies in Utah at the time: Novell and WordPerfect. I suspected that the larger Utah community, perhaps even the Mormon Church, had recognized the state's future was tied to software. And Microsoft's growing dominance threatened that future. For them, Microsoft wasn't just a competitor—it was an existential threat. Maybe Ray had been handed an unspoken mandate: "Stop Microsoft, whatever it takes."

I didn't share this vendetta. I argued with Ray about it. "Microsoft's strength is on the desktop, Ray," I said. "We're about servers and networking. They sell more DOS, and we sell more NetWare. We're partners."

Ray wasn't having it. "They are evil," he declared.

I couldn't resist asking, "How are they any more evil than us?"

But then Microsoft made an unexpected move. They approached Ray about a merger. On the surface, it seemed like a coincidence. But knowing how strategic Gates was in business, it's hard to believe he wasn't aware of Ray's animosity. Bill Gates didn't back down from a fight, and now we had what felt like a chess match between two grandmasters. Ray said yes to the talks, even musing about whether the government might block the merger. But Microsoft reassured him: "We've got D.C. covered."

That's when I was pulled into the whirlwind of negotiations. Ray, always enigmatic, remarked, "We all have to go to the Pearly Gates sometime."

From a strategic standpoint, the merger made perfect sense. Microsoft lacked strong networking capabilities; Novell had them. Together, the companies could've been unstoppable. But that wasn't the real agenda. For Microsoft, this deal wasn't just about synergy—it was about neutralizing the one company bold enough to challenge them head-on. They were willing to pay handsomely to eliminate a potential disruptor.

Then came the twist. Right before the deal could close, Microsoft announced they were acquiring FoxPro for $75 million. FoxPro was a database solution—a glaring gap in Microsoft's portfolio. The ripple effects were immediate: Borland, which had cornered the database market after acquiring dBase, saw its stock price plummet. But the announcement had another unintended consequence. It enraged Ray.

"Why didn't they tell me about FoxPro?" he fumed. In a moment of fury, he killed the deal.

Looking back, I wonder if Ray ever intended to finalize the merger. Maybe he was just playing his adversary, dragging Microsoft into the negotiation. Or maybe it was the other way around, with Gates using FoxPro to provoke Ray into walking away.

As I had warned before, "If you shoot at them, there's a very good chance they'll shoot back."

CHAPTER

17
The Cost of Disruption

THE CARDINAL RULE OF SOFTWARE—AND any customer-focused business—is simple: *thou shall not inflict any pain on the customer.*

Customers are your friends, your lifeblood. Treat them with respect. No update should confuse, complicate matters, or alienate the customer. I wish I could have drilled this into the minds of the engineers behind NetWare 4.0. Unfortunately, I wasn't in the driver's seat when Novell's flagship product took a wrong turn.

By then, Novell had acquired UNIX, and the engineering team in Utah treated it like an unwelcome guest. To them, UNIX wasn't just another product—it was the enemy. This bias wasn't isolated to the engineering ranks; it extended all the way to Ray. He divided the company into two warring camps: California, home to UNIX and TCP/IP, and Utah, focused on DR-DOS and applications.

The result? An internal cold war. I had my suspicions about why Ray acted this way. Something about him had changed after his heart issues and the pacemaker that followed. He was no longer the leader I once collaborated with so closely. Our relationship, once a partnership of mutual respect and shared vision, became strained. Meetings started happening without me—a stark departure from how we once worked.

The internal discord didn't just affect me. Long-time colleagues like Duane Murray and Navin Jain, who had been with me since the early days of Excelan, walked away. They couldn't stomach the chaos. This turmoil trickled down to our product strategy.

NetWare was a juggernaut, dominating the market and driving massive profits. But the new leadership decided the market was saturated—everyone who needed NetWare already had it. Their solution? Force upgrades.

Wrong move. In software, your greatest asset is your customers' familiarity with your product. People rely on what they know. They've invested time learning it, mastering it, and integrating it into their lives or workflows. The moment you disrupt that familiarity—by making their knowledge obsolete—you create friction. You force them to ask: *Is this still worth it? Is there something easier or better out there?*

The NetWare team made this fundamental mistake. They overhauled the user experience in NetWare 4.0, breaking the unwritten contract between us and our customers. It was as if Detroit's automakers had tried to reinvent the wheel every two years. That strategy worked for a while, but it faltered when Toyota entered the scene. Toyota didn't play the obsolescence game. They kept it mostly the same. Instead they refined. They improved. They built loyalty through incremental, meaningful upgrades—better mileage, more reliability. Customers noticed, and the auto industry was forever changed.

The same principle applies to software. Upgrades should feel like gifts, not burdens. When you force users to relearn your product, you lose their trust. Worse, you give them a reason to consider alternatives. That's exactly what happened with NetWare 4.0. Not only was it a flop, but it also opened the door for Microsoft Windows NT and LAN Manager to capture attention and market share.

The NetWare team had violated the cardinal rule of software, and the fallout was predictable. Growth isn't about disrupting your customers' routines. It's about making their lives easier, one thoughtful improvement at a time.

Another Pivot That Never Was

Like the Microsoft merger, this one might have rewritten history, too.

After NetWare 4.0 tanked, Ray came up with another angle to get at the "Pearly Gates"—acquire Apple. It sounds ludicrous now. But back in 1993, it seemed plausible enough that Ray was able to pitch it to Apple CEO John Sculley.

Steve Jobs was running NeXT and Pixar, but his shadow was still rattling around its Cupertino campus, and Apple was in trouble. The PC had emerged as the clear winner in homes and offices; Apple's desktop line was going nowhere. They had launched Newton, a digital message pad, and it was a bust. Ray envisioned a Novell–Apple merger in order to put Apple's elegant operating system on PC hardware and compete with Microsoft.

The idea had merit if not genius. Apple had spent a decade developing this great operating system that only worked on Apple computers. But what if it also worked on PCs? Everybody was manufacturing PCs and putting Windows on them. What if they could put Apple on their PC? What if they had a choice? What if Apple was the better choice?

Anyone who experienced the frustration of Windows and the ease of Apple's OS had entertained this fantasy. Ray envisioned turning this fantasy into a reality—and thereby inflicting a great big hurt on Microsoft if it worked. But Apple's magic was Apple's hardware, Sculley said. The operating system wouldn't work on non-Apple hardware. Ray was undeterred.

"Let's see if we can make it work," he said, and then suggested a dozen engineers from each company get together in secret and try to adapt Apple's operating system so it would work on a PC.

"I don't think so," Sculley said.

It took them thirty days. Apple worked like a charm on the PC hardware.

It was brilliant—too brilliant. Sculley knew most of Apple's business was hardware, and that business would disappear overnight if Apple's operating system was available on a PC. Why buy a Mac anymore? Apple would be a much smaller company. A much different company. But a much more profitable company, Ray argued. I could hear him echoing thoughts I had shared with him for years. With software, you have 100 percent margin. Hardware depends on volume. We would have no disadvantage with Microsoft.

Sculley realized that this was Ray's whole game, taking on Microsoft. There really was no "we" in Ray's vision. In a merger, Apple would be the junior partner and Sculley himself would most likely be out of a job, if not immediately then soon enough. He stopped any further conversation. The deal was dead.

In the years since, I have thought about those deals that fell through. At the time Microsoft approached us, Novell was valued at about $12 billion in the market. Microsoft was worth $20 billion. It was a flat merger. Novell shareholders would have gotten about 40 percent of the combined deal. Microsoft would have gotten 60 percent. Fast forward five years. Novell was worth $2 billion in the stock market. Microsoft was valued at $400 billion. Novell shareholders lost not one but several fortunes.

And if the Apple deal had gone through? History is full of *what ifs*.

But Ray still had one more card to play in his war with Microsoft. Though wearied by the whims of my counterpart, my faith was still intact. I believed innovation would continue to present opportunities for new deals, including one I fully expected—taking over for Ray whenever he retired.

The Wake-up Call

Ray turned on me.

Both of us were grappling with personal challenges that seeped into our professional lives. My lifelong battle with daytime drowsiness often saw me nodding off at my desk or during meetings. Ray, always the concerned colleague, would say, “Go home and get some rest.” He thought I was simply overworked. The truth was deeper. My father, and his father before him, had suffered from the same issue. Eventually, a doctor sent me to Stanford’s sleep clinic, where I was diagnosed with sleep apnea.

With a CPAP machine, my life transformed. For the first time in forty-six years, I could stay awake through an entire day, watch a movie from start to finish, and drive without fatigue. It felt like waking up to a new life.

Ray’s struggles were different and far less solvable. He was forgetful—or at least, he pretended to be. He cultivated this affable, grandfatherly image, which included bouts of convenient absentmindedness. But I knew better. Having traveled with him and worked in close proximity, I saw his sharpness. I also saw that his forgetfulness often seemed a deliberate tactic to avoid unpleasant interactions.

Many years later, he passed away from complications related to Alzheimer’s disease. That diagnosis shed a different light on his behavior. He may have been experiencing early symptoms of the disease. At the time, though, it was clear when he deployed this act against me that my days at Novell were numbered.

Ray was laser-focused on his final gambit—acquiring WordPerfect Corporation and Borland’s Quattro Pro to create a suite of software that could go toe-to-toe with Microsoft. The negotiations were handled entirely by Ray and his Utah team. I was excluded, an unmistakable departure from our previous collaborative dynamic. His vision was to shift Novell from networking to the desktop market, a strategy I considered ill-advised.

"Why do you have to fight with Microsoft?" I asked him directly, as I had done in the past. "This is not our fight."

He looked at me as if I were speaking a foreign language. That blank stare told me everything I needed to know—I was out of the circle.

But Ray underestimated the influence I had at the company. At the next board meeting, I recounted our interaction and voiced my concerns. "Ray's forgetfulness is compromising his ability to lead," I said bluntly. The board listened. My words carried weight, and the message wasn't lost on Ray, either. No one spoke to him that way. I was merely exercising my responsibility as a board member.

Soon after, in November 1993, he announced his retirement, citing minor memory lapses. Official statements insisted his performance wasn't affected, but the writing was on the wall.

Novell was quick to assure everyone that Ray's condition had no impact on his performance. Whether that was true or not, the reality was that Ray gradually stopped attending board meetings, then key company meetings, and eventually, he stopped coming in altogether.

This should have been my moment to step up. Ray had always been a hands-off CEO, leaning heavily on me to run the company. I was the face of Novell on Wall Street. The stock had risen tenfold in just two years. Despite challenges, we had grown from strength to strength under my leadership.

I was certain—100 percent certain—that the CEO job was mine. So, when I heard that the board had hired Bob Frankenberg, a former HP general manager, as the new CEO, I was floored. Shocked doesn't even begin to describe it. I felt betrayed.

It was the same old story—no matter what I achieved, it was never enough. It was déjà vu all over again, as Yogi Berra would say. At home, Ann was my rock, helping me through the sting of disappointment and depression that followed. I wasn't one to talk much about my emotions, but I didn't need to—she understood.

"Look around you—at this house, at the kids," she said. "Those are the things you need to pull yourself out of this funk."

I met Bob at a board meeting before his appointment was public and urged him to reconsider the WordPerfect and Quattro Pro deals. "The papers aren't signed yet," I reasoned. "Let's not saddle you with someone else's strategy. You should carve your own path." Bob's response was blunt. "The only reason I took this job was the WordPerfect merger," he said to the entire room.

He asked me to stay on as an advisor, but it wasn't the same. My role became perfunctory—more symbolic than substantive. I stayed in San Jose, rarely traveling to Utah. Bob would call if he needed advice, and if not, I stayed out of the way. My official last day was January 2, 1995.

I did what I thought was right. In hindsight, though, I should have resigned then and there. By remaining, I locked myself into restrictions as a board member and officer. Selling shares required a ninety-day notice, plus additional restrictions for insiders. When Novell's stock tanked, I was unable to act. That decision cost me dearly.

It was a bittersweet conclusion to an otherwise remarkable run. To some, that journey might appear to have begun when Navin, Inder, and I founded Excelan. But the truth is, it started much earlier—when, like almost every entrepreneur, I asked myself a simple yet profound question: *Why not me?*

Perspective is one of the hardest things to maintain, especially in difficult times. Looking back, my life was a series of transformations. Student to employee. Employee to founder. Founder to CEO. CEO to a top executive at a multibillion dollar tech company. And now, as that chapter closed, I stood on the edge of another shift. I just didn't know what that would be—or that it was already underway.

PART 5

THE GOSPEL OF ENTREPRENEURISM

CHAPTER

18

Building Bridges: TiE and Beyond

MY NEXT CHAPTER HAD STARTED a few years earlier, when I traveled to India to launch Novell India, in 1993.

The success of Onward Novell, my venture with Harish Mehta, inspired me to look for additional opportunities there. Harish suggested setting up a software development center. I did not need much convincing.

Novell was spending $300 million a year on R&D—almost $1 million a day. The cost of an engineer in India was 5 percent of the cost of an engineer in the US. I looked at the numbers and saw we could divert 1 percent of our R&D spend, or $3 million, to India, and I could hire 100 people to develop software. They would also be the smartest people in India.

Novell India, headquartered in the fast-growing tech hub of Bangalore, did extremely well. Eric Schmidt, who joined Novell as chief executive after I left and then became CEO of Google, praised the valuable roots I had planted for the company in India. Harish was absolutely correct about India. It was on the move—moving in an intriguing and positive direction—and I was glad to be riding the wave.

One afternoon, I was at Harish's office in Bombay when it struck me—I was not far from my alma mater, IIT. On a whim, I asked him to drive me there. As we entered the campus, my heart sank. The place that had once been a temple of learning, where I had spent some of the most formative years of my life, was now in shambles. Buildings were crumbling, the paint was peeling, and nature had begun to reclaim the pathways. The campus, originally built with Soviet collaboration in the late 1950s, had aged poorly. It no longer radiated the pride and excellence it once did.

Disturbed by what I had seen, I arranged a meeting with the institute's president. I told him how disappointed I was by the neglect and immediately offered to write a check to repaint the buildings, including my old dorm—the place where I had formed lifelong friendships and dreamed big dreams. To my surprise, he refused. He explained, almost apologetically, that the school could only accept funds from the government. It was the law. Part of his hesitation, I sensed, was pride. But mostly, it was bureaucracy.

I wasn't going to take no for an answer. I told him this wasn't just a donation—it was an investment. I knew that if I could give, so could many other IIT alumni who owed their success to the education they had received here. We all understood the power of an IIT degree, and I was certain they would be willing to give back.

Determined to change the system, I lobbied the government. It took effort, but eventually, the law changed to allow private donations. This was just the beginning. I argued that while the government should continue supporting IITs, alumni and industry should play a bigger role in funding them. That way, the government could focus on building a thousand new IITs instead of just maintaining the existing ones.

It was a radical idea at the time and sparked heated debate, but one thing was clear—giving more students access to a world-class education was an investment India could not afford to ignore.

India on the Move

The school aside, I remember driving through the city with Harish and feeling waves of pride as I saw and heard about the way India was being transformed by tech—and all during my relatively brief lifetime. When the British departed in 1947, India was in extremely poor shape politically and economically. Its share of the world GDP had dropped from 25 percent to less than 2 percent. At the time of Independence, 90 percent of Indians were illiterate.[1]

The British had skillfully exploited India's diversity—thirty sub-nationalities, nearly 500 princely states, and 30 percent Muslim—and used the "divide and rule" policy to maintain an iron-fisted control. They developed a privileged class of English-speaking Indians, the so called "Macaulay's children," named after Thomas Babington Macaulay, who had seen the need for them. These Macaulay's children became well-versed in English liberal tradition and proved to be very useful in the beginning but with time came to see the unjustness of the alien rule of the British.

The Indian freedom movement was led by these English-speaking Indians and was universal and very peaceful in nature. Even with that, when the British decided to depart, they partitioned India into two countries: a Hindu majority country and a Muslim majority country. The partition caused a violent convulsion where about a million people died and ten million were uprooted in the world's largest population migration.

Despite all that, India chose to become a constitutional democracy with universal franchise. On the economic front, Indian founding fathers trained in British Fabian socialism chose the Soviet model of planned economy with the state in control of the economy. Five Indian Institutes of Technology were set up to produce world class technocrats to man the industries being planned.

While Indian democracy worked like a charm, as it went through eighteen election cycles with peaceful transfer of power, the economy stagnated, as it did the Soviet Union. Most of the engineers being produced by IITs migrated to the US when the US opened to immigration from India in the mid- to late-'60s.

By the late 1980s, democracy finally forced economic change. The old socialist framework collapsed under its own weight. Most government controls were rolled back, and by 1991, India fully embraced liberalization. The floodgates opened. Entrepreneurs like Harish stepped forward to build companies in IT and pharmaceuticals, unleashing a new wave of economic energy.

It was exhilarating to see India shake off the shackles of socialism. The new Prime Minister moved swiftly—abolishing price controls, slashing tariffs, opening markets, and welcoming foreign investment. The old business elite, used to operating in protected silos, suddenly had to compete—not just with each other, but with global giants from the US and Japan. Indian businesses scrambled for expertise, and their search for guidance stretched all the way to Silicon Valley.

A Meeting of Minds

India's Department of Electronics Secretary, Mr N. Vittal, was a man on a mission—a visionary committed to modernizing India through the power of information technology.

Arranging a fact-finding trip to Silicon Valley, he tapped Kailash Joshi, then president of Oryx Tech, to gather a select group of Indian-origin entrepreneurs, executives, and thought leaders for a discussion. The goal? To explore how we could contribute to India's growth and transformation.

About twenty of us met for lunch at the Marriott Hotel near San Francisco Airport. Among those present were AJ Patel, CEO of Odyssey Enterprises; Suhas Patil, founder of Cirrus Logic and a former professor at the University of Utah; Roy Prasad, CEO of Propell Micro Systems; and Chan Desaigoudar, chairman and CEO of California Micro Devices Corporation. It was an impressive lineup of trailblazers who had carved their own paths in Silicon Valley. Yet, the man who had orchestrated the meeting was conspicuously absent.

Word came after an hour: Mr Vittal had missed his flight from Los Angeles. While such a delay might have derailed a typical gathering, this was anything but ordinary. Instead of dispersing, we stayed. Most of us knew *of* each other but had rarely interacted personally. What unfolded over the next few hours was transformative.

We began sharing our stories—our origins, our journeys from small towns and cities across India to the United States, and the challenges we faced along the way. There was a powerful sense of connection as we discovered shared experiences: the loneliness of being pioneers, the pressure to perform exceptionally, and the uphill battles to prove ourselves in environments that rarely gave us the benefit of the doubt.

The hours flew by. By the time Mr Vittal finally arrived, the seeds of something much larger had already been planted. Before we parted ways, AJ Patel suggested we meet regularly to continue these conversations. The idea resonated deeply, and we committed to monthly dinners. What began as casual meetups soon became a forum for sharing wisdom, support, and camaraderie.

During these meetups we realized we were bound by common traits—a relentless drive to solve problems, a refusal to accept mediocrity, and an unyielding desire to control our own destinies. Many of us had chosen entrepreneurship as our vehicle for achieving this independence. Corporations, with their rigid hierarchies, felt stifling. Building something of our own—that was freedom.

As we reflected on our journeys, one theme emerged repeatedly: we had no role models, no mentors, and no roadmap. Each of us had navigated this path alone, often against formidable odds. "It shouldn't be this hard for the next generation," Suhas Patil observed. His words struck a chord. The idea of mentorship took root.

Kailash suggested we focus on supporting entrepreneurs. I couldn't have agreed more. "Entrepreneurship is the ultimate path to independence," I said. "When you build something yourself, you're not just making a living—you're living the dream that brought you here in the first place."

What started as a delayed lunch became a catalyst for lifelong friendships, a shared vision, and a commitment to pave the way for future generations. We were no longer just individuals navigating our respective journeys; we were a community, united by purpose and bound by a common mission to give back and lift others up.

A Revolutionary Idea

From simple dinner conversations, a transformative idea was born—a formal organization aimed at fostering the next generation of entrepreneurs from the Indus region.

This wasn't just about India. We sought to include Pakistan, Bangladesh, Sri Lanka, and the entire diaspora. The goal was straightforward yet profound: to serve as role models and mentors while keeping politics and religion at bay. Our message was clear—embrace wealth creation, succeed, and then help others succeed. When one prospers, everyone benefits.

As we deliberated, I found myself reflecting deeply, revisiting the winding path that brought me here. Growing up in Kanpur, I was an unremarkable student, overshadowed by brighter peers, and dismissed by my father. My journey began without fanfare—shy, poor, and burdened with self-doubt. At IIT, I wasn't among the star students. Many classmates, including one who rose to prominence at Bell Labs, seemed destined for greatness.

So, what drove me? How did I navigate these waters?

It was a blend of circumstances and inner resolve. Being left to my own devices as a child shaped my ability to chart my own course. Facing layoffs—three in total—ignited a fire within me, a vow that I would never again be at someone else's mercy. Hard work and self-improvement were constants. But two factors stood out above the rest.

First, independence. Each time I was left on my own, my instincts took over. At IIT, Singer-Link, Zilog, and eventually Excelan, the same pattern emerged: *If no one else can, I will. And I'll do it my way.* That mindset became the foundation for Excelan's success.

Second, Ann. Her belief in me was life-altering. When she accepted my proposal, she became the first person to truly believe in me. That belief gave me a confidence boost that fueled everything that followed.

Could all or some of that be understood and shared with others in a meaningful way? Could it help other people produce results?

A core team of seven—AJ, Kailash Joshi, Roy Prasad, Narpat Bhandari, Bipin Shah, Ray Vradula, and Sam Satya—began shaping the idea into reality. We envisioned workshops where those of us who had succeeded would guide aspiring entrepreneurs. We came up with questions that would illustrate the topics we wanted to address and the answers we thought were important to provide new entrepreneurs: *Am I cut out to be an entrepreneur? How do I write a business plan? Raise funds? Build a team? Define my product?*

Because I was still in my role at Novell, my involvement was relatively limited but it was still meaningful. I suggested the name The IndUS Entrepreneur (TiE)—to highlight both our roots and our identity as Americans. The logo was red, white, and blue logo to further reinforce our connection to America, a country born of an idea that afforded us the freedom to dream and create.

TiE embodied this ethos. The first workshop was scheduled. AJ herded everyone to the early meetings, Kailash ensured commitments, and Roy incorporated TiE, doing much of the heavy lifting. We pooled resources to cover expenses—Suhas Patil alone contributed $15,000.

He became TiE's first president, setting a high standard for everything we did. At the time, none of us could have foreseen the global impact this idea would have. But we knew we were on to something powerful. As Victor Hugo once said, "You cannot suppress an idea whose time has come." TiE was that idea. And the time was now.

A Game-changer in the Making

The weekend of March 26, 1994, at the Fairmont Hotel in San Jose marked a turning point for TiE—and perhaps for the entrepreneurial community at large.

We had modest expectations for our first-ever Entrepreneurial Seminar and Workshop, predicting an attendance of fifty, maybe a hundred. That number turned out to be laughably low. Over 500 people—entrepreneurs, venture capitalists, Stanford professors, and top-notch lawyers—packed the conference rooms, eager for insights into marketing, operations, finance, and legal strategies.

By Sunday evening, the buzz wasn't just local; it stretched from Berkeley to Bombay. TiE had officially arrived.

In those early days, TiE was more of a weekend social club than the powerhouse it is now. Our twenty charter members, each contributing $1,000, gave us a modest war chest. We rented an office in Santa Clara, open only on Saturdays and Sundays when our core group could meet. During the week? The office sat empty. Everyone had jobs—except me.

I had recently stepped back from Novell, which left me at home full-time, much to my wife Ann's frustration. We navigated our days like two people performing mismatched dances. Finally, one day, Ann gave it to me straight: "Find something to do during the day." Translation? Get out of the house.

The next morning, armed with my usual stack of newspapers—*The New York Times*, *Wall Street Journal*, and *San Jose Mercury News*—I headed to the empty TiE office. I made coffee, read the papers, tackled crosswords, and answered the phone when it rang. If friends wanted to meet me, I invited them to come over. My schedule was open, and so was the door.

Slowly but surely, word got out: I was in the office every day, and anyone could swing by for a quick meeting without much hassle.

The drop-ins began. Entrepreneurs showed up to pitch their startups, share business plans, and seek advice. I listened, asked questions, and offered feedback. With each conversation, the TiE office transformed from a quiet space into a dynamic hub—a clubhouse for smart, driven entrepreneurs eager to turn ideas into thriving businesses. This was exactly what we had envisioned when we first conceived of TiE.

But here's the thing: mentoring these entrepreneurs rejuvenated me as much as it helped them. After the grind of corporate life at Novell, I found myself rediscovering the joy of creation. There was no corporate politics, no bureaucratic inertia—just raw ideas and the people passionate about bringing them to life. My days were filled with a sense of purpose once again.

I found myself asking the entrepreneurs same fundamental questions I'd asked myself throughout my career: *What problem are you solving? Who is your customer? How will you reach them? What sets you apart?* If they couldn't answer, I pushed them to refine their thinking. And if the numbers didn't add up, I channeled John Bosch, the former board member at Excelan: "Spare me the story. Show me the numbers."

One lesson stood out: while every conversation began with the idea, it always circled back to the person behind it. Success in startups isn't just about the plan—it's about the person driving it.

In the months and years that followed, TiE would grow beyond our wildest dreams. But for me, those early days in that empty office, connecting with hungry entrepreneurs, remain some of the most fulfilling of my life.

Taking the Baton

In 1995, I became president of TiE, the first of six years that I served in that position. My predecessor Suhas Patil had set a high bar in our inaugural year. Getting a person of Suhas' stature to join TiE's founding team in the first place had been a real coup. As a president, he was a taskmaster, the epitome of rectitude. He demanded quality and punctuality. He made sure our events ran like clockwork, and I set out to build upon that high standard.

Why did I throw myself into it with such relentless energy? Why did it feel so personal from the start? For years, I chalked it up to destiny meeting opportunity—lightning in a bottle. But I was a cutthroat businessman, the kind who believed, "You can't be a CEO if you can't fire your own brother." There had to be more to it than just fate.

Over time, I realized it was something deeper, something rooted in who I was. In many ways, I am a product of India's freedom movement. I grew up in the 1950s, a time of unshakable optimism and idealism. We were poor, but we believed we would be rich. We were uneducated, but we knew we were the smartest people in the world. We had been under foreign rule for 200 years, but now we were free—and we were convinced we would thrive.

Even though I was a hardcore businessman at the time, the idea of entrepreneurship struck a chord with both sides of my brain. TiE wasn't just an organization—it was a movement—the freedom movement of my youth. It filled me with idealism. It let me see possibilities.

So I took the baton and ran with it. Kailash Joshi and I collaborated on a code of conduct that we distributed to all charter members. (*Thou shall return calls from fellow charter members.*) Suhas, Roy Prasad, and I spent an evening writing a philosophical framework. (*Emphasize value-creation through informed entrepreneurship. Be intolerant of pettiness, divisiveness, and corruption.*) Prabhu Goel, who founded Verilog, helped Suhas finalize the by-laws.

Nitin Mehta, a Harvard MBA and VC/PE investor, helped structure TiE as a 501c(6) organization, which categorized it as a business league. And Bakul Joshi, a PhD in agril entomology with a fierce sense of humor, ran our members' meetings the third Wednesday of every month. He planned the program, secured a speaker, arranged the menu, and kept things interesting. Access to these monthly TiE meetings was highly valued. The networking was priceless. People found mentors, partners, and angel investors.

One of the early issues was that everyone would sign up at the last moment. Many just showed without signing up. Since these meetings included dinner, it was hard to order the right amount of food without knowing how many were coming. Bakul finally devised a market solution to the problem. The meeting fee was $35 if you signed up forty-eight hours ahead of time. If you signed up only twenty-four hours before, the fee went up to $45. The price for showing up without a reservation was $55. Problem solved.

Bipin Shah, part of the senior management team at Altera and later the president of Altera Japan before founding Kovair Software, convened the second annual TiEcon. Ramesh Yadav marshalled an army of nearly 100 volunteers into an efficient team that took care of registration, badge printing, room staging, and the myriad other tasks that made the trains run on time. After the conference, membership grew by leaps and bounds.

Afterward, I heard Ramesh sing the Shree 420 song "Dil ka Haal Sune Dilwala" to his exhausted team. The loose translation: Listen to your heart.

People were clearly listening. That year was a turning point for TiE. It had an office, a full time president, and monthly events that were very productive. TiE inspired a large number of successful entrepreneurs starting that year. There was also a lucky break: it was just in time for the Internet revolution.

Taking It a Step Further: Angel Investing

Mentoring, I quickly realized, was only part of the solution.

Entrepreneurs didn't just need guidance; they needed capital. I understood this all too well from my own experience. For a startup, money wasn't just a resource—it was survival itself, as essential as oxygen is to life. Without it, a venture suffocated and died.

I tried sending some of these hungry, driven entrepreneurs to my venture capital friends, hoping they'd see the potential I did. But the response was disheartening. The rejections piled up, and it became clear: the VC world still hadn't adapted to the idea of Indian entrepreneurs, despite the successes a few of us had achieved.

This wasn't just a hurdle—it was a wall that needed breaking. If change was going to happen, someone had to make the first move. That's when an idea struck me: if I truly believed in the advice I was giving, why not back it up with my own money? Angel investing wasn't something I'd planned, but that year, I dove in headfirst. I wrote checks for eight companies: Zeitnet, Ambit, Exodus, Cybermedia, Apptivity, Mediaway, Intellimatch, and Versata.

Each investment felt like a gamble. The Novell stock I'd once relied on had taken a nosedive, leaving me with far less financial security. Every time I wrote a check, a little voice in the back of my head asked: *Are you throwing money down the drain?* But then, something remarkable happened. Zeitnet, a small networking startup led by Amit Shah, began showing promise. Its sharp focus as a LAN alternative reminded me of my own Excelan days.

Yet, as startups often do, Zeitnet hit turbulence. The technology didn't gain the traction we'd hoped for, and a year later, Amit faced a tough decision: find a buyer or shut the company down. Most of us on the board were ready to write it off as a loss. But Amit—an extraordinary sales guy (and I've always had a soft spot for great salespeople)—pulled a rabbit out of the hat. He convinced Cabletron to acquire Zeitnet for nearly $140 million.

I recovered not just my investment in Zeitnet but all of the investments I had made, with seven other companies still in play, so everything from then on was house money. Besides a tidy profit, that win gave me something priceless: confidence. Investing, much like entrepreneurship, requires a mix of skill, timing, and yes, a little luck. I'd just gotten mine. From that moment, I was all in as an angel investor.

This wasn't just about my own journey, though. Around the same time, TiE began transforming into more than a mentoring platform. It became a place where entrepreneurs with great ideas—but no access to capital—could find angels like me. That synergy between mentoring, networking, and funding became TiE's magic formula.

TiE wasn't just about building startups; it was about building wealth, passing it forward, and creating a virtuous cycle of success. Once someone achieved financial freedom, TiE gave them a higher purpose—helping the next entrepreneur take their shot.

And that, I believe, would become TiE's most impactful legacy: it wasn't just about supporting businesses. It was about starting a movement.

A Lesson in Financial Economics

In 1994, the Mosaic browser opened a floodgate of change and opportunity.

Up until then, the Internet was a niche tool—a glorified file-sharing system used mostly by the military, corporations, and universities. Mosaic turned it into something anyone with a PC could use, and by 1995, the revolution was in full swing. Mosaic soon rebranded as Netscape, and the rest is history.

By the end of 1995, forty million people had downloaded the Netscape browser. Giants like Microsoft and Novell, initially caught napping, scrambled to respond. Microsoft pivoted aggressively, launching Internet Explorer, and by early 1997, it had overtaken Netscape.

As the Internet gained traction in the mid-90s, America Online (AOL) became the dominant player, offering dial-up connections and, most importantly, the wildly popular AOL Instant Messenger. In 1998, AOL was powerful enough to devour Netscape and bold enough to buy Time Warner—a move that would become a textbook example of corporate hubris when it ended disastrously in 2000. Meanwhile, the Internet was spawning titans like Yahoo, eBay, Amazon, and Google, making household names out of tech nerds like Jerry Yang, Pierre Omidyar, Jeff Bezos, and Larry Page and Sergey Brin.

Amid this gold rush was a young entrepreneur named Sabeer Bhatia, who had an idea: email on the web. Until then most people's email was tied to your company ID—if you switched jobs, you lost your email. Sabeer launched Hotmail, offering free email to the masses. I wasn't impressed with the business model. Giving away such a useful service for free? It seemed unsustainable. But the numbers didn't lie—at its peak, 60,000 users were signing up every day. The problem was, as users flocked to Hotmail, expenses piled up just as fast. Sabeer was running out of money, and his investors weren't sure he'd ever make any.

I met Sabeer during this time. He told me his goal was to reach ten million users; at that point, he believed Hotmail would be golden. He talked about monetizing that user base, but I was skeptical. "Sabeer," I said, "you have nothing to upsell." I advised him to start charging $10 a year and promised to invest $1 million if he did. Reluctantly, he agreed. I was heading to India at the time and told him we'd finalize things when I returned in two weeks.

Barely a week into my trip, I got the news: Microsoft had acquired Hotmail for $400 million. I was stunned. Hotmail didn't have a product to sell, but Microsoft didn't need one—they had MSN, a $2 billion investment with just 1 million users. By acquiring Hotmail's 10 million users at $40 per user, Microsoft turned their struggling service into a powerhouse.

For Sabeer, it was the deal of a lifetime. And for me, a lesson in financial economics. An asset's value isn't fixed—it changes depending on whose hands it's in. I had offered $1 million for 10 percent of Hotmail. In Microsoft's hands, it was worth forty times that.

CHAPTER 19

Betting on People

INVESTMENTS ARE PERSONAL. AS HARD as you try to base decisions solely on numbers, it is nearly impossible to completely close the door on gut feelings about people.

That's one of the things that made TiE so hot: the networking possibilities. Everyone wanted in on the monthly workshops. Sponsors now included Valley A-listers like the VC firm Kleiner Perkins Caufield & Byers, Silicon Valley Bank, and the law firm Wilson, Sonsini, Goodrich & Rosati. Successful startups like CyberMedia and Junglee, which sprang from TiE support, not only added credibility but also access to those who struck it rich.

These were stars of the business section. They were written about in the *Wall Street Journal*, *Forbes*, and *BusinessWeek*. You could speak with them and then walk away, as many did, asking yourself, "If they can do it, why can't I?"

I spent these meetings standing in the back, talking to whoever wanted my attention. My responses were always quick and direct. I remember one guy pitching me an idea for computerizing warehouse services. He went on and on until I finally cut him off. "You have a nice story, but you're not telling me what you're doing," I said. "You spent twenty minutes beating around the bush; let me tell you what your business is."

It took me ten seconds to describe it. He was dumbfounded. "Yes, that's exactly what I want to do!" he exclaimed. "Can I have your card?" Rather than explain I was most easily reached through TiE, I took his card. I usually went home with my pockets filled with business cards. One night, toward the end of December, I was going through the box of business cards I had collected the past few months. A handwritten note on the back of one card caught my eye.

Because the card was on top of the pile, I must have been given it at the most recent TiE meeting two days earlier. I had no memory of receiving it or writing that note. It was definitely my handwriting, though. It said, "Call this guy back." The name on the card was K.B. Chandrasekhar. I dialed the number. Chandrasekhar answered immediately.

"Hello, this is Kanwal Rekhi. We met, and I have your card and—"

He cut me off before I finished.

"Can I come over to your office?" he said.

"I'm at home," I said. "How about tomorrow or the day after?"

"I'll come to your home then."

"I'm busy."

"I need to see you today."

Within half an hour, K.B. Chandrasekhar was at my house. We sat opposite each other in my office. Before he even sat down, he started telling me about his company, a web-hosting business called Exodus Communications. Chandrasekhar had come to America from India in 1992. Two years later, he and B.V. Jagadeesh started Exodus from his bedroom after recognizing a giant need in the marketplace. Millions of people were on the Internet and more were signing up every day. Businesses would inevitably follow.

"Businesses go where people are, and people are on the Internet," he said with the urgency of a novelist trying to summarize a 500-page book in two minutes. "Businesses will need help getting on the Internet, storing information, backing up data, and executing their transactions. They will be willing to pay tens of thousands of dollars a month for flexible, reliable Internet connections and lots of bandwidth. We will build data centers all over the country. Here. New York. All over."

Chandrasekhar was a superb salesman. He had a gift for crafting a story and a hustler's energy and determination. He made it easy for me to see that he and his partner had come up with a solution to a problem that people had not yet realized was going to arise. He was smart. And he was also desperate. Exodus was out of money. They hadn't paid rent and he hadn't paid his employees for a month or two.

"If I can't come up with the money," he said, "I'm shut down tomorrow."

Something about Chandrasekhar resonated with me. It wasn't his desperation. I had seen my share of that in entrepreneurs who moved me to shake hands and wish them good luck. This is why I say some decisions are personal.

Let me cite a parallel. In 1989, I was at a Palo Alto VC firm, helping to close a deal with some Chinese investors. Suddenly, the building started to shake violently. It was an earthquake. A big one! I got under the large conference table while the Chinese investors ran out on to the street. Once the shaking stopped, the Chinese investors refused to sign the deal. They said the earthquake was a signal from God that the deal must not be done.

It is no different when it is just people. You project your thoughts and beliefs on to this other person. Do I like this entrepreneur? Can they make it happen? Do they have the right approach? A winning strategy? Are they focused? Do they have the energy it takes? Can they sell?

Ultimately, the human element is the most important part of the equation. I always bet on the person rather than the business plan. I can help change or improve a business plan. I can't do much with a person.

Chandrasekhar had my attention. I could see he was drowning, and I understood what a waste it would be if he and his company went under. I saw it had the potential to be big, very big. I asked Chandrasekhar about his business plan. Finally, I heard enough and did something completely out of character for me. I wrote Chandrasekhar a sizeable check on the spot. There was no time to do any more due diligence than I just had by talking to him. I liked the idea. I had a feeling. We sketched out the terms with a pen and paper and both of us signed it before he left my house.

It was the last of the eight investments I made in 1995, and it turned out to be the biggest one of my life.

Purposeful Simplicity

Startups don't have the resources to do more than one thing.

This was something I repeatedly explained to Chandrasekhar. An entrepreneur needs a sharp focus on what he's doing, and they need to be extremely focused doing it. Anytime you look at other opportunities, you get distracted from the opportunity at hand. Every opportunity has an associated cost. Chandrasekhar was one of those entrepreneurs who chased opportunities one after another until he was so tangled up in YAFOs (yet another friggin' opportunity) he lost his focus entirely.

The day after I signed the check, I visited Chandrasekhar and his partner. They had a small operation in Sunnyvale. We sat down and I listened. Chandrasekhar was full of plans for the services Exodus would provide. The network, the bandwidth, servers, applications, managing applications, and so on. He sounded like a waiter explaining the menu at one of those restaurants that have everything. So many choices and specials made you wonder if anything was good.

"No, no, no," I said to Chandrasekhar. "Let's simplify things. You don't have to do any applications. No managing anything. Build the data centers. Period."

I saw Chandrasekhar's business partner smile. I glanced around the makeshift office. Servers were stacked on top of more servers. Employees sat shoulder to shoulder in front of computers. I noticed the temperature in the room. The room was hot, crowded, and uncomfortable. But everyone was focused on one thing, the same thing. Exodus Communications was doing what it was supposed to be doing, nothing more and nothing less. I pointed that out to Chandrasekhar.

"Look around this room," I said. "This is your business."

Businesses could not get on the Internet easily and quickly. The required bandwidth was not available. T-1 lines were expensive, and even if you could afford the cost, phone companies had a six-month wait to get them installed. Exodus offered a solution. It could have ten T-1 lines in its data center and businesses could put their server there and be on high speed Internet in practically no time.

The purposeful simplicity of this reminded me of the way I had focused Excelan as a solution to a company's networking problem. Chandrasekhar could sell that: Exodus will provide you with fast, reliable Internet and a place to locate your servers. In subsequent meetings, we honed the business model, the language, and worked on projections. The potential market was enormous. Yet again, when considering who might want this service, I wrote down a single word: everyone.

Lightning in a Bottle

Predicting success in this game is like catching lightning in a bottle.

Starting in 1996, I dove headfirst into angel investing, making fifty-four bets on companies that came through TiE—The IndUs Entrepreneurs network. The results? I had twenty-three exits—

including six IPOs—and thirty-one write-offs. On a cash-on-cash basis, my returns were over 10x the money I put in, with the lion's share coming from a handful of investments. NexTag, a comparison-shopping site, was one. Another standout was The Great Unwashed, a self-publishing platform. I handed the founder a check, and before we even finalized terms (a handshake deal for 10 percent), Amazon snapped up the company for $10 million.

But none of these stories compared to Exodus.

Exodus, led by Chandrasekhar, was a case study in flawless execution. The business plan we drew up was ambitious, but he delivered beyond expectations. The first data center, expected to take a year to fill, was bursting at the seams in just three months. Demand forced us to expand rapidly, building new data centers in New York and Dallas. To fund this growth, I brought in heavy hitters like Prabhu Goel, Suhas Patil, and former Excelan board members Ed Shea and John Dougery. Together, we raised $3 million, setting Exodus on a path to scale.

Timing, as always, was everything. The Internet was exploding. By 1996, the number of users had tripled to forty-five million. Companies like Hotmail were adding 60,000 new users daily, expanding their servers in Exodus' data centers. Chandrasekhar's customer list read like a tech hall of fame: Yahoo, Netscape, GeoCities—and later, Oracle and HP. These companies formed a symbiotic ecosystem, driving Exodus' capacity to double every six months. At one point, 50 percent of the world's Internet traffic flowed through Exodus data centers. Their audacious tagline? "We are the Internet."

Revenue followed demand. Exodus went from $1 million a month to $10 million a month, eventually reaching $100 million a month in just three years. Bill Clinton declared Exodus a national asset and ordered heightened security around its data centers. By 1998, 147 million people were online, tolerating slow speeds and shaky connections because everyone believed the tech would only get better.

I pushed hard for Exodus to go public. The numbers were dazzling: 40 percent quarterly growth over thirteen quarters and forty data centers nationwide. With those types of numbers you have to go public. The Internet sector was commanding astronomical valuations, and I knew Exodus had a story that Wall Street couldn't resist.

The IPO in March 1998 was a smash hit. Initially priced at $15 a share, the stock opened at $25 and soared to $42 within weeks. By 2000, Exodus' valuation hit $30 billion, with shares peaking at $80. On paper, my net worth ballooned to unfathomable levels. I shared my good fortune, giving stock to friends and family who suddenly found themselves wealthy.

But the Internet boom had its quirks. Exodus, like many other tech darlings, had revenues but no profits. Rapid expansion outpaced income, with 80 percent of revenue lost to selling and marketing costs. If Exodus did $1 million a month, it lost $800,000. If it did $10 million a month, it lost $8 million. The market didn't care. Growth trumped profitability. Hotmail had zero revenue but was acquired by Microsoft for $400 million. That was the era's playbook.

For me, the IPO brought riches but also a sobering perspective on wealth's limitations. My mother, who had lived to see the family prosper, though she often lamented that my father hadn't been there to witness it, passed away. Three generations of her family were in the room with her, holding her hand, as she took her final breaths. It was a beautiful reminder of a core value: family gives life its meaning.

But family also presented challenges that logic couldn't solve. My wife struggled with the success of Exodus and TiE. She feared that my dedication to TiE meant I was unhappy at home. When sudden wealth came into our lives, her fears only deepened, all fueled by her depression. Ironically, because I sat on the Exodus board, much of my stock was locked away, out of my reach. Ann's suffering was locked away too—also beyond my grasp.

I tried to reassure Ann—not just about money but about what we had built together as a couple, as parents, as a family. But logic was no match for the darkness of her illness. She was trapped in her suffering.

Years earlier, at her suggestion, we had gone to couples therapy and Al-Anon meetings, which offered support for family and friends of people with alcohol problems. Ann courageously sought answers to her struggles, and she wanted me to have the tools to support her. Those experiences taught me that the analytical mindset of an engineer had its limits. A wounded heart didn't respond to reason. I did everything I could to comfort her, to understand her pain.

Through it all, work became my refuge. I never wanted a life of luxury—jets, yachts, and excess held no appeal. To me, the Exodus IPO wasn't only about adding to my bank account; it was validation. It proved the impact of TiE, the strength of the network we had built, and the transformative power of collective ambition.

The success of Exodus and other ventures didn't just change bank balances; it shifted perceptions. In an article about me titled "The Venture Capitalist from Kanpur," *Forbes* declared, "The former conventional wisdom—that Indians were great technical minds but lousy marketers and executives—no longer holds water."

Recognition—this was the holy grail. It wasn't about money anymore. My passion for TiE soared because I knew our work mattered more than ever. Wealth had its perks, but it was secondary to the real mission: empowering entrepreneurs.

Why entrepreneurs? Because they are the engines of progress. This is a song I have sung countless times. Entrepreneurs see a problem, come up with a solution, and move things forward. They are society's change agents. An entrepreneur doesn't just build a company; they pull along an entire ecosystem—workers, customers, suppliers, and whole industries. They create jobs, drive innovation, and lift entire communities. Wealth creation isn't about a few people getting rich; it's about expanding prosperity for a great many people.

Most successful entrepreneurs I know and have invested in aren't in it just for the money. They are driven by a burning desire to make something work—to prove their ideas can change the world. Profit is just a scoreboard, a way of saying, "See? I told you it would work."

When Excelan merged with Novell, about 100 people became millionaires. And what did they do? They reinvested in their communities and their children. They bought more goods, used more services, and pumped more money into the economy. They funded new startups, mentored the next generation, and paid it forward. This is the part of wealth creation that too many people overlook—it has a ripple effect. Entrepreneurship isn't a zero-sum game. When one succeeds, many benefit.

This was the foundation of TiE, the gospel, and it was working. And for me, it was just the beginning of an even greater journey.

CHAPTER

20

Tough Love: Sparking India's Second Revolution

TiE HAD BECOME A PHENOMENON. It wasn't just an organization anymore—it was a movement. For me, it marked the start of another uphill climb, with new challenges and responsibilities that kept me busier than ever.

We opened chapters in Los Angeles, Boston, Atlanta, and Dallas, and I made it a point to attend each one. During my tenure as TiE president, I would travel to the openings of forty-six chapters. Indian entrepreneurs. lined up, eager to join the organization. I said, "Here are our bylaws, the way we operate, and the values we have enshrined in our philosophical network. You will have to buy into that if you want to be part of TiE."

In the process, I realized the politics and in-fighting at Novell had taken a toll on me. Now, in my third year as TiE president, I felt alive and vital again. I was mentoring hundreds, if not thousands, of entrepreneurs, and through TiE, we were impacting even more. I was constantly giving interviews to newspapers, magazines, and TV networks in the US, Europe, and India.

My rising profile drew nearly 1,000 people for a speaking engagement at the Harvard Club in New York City. My son Ben was studying at NYU at the time. I invited him to the talk. Afterward, he turned to me, astonished.

"Dad, everybody here knows you," he said afterward.

"Yes," I said.

"I had no idea."

The growing demands on my time led me to hire my former Novell administrator to manage my schedule. But looking at my calendar, you could sum up my activity in one word: India.

India was on the brink of transformation. Its size, population, and growing emphasis on tech represented boundless opportunity. In 1998, India's Prime Minister Atal Bihari Vajpayee took his third oath of office and spoke passionately about the importance tech was going to play in the country's future. He referred to IT (information technology) as "India's tomorrow." It was not just his clever wordplay that caught my attention. It was his vision and dedication to technology.

He echoed Prime Minister Nehru's reference many years ago to the IITs as "India's future in the making." Vajpayee's conviction inspired me to request a meeting. Naturally, something like that takes time to arrange. Meanwhile, those of us who had benefited from an IIT education but left India felt the obligation to repay our debt and contribute to history.

In December, Saurabh Srivastava, NASSCOM Chairman at the time, was launching the TiE Chapter in Delhi and helped organize the first TiE workshop in India, titled "Wealth Creation and Entrepreneurship, Silicon Valley Style." Twelve charter members, including me, flew to Delhi for the event at the Taj Mansingh Hotel. More than 300 people showed up, including senior government bureaucrats. The level of intensity in the sessions and eagerness to network was palpable. It wasn't just ambition—it was a hunger to redefine India's economic future.

The event served as an informal launch of the TiE Delhi chapter. TIECON events would follow every year with an ever-growing mix of Silicon Valley stars, Indian entrepreneurs, investors, and government officials. We called this India's second independence movement, this time for economic freedom. For many, TiE wasn't just about business. It was a higher calling. There was also appreciation for the attention we were paying to India.

One government official pulled me aside to ask a pointed question: *After thirty years in America, did I still feel Indian?* His question made me smile. It was something I had been forced to think about many times. I told him wherever I was—whether at the grocery store or the New York Stock Exchange—people asked where I was from.

"The Bay Area," I would say.

"No, before that."

"Florida. Before that New Jersey. And before that Michigan."

Finally, they would ask, "No, where are you from originally?"

The truth was, I could never distance myself from India. My identity was intertwined with India's journey. To understand India, I had to examine my own life. To understand my life, I had to look at India. The TiE members with whom I had traveled halfway around the world felt the same way. Yet there were hard questions we needed to face: Why do Indians have to leave India to succeed? Why do we succeed in Silicon Valley while people as smart and much smarter than us fail in India? Why have first-rate thinkers in India produced a third-rate country?

These were uncomfortable truths. But if we were going to bring about change, we had to confront them head-on. And that's exactly why TiE had come to India.

Tough Love: The Case for Entrepreneurship in India

When I took the stage, I didn't mince words. "India's biggest challenge is poverty," I began. "And the only cure for poverty is wealth.

Wealth doesn't come from governments or policies; it comes from entrepreneurs. If India wants to rise, it needs policies that actively promote entrepreneurship."

The room was quiet, save for a few hesitant claps. I knew I was treading on sensitive ground. Very few people dared to say that the government was a hindrance to progress. But facts are facts. If India's future was tied to its IT prowess, we had to confront the issue head-on, without excuses or delay.

"Why are we poor?" I asked. "We're poor by choice. By not doing what's necessary to create wealth! It's not our DNA. It's not our intelligence. It's the environment. We must make India a place where entrepreneurship thrives."

I paused to let that sink in, then continued. "Think about it. In 1947, we gained independence. Politically, we were free. Economically, we were destitute. And what did we do? We embraced socialism. Our leaders believed distributing wealth was the solution, but what we ended up distributing was poverty. The only path to economic freedom is wealth creation."

I could see heads nodding now. "Unless you're sitting on a sea of oil like Saudi Arabia, the only way to create new wealth is through entrepreneurs. Governments don't create wealth; they destroy it—sometimes quickly, sometimes slowly. The best governments understand this and focus on creating an environment where entrepreneurs can dream, build, and succeed.

"That's what TiE is all about," I said, my voice rising with an evangelical fervor. "It's about creating a cycle of entrepreneurship. One generation succeeds, lifts the next, and the cycle continues. That's how it happened in Silicon Valley, and that's what needs to happen here. For India to thrive, it must embrace this virtuous cycle."

The applause this time was louder, more confident. But I knew criticism would follow. It always did. And sure enough, the detractors came—some of them old friends, even classmates from IIT. "You're wrong about socialism," they argued. "It's the best way to ensure everyone gets their fair share."

This debate isn't new. It's been raging for centuries, and it won't end anytime soon—not in India, not even in wealthy nations like the US. The clash between capitalism and socialism boils down to this: capitalism rewards creators and innovators; socialism focuses on equality. As Marx said, "From each according to his ability, to each according to his needs." But here's the problem: who's going to work hard if everyone gets the same, no matter what? Where's the incentive to innovate, to take risks?

Socialists believe governments can decide what's best for everyone. But no single person or committee is smart enough to predict all the ways wealth can be created. That's why I avoid the terms capitalism and socialism. Instead, I frame it as the politics of wealth creation versus the politics of wealth distribution. In democracies, the pendulum swings between these two poles. Wealth creators rise, but eventually, those left behind demand redistribution. Back and forth it goes.

The trouble with focusing on wealth distribution is that it breeds stagnation. Look at the US in the 1970s. Social programs expanded, people got comfortable, and innovation slowed. Meanwhile, Germany and Japan surged ahead. It wasn't until the pendulum swung back—toward wealth creators—that America regained its edge.

India's story isn't so different. For decades, socialism stifled entrepreneurship. The brightest minds left for greener pastures. It took a near-economic collapse in 1991 to force liberalization. The result? A wealthier, more dynamic India. But even today, the entrepreneurial spirit isn't fully unleashed.

"What about the poor?" someone asked me afterward.

"There are poor people now," I said. "What have you done for them in the past ten, twenty years? Let entrepreneurs build wealth. They'll create jobs, opportunities, and solutions that lift people out of poverty. That's how you solve the problem—not by clinging to failed ideologies."

The message was clear: India needed tough love. It was time to stop making excuses and start building the future it deserved.

The Prime Minister's Challenge

Before leaving India, I was granted a meeting with the Prime Minister.

Thanks to my friend and colleague Harish Mehta, the right strings had been pulled and I was able to get time with Prime Minister Vajpayee. We met in his office, with several of his aides and Harish seated close by. Never short of opinions or the moxie to share them, I told the PM that if he truly believed the IT industry was India's tomorrow, there were a few things he needed to do quickly.

"A large, modern IT industry cannot be built on India's Third World telecom infrastructure," I said. "It's all very old, outmoded dial-up line. There's no cellular phone, no Internet."

The PM, a man who spoke in flowery, poetic sentences but rarely uttered more than a few words, merely raised an eyebrow in the direction of one of his aides, who nodded in confirmation. I took that as a cue to continue.

"You also need to foster entrepreneurship and allow the VC industry to emerge here in India."

"Are you able to tell me what is needed to do this?" he asked.

"Yes," I said.

"Please come up with a plan of detailed recommendations," he said. "I will look forward to it."

Big Bang Liberalizations

The timing was fortuitous.

After I returned from India, Anne Krueger reached out to me about her desire to research India's economy. Anne was a brilliant economic professor who went on to become the first deputy director of the International Monetary Fund. As a graduate student in the

1970s, her passion was to study India's economy. But India, perhaps too sanctimonious for their own good, denied her a visa. She went on to become a specialist in the Turkish economy.

But her passion was India, and with the country's liberalization, she wanted to set up a program at Stanford to study India's changing economy. I agreed to fund and help organize a group to develop policy recommendations for telecom liberalization in India. We came up with a stellar, motivated group of experts. They studied thirteen countries where liberalization of the telecom industry had taken place, including England, Hong Kong, and New Zealand. They also looked into FCC regulation in the US.

It didn't take a Stanford think tank to identify the problem was India, not a lack of technology or know-how. The government had a monopoly on the telecom services. The two largest employers in the country were the Departments of Railways and Telecom. Both were treated like bottomless wells for patronage. The jobs were for life. Between the government's monopolistic hold, the dense bureaucracy, and a more imperative concern of feeding the populace, the industry idled in the past.

India was strapped with technology from the 1930s and '40s. Meanwhile, the world went digital with modern chips, wireless, and fiber, and everything changed.

But our study surfaced additional problems. When India began to open their telecom industry, the government sold the bandwidth as a licensed property. Say it cost a provider $20 million. But after a company used their capital to buy bandwidth, they did not have enough money left to build a network. The government got rich but nobody got service. Another issue was corruption. When a few people have the power over granting the right to do business, as they did in socialism, it almost always bred crooked dealings, bribes, and payoffs.

And that's what our research, done over eighteen months, concluded: licensing, the way it was being done in India, almost always failed.

We proposed an alternative. The central idea was a revenue share between the government and the private operator, what I described as "big bang liberalization." Invite everybody in the world to build a network, competition being the best way to create efficiency. Give them a license for free or a nominal fee. But stipulate that 7 percent of their revenue would go to the government. Competition would cause prices to drop and take the bandwidth from the cities to the villages.

Also, we were recommending there be no limit to the amount of competition, yet once permission to do business was granted, they had to start a service within eighteen months. They could not sit on the opportunity. They had to start right away. Our report was only three pages in length. Its simplicity alone was revolutionary. It could be adopted overnight.

DoT Hatao Desh Bachao

In early 2000, I led a small team back to India to present our telecom policy recommendations to the then minister of telecommunications, Ram Vilas Paswan.

I arrived brimming with optimism, buoyed by the entrepreneurial spirit that seemed to be taking root in India. TiE chapters were sprouting across major cities—Delhi, Mumbai, Hyderabad, Chennai, and Bangalore, the latter rapidly becoming the heartbeat of India's IT revolution.

The air was electric with possibility, a collective sense that India was ready to rise. But my meeting with the telecom minister was a jarring exception. It was over almost before it began.

"You are wasting your time," he said curtly. "Telecom is not India's problem. The population is."

I couldn't hold back. "You're not the health minister. Your job is to focus on telecom, not population growth."

He wasn't moved. "What you're proposing will never happen. Telecom is a national defense issue."

"And you're not the defense minister either," I shot back, trying hard to contain my frustration.

I walked out of that meeting hopping mad. A year's worth of effort—and significant personal expense—was wasted. Before leaving India, I vented my anger in an op-ed for *The Economic Times*. "IT has become the great hope of India," I wrote. "The Indian spirit is reawakening. We're regaining the confidence to compete on the world stage." But I didn't mince words about the telecom ministry, accusing it of behaving like a monopoly prioritizing its own profits over the national interest.

I had learned the importance of catchphrases and marketing. I wanted to ensure I had people's attention. So I gave the piece a provocative title: "DoT hatao, Desh bachao"—*Get rid of the Department of Telecom, save the country*.

The op-ed caused a stir. Friends warned me about potential repercussions. "Aren't you afraid of speaking out against the government like that?" they asked. I shrugged. "Am I doing something that warrants fear?" My intent was clear: to shift the debate from closed-door meetings to the public square, where change couldn't be ignored.

Back in the US, I received a call from N.K. Singh, a principal secretary in the Prime Minister's Office. "The Prime Minister read your article," he said. "He wants to meet you." Within days, I was back in India.

The meeting was brief but unforgettable. The Prime Minister received me at his heavily guarded residence, a stark reminder of the region's ever-present tensions. He entered with a calm, almost spiritual demeanor, his expression unreadable.

"Why did you write such an intemperate op-ed?" he asked, his tone more inquisitive than reproachful.

I reminded him that he had tasked me with developing a plan, only for it to be summarily dismissed by his telecom minister.

"I understand your anger," he said, then asked, "What's your sense of India and Indians?"

"Our future is incredibly bright," I replied. "But we need leadership to show us the way."

With that, the meeting ended. It had lasted all of five minutes. Outside, I turned to N.K. Singh, puzzled. "Why did I have to fly all the way back for this?"

"He heard you," Singh said, placing a reassuring hand on my shoulder.

"But he didn't say anything."

"Just wait."

Not long after, Telecom Minister Paswan was replaced by Pramod Mahajan. Our recommendations were adopted wholesale and implemented without a single change as the new telecom regulations, effective January 1, 2001. At the time, India had a mere one million mobile subscribers. Within a year, that number skyrocketed to eighty million. Today, with over a billion subscribers, India boasts the second-largest telecom market in the world.

This shift set the stage for India's world-class digital backbone and its $300 billion tech industry. The growth has been nothing short of extraordinary. Many forces drive such a cultural and technological revolution, and I wouldn't claim sole credit. But there's no denying that persuading the Prime Minister to rethink policy played a pivotal role in the massive transformation still unfolding today.

So when people ask me, "Can one person really change the world?" my answer is always the same: "Absolutely—if you care enough to make it happen."

CHAPTER

21

The Crash and a Personal Reset

WHY WERE VALUATIONS SO HIGH when companies didn't make any money? It was madness—and I ignored it.

Actually, that's not entirely true. In early 2000, I gave a speech warning that the dot-com phenomenon was a flimsy bubble, a house of cards waiting to collapse. At the time, I felt smug about being a value investor, steering clear of the speculative frenzy. I had avoided pouring money into dot-com startups, preferring instead to back companies offering the "picks and shovels" to these digital gold diggers. I predicted that 99 percent of dot-coms would fail because they lacked solid business models. Some of the most celebrated names, like Pets.com, were losing money hand over fist without a clear path to profitability.

"Revenue can be manipulated to glow in the dark," I said in that speech. "Profit is proof of life."

Exodus Communications became the poster child of both the dot-com boom and its inevitable bust. The company's valuation soared to $32 billion despite never turning a profit. Growth was there, sure, but stability and sustainability were not. Months after its IPO, founder and CEO K.B. Chandrasekhar stepped down. Ellen Hancock, a seasoned executive from Apple and IBM, took the reins. She made bold moves, including acquisitions that expanded Exodus' footprint into Japan. For a while, it seemed like the company might find its footing.

In March 2000, the NASDAQ hit an all-time high. Upstart AOL acquired media giant Time Warner in a deal that seemed to defy traditional business logic. The Valley buzzed with talk of startups rewriting the rules. It felt like a casino where everyone was rolling the dice, and a few lucky ones were hitting jackpots.

Then came the wobble. At first, no one took it seriously. But by October, the NASDAQ had plummeted 76 percent. Fortunes evaporated overnight, including mine. Publicly, I tried to maintain a stoic, philosophic demeanor, cool but in control, while inside I was reeling. I stayed in touch with Chandrasekhar's co-founder, B.V. Jagadeesh, and others, advising them to disengage emotionally and financially. To this day, B.V. says that is some of the best advice he has ever received.

But for me, it wasn't so simple. I was on the board and tied to a lock-in period. I couldn't sell my shares and was forced to watch as Exodus' stock nosedived.

In January 2001, just months after the bubble burst, Exodus closed its acquisition of GlobalCenter for $6.5 billion in stock. By then, the company's market cap had fallen below $2 billion. The billions of debt it carried had become a metastasized cancer. The board began to unravel, with key members resigning. Then the CFO quit. In March 2001, Ellen Hancock stepped down abruptly. It became clear to me that Exodus' challenges weren't just about leadership. The market itself had changed. As one dot-com after another—Webvan, AltaVista, Broadcast.com, eToys—collapsed, Exodus' customer base disappeared. So did its revenue streams. The company eventually declared bankruptcy and was sold for a mere $1.

How could a company generating $100 million in monthly revenue fail to make a profit? A business must sustain itself. If it's reliant on external capital that suddenly disappears, the game is over. The lights go out. The party ends.

Looking back, I can say the experience humbled me. But the truth is, I was devastated. My fortune disappeared. Worse than the financial loss, though, was the blow to my confidence. I had always prided myself on being a savvy businessman, a mentor to others. Yet here I was, blindsided. How had I not seen the signs? Why didn't I sell my shares when I had the chance? Was I as smart as I thought I was, or had I been fooling myself all along?

For a good bit of time, I was plagued by self-doubt. I'd always started my days by asking questions about my priorities and figuring out the answers, but now I had too many questions and too few answers. I was overwhelmed by the facts and the emotions. My son Ben was a recent NYU film school graduate and in Los Angeles. One day he had lunch with a friend of mine, a former colleague, who spoke about the financial loss like it was a death in the family. "It's all gone. What are you going to do?"

Ben called me. "Life goes on," I told him.

That was true even if it didn't feel like it at the time. My son pressed me further, worried that I was stiff-upper-lipping it. He wasn't wrong. I've always been the kind to grit my teeth and push forward. I got that from my father, who was the same way. Survivors don't waste time lamenting setbacks. They focus on what's next. My wife, Ann, shared that same sober mindset. One day, as I sat in front of the TV watching CNN, she walked past and gave my shoulder a squeeze.

I looked up and, in that moment, I understood: perspective. That's true partnership. When one person is down, the other maintains perspective, provides stability, buoyancy. I knew right then that we would be okay.

Indeed, the gradual passage of time brought clarity. I came to understand a fundamental truth: There's a difference between wealth creation and wealth preservation. The first requires bold risks; the second demands caution, diversification and prudence. I had focused too much on creating wealth and not enough on preserving it. That mistake cost me dearly.

In that regard, it was a self-inflicted blunder. Exodus was too personal. I had invested in it, mentored its leadership, helped them navigate pitfalls, and pushed for their IPO, a crowning achievement by any standard. Perhaps that clouded my ability to see. As the saying goes, love is blind.

But I wasn't alone. I came to see that my mistakes weren't unique. The beauty of free markets is that everyone assumes the same risks; it punishes and rewards without bias. Countless others made the same mistakes during that era. I had no reason to believe I should have been the exception. I realized that much of my frustration stemmed from comparing myself to Valley titans like Bill Gates, Vinod Khosla, and Larry Ellison—all billionaires whose path had crossed mine.

Still, despite my reduced wealth, I was by no means a pauper. But chasing those comparisons was a fool's errand. There will always be someone bigger and better. What matters is recognizing how far you've come, not obsessing over how far you could have gone.

The dot-com crash taught me lessons I couldn't have learned any other way. It forced me to pause and reflect on my journey—to appreciate where I started and where I'd arrived. Perspective, I've learned, is everything.

India and Pakistan: A Waste of Resources

By 2001, TiE's center of gravity had started to shift to India from the Silicon Valley.

It made sense. Indians were established in the US by this time. A dedicated organization like TiE was helpful but not needed the way it had been when the idea for it was first hatched. But entrepreneurs in

India and other subcontinent countries were still aspiring to achieve their potential.

Though I had resigned as president the previous summer, I retained my title as global head. I was the point person when the US State Department brought a delegation from Egypt to meet with me and observe TiE in action. I also traveled to conferences in the former Soviet Republic of Georgia, Germany, and England.

The State Department loved TiE. The pureness of our message was irresistible. We avoided politics and asked only that those who achieved success pay it forward. The goal was to create wealth that would benefit everybody. It was hard to find fault with our message of self-help, entrepreneurism, free markets, and giving back. After one talk, a State Department official gushed, "What you're doing is America!"

In April 2001 I took a delegation of Indian Americans and Pakistani Americans from Silicon Valley to Pakistan to launch chapters in Lahore and Karachi. I arrived in Bombay, where the US Council General hosted a dinner for me with all of Bombay's business elite. He told me that an American diplomat would accompany me to every meeting I had in Pakistan, ensuring my safety as the Pakistan army would have to provide protection to the delegation if it included a US official.

I had no objection.

Then it was off to Delhi, where I rendezvoused with my group. While I was there, India's deputy foreign secretary came to see me at my hotel. It was an unscheduled meeting, so I didn't know what was on his agenda. From his demeanor, I assumed it was serious.

"You're very well thought of in India," he said. "You are a prominent Indian, and we strongly advise you not to go to Pakistan."

I knew his concerns. It was a dark time in India–Pakistan relations as the Kargil War of 1999 was still fresh in everyone's minds. I did not mention the arrangement I had with the US State Department. But I did explain that we in TiE believed that focusing people and countries on entrepreneurship and wealth creation was the best way to make peace. Also, I had traveled too long of a distance with too many important people to be given this warning at the last minute.

"I am an American, and I am glad the Indians like me," I said. "But I am going to Pakistan."

"Even if we advise you not to go, you will still go?" he asked.

"Yes. I carry an American passport," I said. "I travel on an American passport. And I am on a personal mission of wealth creation."

"Why not create wealth in India?"

"I am. But why are you worried about Pakistan?"

A political debate was not on his agenda. He left. But a few hours later I received a call from India's Prime Minister.

"I hear you're going to Pakistan," PM Vajpayee said.

"Yes," I replied.

I knew PM Vajpayee must have been briefed on the mission of TiE, but I took a moment anyway to reiterate that TiE stood for the *Indus* entrepreneurs, not just Indians, meaning that our vision was expansive and included Indian, Pakistani, and Bangladeshi people. In terms of India and Pakistan, we did not want to be stuck in the mud of an old fight that seemed to be a waste of both India's and Pakistan's resources. We wanted to be a peace-making bridge between the two countries.

"It is my opinion that India and Pakistan should not be enemies forever," I said. "India is far ahead of Pakistan. But you have to bring them along. How do you do that? How do you stop the waste of resources and bring the countries together? I believe the answer is wealth creation."

"I am very glad to hear about your trip," the Prime Minister said. "We wish them well. We want to be friendly with them. I'm happy you're going."

I was fearless when it came to sharing my opinions with the Prime Minister. I believed I had right on my side. I was also using TiE to help me rebound from the Exodus debacle. Helping other people learn from these successes and failures was therapeutic. I could have been at home, singing the old tune, *woe is me*. But I was talking to entrepreneurs and world leaders. I did not lose standing in the community. Life for my family did not change. It was all in my head. But doubt is a battle you fight alone. The path to victory is simply onward. I pushed myself hard, maybe too hard.

The rest of the week-long trip was spent in Lahore, the cultural capital of Pakistan. We met with a delegation of government officials and a smattering of military officers who were clearly keeping tabs on everything discussed. My message was both personal and big picture. I recalled that my mother and father were both born in Pakistan, as was I two years prior to Partition. Peace and cooperation between the two countries had been an elusive dream for as long as I had been alive. It was time to turn that into a reality—and the way to do that was through the creation of wealth.

"India is growing its IT industry and its future through entrepreneurship," I said. "Pakistan should do the same thing."

I thought the message played well, but it was hard to tell considering none of them could tell me what they really thought. All the shots in Pakistan were called by its leader, General Pervez Musharraf. But something I said must have been passed through the Pakistani halls of power. The next day we were summoned by Musharraf. We met him in Rawalpindi for a surprisingly informal lunch. I provided an overview of TiE and expressed our excitement about the two chapters opening in his country.

"This is going to make a difference," I said. "The entrepreneurs are the people who move society forward. It will help you catch up to India."

"Surely India is not that far ahead of us in Pakistan," he said as if it were a matter of fact, before turning to several of his officials who had been traveling with us and asking, "How far ahead of us are they?"

"About six months to a year," one of them said.

I shook my head. "That's not correct. They are twenty years ahead of you."

"That is a joke, right?" Musharraf said.

"No, India has been at IT for twenty-plus years."

My frankness did not go over well with the general. He was not accustomed to being criticized or corrected.

I continued, "Pakistan needs to develop a positive narrative. Right now the story is jihadi, and jihadi is dark. Pakistan appears to be a country looking backwards. Is there a positive step forward? I believe it is through entrepreneurialism."

"Pakistan is very forward looking, very positive, and its people are very positive," Musharraf said, and with that, he got up and left, followed by his entourage, which made our room feel empty.

Later, several of the Pakistanis traveling in our group let me know that they agreed with me. They were afraid to voice their opinions out of fear for their families and their own lives. That made me appreciate America and my US passport even more. A few months later, I returned to Pakistan without the large delegation. I floated an idea I had: India and Pakistan would set up a trade zone at the border—5,000 acres on each side. It would be an entrepreneurial free trade zone, where anyone could set up an IT business as long as it was available to both countries.

I saw it as a way to bring people on both sides together. Prime Minister Vajpayee liked it. My contacts in the Pakistani government were also intrigued.

Encouraged by the positive feedback, I wanted to devote myself to making this free trade zone happen. The possibilities were monumental. If it worked, I thought peace and prosperity would be possible in my lifetime and beyond. It would be a tremendous legacy for TiE. Then on December 13, 2001, five Pakistani terrorists attacked the Indian Parliament and overnight things came to a screeching halt. After that, you could not talk about Pakistan in any way other than as "the enemy."

9-11-2001

The phone rang at 6.30 a.m.

Calls at this hour were rare, and they were never for casual chatter. I picked up. It was Roy Prasad. His voice was clipped. "Turn on the news," he said.

I switched on the TV just in time to see the second plane crash into the other tower. There was no doubt in my mind—this was terrorism.

At that moment, like millions of Americans, I became a New Yorker. Shocked. Angry. Thinking of my deep connections to that city. I had landed in New York on my birthday in 1967, stepping into America for the first time. I had watched the World Trade Center rise in the '70s. I had walked those streets for business, raising capital and preparing Excelan for its IPO.

My son had graduated from NYU just three months earlier. My daughter, who studied at Syracuse University and got her graduate degree from the London School of Economics, lived on 23rd Street and worked near Central Park. I called Raj-Ann—she was at work, safe for now. Ben was shaken—many of his friends were still in the area. One worked at Merrill Lynch, just south of the towers, and had to be evacuated to New Jersey by ferry.

I was emotional about the attack for a long time and still choke up every time I visit the 9-11 memorial. Violence never ends with a single act. It ripples outward, leaving more suffering in its wake. The wisest leaders understand that prosperity, driven by a free market, with the freedom to dream and create, benefits everyone, and is the only lasting path to peace.

A Necessary Reset, Finally

I struggled to keep up with my schedule.

In December, I took my family to India for the groundbreaking of the Kanwal Rekhi School of Information Technology (KReSIT). It was a proud moment, made even more special by the presence of Ann, Raj-Ann, and Ben. At the US Consulate in Worli, I was honored, but what truly moved me was seeing my grown children reconnect with India and their heritage. That trip turned out to be Ann's last, making it all the more poignant.

The following month, I was in Kuala Lumpur for the launch of TiE Malaysia, the thirty-ninth chapter, with more on the drawing board. The organization now spanned eight countries and boasted 10,000 members. The multi-day event in Kuala Lumpur, highlighted by the Malaysian prime minister, brought nearly a thousand people to the Palace of the Golden Horses in Sri Kembangan.

The prime minister understood what we were doing and backed the effort to organize and support Malaysia's entrepreneurs. He was all for economic progress and recognized the role entrepreneurs played. They were a small country, but in terms of per capita income, their people were doing ten times better than India.

At the hotel, I was given a palatial suite with a grand staircase up to the bedroom. I had to go up and down the stairs multiple times a day. The morning trips had me breathing hard. By the end of the day, I was nearly out of breath. At fifty-seven years old, I was too young and vibrant to feel this way, yet my grandfather, my father, my uncle, and several cousins all had heart attacks or strokes in their fifties. One day, after huffing and puffing my way upstairs, I looked in the dressing room mirror and saw a man I did not want to recognize as myself. I was morbidly obese and unfit.

I had no doubt the man I saw in the mirror was going to die if he kept going like this. This man was outright stupid. He could not have been me, could he? I was smart. People came to me for advice. How could I ignore my own family history? A stroke had paralyzed my grandfather. Coronary disease had killed several family elders. How had I ignored my own first principles? Education. Family. And *health*. These were my pillars. Education makes your mind sharp. Health makes your body strong and capable. And family gives you emotional strength and purpose in life.

Where was I, the man I thought I knew? What had happened to me? How could I lecture people when I wasn't smart enough to take care of myself? TiE was lauded in the US and abroad. A writer noted it was widely envied by immigrant groups. But I asked myself, "Who would envy a man out of breath from walking up a flight of stairs?"

The dissonance scared me. Though I was in the middle of this important retreat, I sat down on the edge of my bed, picked up the phone, and cancelled everything on my schedule. I told my contact in the Prime Minister's office that I was not feeling well and had to go home. He wanted me to see a doctor, but after I insisted on going home as soon as possible, they got me on a flight that night and arranged for a police escort to the airport, with lights flashing and sirens blaring.

It was time to push reset. I had to make a change in my life … or face the consequences.

CHAPTER 22
Rebuilding

AFTER I RETURNED HOME FROM Kuala Lumpur, my doctor scheduled a battery of medical tests. The distressing news started as soon as I stepped on the scale. I weighed 275 pounds (about 125 kg). I had learned long ago that numbers told the only story that mattered, and this one was not good.

My blood pressure was elevated and my cholesterol was very high. My doctor didn't mince words—the red danger lights were flashing.

In business, when the numbers are bad, you face the reality head-on. That's what I did with my health. I embarked on a medically supervised diet and started working with a personal trainer. My brother-in-law, Mark, joined me on this journey, and we trained together both in and out of the gym. We worked out with weights, did a variety of aerobic exercises, and bicycled for miles.

The process wasn't easy, but I approached it with the same discipline I would a struggling business. When I visited Raj-Ann in New York, I eschewed the city's ubiquitous yellow taxis and insisted on walking, even if we were going thirty or forty blocks. My goal was achieved. Over six months, I shed 75 pounds. A year later, after countless hours of cardio, weight training, and biking every trail in the Bay Area, I felt like a new person. My health was back on track. I saved my life.

People often asked me how I achieved such a transformation. My answer was simple: I treated my health like a business. I tracked the metrics—calories in, calories out, weight up, weight down. I became the CEO of my body, making the hard decisions necessary for success.

The principles that guide us in building successful ventures can hold the key to personal transformation as well and vice versa. A case in point: During the dot-com bust, I wrote off several of my non-Exodus investments. Among them was NexTag, a price comparison search engine whose founder I had connected with through TiE. Like many startups of that era, I assumed NexTag had succumbed to the storm. Then, in 2003, I came across an article in *San Jose Mercury News* that described how the founder had navigated the turmoil. He had slashed the company's burn rate by 90 percent, reduced headcount by two-thirds, taken pay cuts alongside his leadership team, and outsourced product development to India. He trimmed the fat and focused on survival.

That story struck a chord because it mirrored my own experience—not just in business, but in life. It all comes down to first principles: you can't take care of anyone else if you don't take care of yourself.

Swagger

I took this theory to heart when I stepped in to run Ensim Corp., a Silicon Valley startup tackling web hosting automation.

Like many Valley companies, Ensim had a solid idea, plenty of buzz, and leadership that was struggling to turn potential into success. That's where I came in—brought in as the veteran fixer, the guy who had been around and could still swing the bat. I wouldn't argue with that, but truth be told, I took the role because something inside me wasn't settled. I felt like I still had something to prove—to myself more than anyone else. Value. Relevance. The simple satisfaction of knowing I still had it.

I once told my son that after leaving Novell, I should have jumped into another startup sooner. "That was my window for another big hit," I said. Ben looked at me like I was crazy. "It's not like you sat around," he shot back. "You put TiE on the map, changed the trajectory of telecom, endowed a building at IIT, and helped countless entrepreneurs thrive. You had an impact far beyond what another startup could have given you." He had a point. But now, seven or eight years after Novell, I wanted back in the driver's seat—if only for a little while—to leave a mark.

And that happened fast. When I arrived, Ensim was hemorrhaging cash—$33,000 a day, burning through a million a month, and barely making revenue. Worse, they were giving away their software for free. "We'll charge when the economy improves," they said. Nonsense. No customer would pay later for something they were trained to get for free.

Six months in, I had to let go of most of the executives who had hired me. Then, I cut a deal with Microsoft, and together we built Ensim Unify—a focused, practical solution that solved a real problem: managing multiple hosted services on one platform. It was Excelan redux but without the personal connection. Unlike Novell, too, I was able to play the game on my own terms, which meant partnering with Bill Gates.

I also got the chance to call out the Stanford and Harvard MBA types who were wrecking Valley culture with their "profits don't matter" nonsense. Since when does a business survive without making money? This isn't tee-ball, where everyone gets a trophy.

I stayed at Ensim a relatively short time, just long enough to make the simple but tough decisions that turned it around, before handing the reins over to a handpicked successor. For me, it was a good paycheck and the company got its swagger back—and so did I. But deep down I knew it wasn't what I wanted to do.

A Near Loss

When my daughter was struggling with a difficult relationship, I had only a few simple words for her.

"This doesn't define you," I told her. "We will never blame you for making a mistake. We only look for ways to help you learn and grow. You will get through this. Your mother and I are always here for you."

Giving advice has always come naturally to me. I've shared it with my children the same way I've shared it with entrepreneurs—*be forward-looking, don't dwell on the past, and never let setbacks stop you.* But empathy? Sensitivity? Those didn't come as easily. Ann helped me with that. I spent my life investing in people and ideas, believing that, in turn, they would invest in others.

Ann, in her own way, invested in me—through her belief, through her quiet strength, through her willingness to be vulnerable—and in our family, raising our children and caring for our home. I didn't fully grasp how much that meant to me until the moment I almost lost her.

It was an ordinary morning in every way but one: Ann was nowhere to be found. The day before, she had done something rare for herself—purchased a new dress and had her hair done. She had indulged in herself, and I was happy for her. That night, I told her that I wished she indulged like that more often. Then I went up to bed while she stayed behind, watching TV.

When I woke up, always much earlier than her, Ann was not in her usual spot next to me. If she had got up before me, I hadn't noticed. I went downstairs and checked the kitchen. Then the family room. I also looked in the backyard; maybe some critter had got into her rose garden. But no, there was no sign of her. I was puzzled. Could she have gone somewhere?

I opened the garage. Both cars were still there. She hadn't left. Relief washed over me—but only for a moment. Then I had a thought, which quickly turned to fear as I checked one last place: the downstairs guest room.

There she was. When I opened the door and looked inside, I saw Ann lying on the bed. She was wearing her new dress. Her hair was still neatly coiffed. At first, this scene didn't make sense to me. Then something odd caught my eye. There was a note on the pillow next to her. I felt like I had been hit by a lightning bolt. I checked her pulse. She was alive, but her breaths were soft. I called 911.

Within minutes, she was being treated by paramedics. I explained what I had read in her note: she had taken an unknown quantity of sleeping pills in an attempt to take her own life. I will spare the more personal details she penned lest I unfairly reduce her to the silhouette of a troubled soul. Trust me, like so many suffering from depression, she was involved in a deeply complicated struggle with multiple demons.

The paramedics rushed her to the hospital, where the ER doctors and nurses brought her back to consciousness.

I will never forget the aloneness and sadness I saw in her eyes when she looked up at me. It was like staring into a well with no bottom, just despair and darkness. I felt an equal amount of helplessness and powerlessness, something that was so rare to me that I did not know how to react. I am ashamed to admit it but I got angry with Ann. "How could you?" I asked. She had gone to therapy. We had gone to therapy together. We had attended Al-Anon meetings in the past. I was getting fit. We were doing so well. Anything we wanted was ours.

I did not see that I was violating one of my own foundational beliefs: it's impossible to learn when you blame others.

Breaking the Silence

Ann embodied the silent battles so many fight alone. There's a well-known saying about depression: "Sometimes the strongest people are the ones who fight battles you know nothing about." That was Ann.

This silent, sinister scourge of a disease had knocked Ann down again and again and left her flailing in the dark until she was unable to tread water anymore. But her longtime struggle with mental illness and her suicide attempt is something we hid from family and friends. We chose to treat it as a private matter, which is typical of those battling mental health issues and of their loved ones.

We don't talk about it because we don't know how to talk about it. We fear being stigmatized. We feel like no one understands. We're ashamed. We simply don't know what to do or say.

As a family, we followed that path until it was nearly too late. Secrecy does nothing to address the pain. Recognizing we needed help, we admitted Ann into the Menninger Clinic in Houston, one of the world's top psychiatric hospitals. It was among the few with a program dedicated to addressing severe depression and suicidal tendencies. Admitting her was a hard decision but the right one.

The first two weeks were brutal. Ann felt abandoned and resisted treatment. But slowly, things shifted. The therapy began to work. She got with the program, as she later put it, and eight weeks later, she was discharged in much better shape.

The intensive treatment changed both of us. Ann learned that she couldn't fight depression. It was something she had to manage. It was wired into her biology. Medication helped. Therapy helped. Family helped. Destigmatizing it helped. I also had my own realization. I was powerless to change or fix her. I saw that some people never escape their torments. Some battles are intensely personal.

Strangely, I understood this in business but failed to see it at home. Could my success or renewed fitness have in some way triggered her fears and led to her depression? It didn't make sense to me. But my logic didn't matter. What mattered was what she was telling herself.

Ann had grown up in a home of chaos—two alcoholic, abusive parents. She was conditioned to expect disaster. That was her default, her comfort zone, even when life was objectively good. We had been married thirty-two years. Our children were thriving. We had no financial worries. And yet, in her mind, catastrophe was always around the corner.

All I could do was stand beside her. Love her. Try to understand this invisible weight she carried.

This was another gift Ann gave me—the gift of empathy. Around this time I remember my son mentioning that he hadn't heard from a friend of his for a few weeks. I asked if his friend was all right. "Maybe he's hurting. Maybe you want to give him a call." Before Ann's journey, I probably wouldn't have said that. If there's a lesson here, it's that growth never stops. Life keeps teaching.

So with Ann's support, I'm breaking our silence. If sharing our story helps even one person find the courage to seek help, then it's worth it. With TiE, we changed the environment for Indian entrepreneurs by fostering knowledge and support. Maybe, in some small way, Ann and I—and our family—can do the same for mental health.

No one goes through life without falling, and there's no shame in reaching for a hand up. I know this because I would never have achieved half of what I did without Ann by my side. And as I always told her, she would never be alone either.

PART 6

WHY NOT YOU

CHAPTER

23

Purpose, Family, and New Beginnings

AT SIXTY, I FOUND MYSELF facing a challenge I hadn't encountered before: defining a purpose beyond ambition.

I wasn't exactly idle—I was speaking to students at Michigan Tech twice a year. Dave House, a fellow Silicon Valley veteran and Michigan Tech alumnus, and I had been urging the school to adopt a more entrepreneurial mindset. Dave focused on updating the tech and management curriculum, while I pushed for fostering a spirit of innovation. The university president, to his credit, didn't just listen—he challenged us to share our ideas directly with the students.

Our Q&A sessions became standing-room-only events. In 2005, the dedication of the Kanwal and Ann Rekhi Hall further deepened my connection to the school. But those weren't the only roots I reconnected with. That same year I returned to Sukho, the village in Pakistan where I was born, for the first time since 1947—when my father carried us away during the Partition. My parents were married there. Almost every story I heard from my parents and aunts and uncles was about their experiences in Sukho. Standing on that soil was more profound than I anticipated.

My son Ben was with me. I also had a map that my mother's youngest brother had drawn for me years before. We found my parents' old house, the local school, and other sites. Incidentally, I had to go back to Sukho in 2007, this time with my daughter Raj-Ann. She had complained loudly about missing out on the visit to the ancestral village. The distance between that humble village and the life I had built in America was no longer abstract. It was tangible.

And with that realization came a sense of calm. I felt, for the first time, that I had nothing left to prove, though that is very different than wanting to do something, to tackle new challenges, to continue to make a difference. I had no idea what that might be, only that another transformation was ahead of me.

The future is more of a puzzle than a clear picture. But I did find it profoundly symbolic that, at that moment, I was standing where it all began, while holding a map in my hand.

Sometime after that trip, an unexpected opportunity came knocking. John Dougery Jr approached me with an idea. His father, John Sr, had been one of Excelan's original investors, and John Jr was carving out his own path as a sharp investor. After obtaining his MBA from U.C. Berkeley, he worked for Sun Microsystems and Silicon Graphics before getting bitten by the startup bug and entering the venture capital side.

We met for lunch and reminisced briefly about the last time we had seen each other in April 2000. It was at a board meeting of a company both of us had invested in, and the previous Friday the market had crashed. It was a tough meeting, at the beginning of a very tough time. We were still licking our wounds in one way or another. John said his firm was pivoting from early to late stage investing and he was unsure of what he wanted to do going forward.

"Do you want to get back into angel investing?" he asked.

He wanted to start a venture capital fund—a small, seed-stage venture firm with $50,000,000 to $100,000,000 that would invest in Indian Americans in America and startups in India. Privately, I noted how far this was from his father's comment back when Excelan was experiencing growing pains that Indians couldn't be trusted. Of course, all that was ancient history, not forgotten but rather proven wrong. Ground had been broken. Ceilings had been shattered. Indian Americans were thriving in the US, John said. The US has always been the land of opportunity.

"Now that same kind of opportunity is available in India," he said. "It's wide open. Nothing but white space. With India emerging as a global entrepreneurial hub, we can do great things."

John said he would handle the operational work of the new fund, while my reputation in both Silicon Valley and India would attract the deals.

"In the Valley, you meet an entrepreneur and they're full of bravado," he said. "They're pumping up everything. Everything is going to be dramatic and big. In India, the entrepreneurs talk small. You'd be amazed at how conservative they are, how overly realistic they are. You have to be a completely different investor there. You have to be the person who expands their point of view, who helps them aim high."

John's pitch was hard to resist. The dual focus on India and the US struck a personal chord. India was my *janmabhoomi*—the land of my birth. The US was my *karmabhoomi*—the place where I had built my life and career. The idea felt like a natural extension of who I was.

But this wasn't just about personal alignment; it was also a challenge. I had been an entrepreneur and an angel investor, but venture capital was a different game. Angel investing is intuitive—you follow your gut, and it's your own money on the line. Venture capital is institutional. You raise funds from others, promise returns, and answer to them. It's more mercenary, more formal. The stakes are higher, the structure more rigid, and the responsibility far greater.

It was a new mountain to climb—exactly what I needed at this stage of my life.

Risks and Rewards

Steve Jobs was angry and embarrassed when he was fired from Apple, the company he had co-founded, at thirty years old, but time and one of the great second acts in entrepreneurial history gave him perspective. "I didn't see it then, but it turned out that getting fired from Apple was the best thing that could have ever happened to me," he told a graduating class at Stanford. "The heaviness of being successful was replaced by the lightness of being a beginner again, less sure about everything. It freed me to enter one of the most creative periods of my life."

I felt similarly as soon as John and I opened our fund, Inventus Capital Partners, with one office in Silicon Valley and another in India. Our focus was on early stage startups in software, mobile, and Internet. We put our toe in the water with Credit Sesame, a consumer financial information company that helped track personal finances, then notched our first big hit in India with redBus, an online bus ticketing company that solved the mind-boggling problem of bus travel in India.

The story behind redBus was one I had lived myself. A problem exists, an entrepreneur comes up with a solution.

Phanindra Sama was that entrepreneur. He was in Bangalore, trying to take a bus back to his hometown Nizamabad about 500 miles away. He was literally standing in the mud unable to buy a ticket. There were lots of small, regional bus companies in India but no direct, nonstop bus from Bangalore. India lacked a single company like Greyhound that could take you from New York to San Francisco. He had so much trouble buying tickets from one bus to the next, and figuring out the schedules of each, that he almost missed his vacation.

"Why can't I just buy one ticket that works for the whole journey?" he asked himself. That simple question led to redBus. It was a problem that could have stumped even Einstein, but redBus cracked it. We wrote the first check, backed the team, and watched it grow into a $10 million business in just a few years. When we exited, it accounted for nearly 40 percent of our fund—a fantastic return, but in hindsight, we sold too soon.

We kept going. IT and software (Sierra Atlantic), health and fitness (Healthify), insurance (Policy Bazaar), and more—we were bringing Silicon Valley discipline to India, but with an Indian twist. It worked well, but we were still looking for a major breakthrough.

Then in 2011, Manish Chandra walked in with a new idea. John and I had both backed his earlier venture, Kaboodle, a women's shopping platform. Kaboodle had been ahead of its time—pre-smartphone era, hard to scale—but it still gave us a good exit when Hearst acquired it in 2007. More importantly, we liked working with Manish.

Now, he had something new—Poshmark. "This time, I want to focus on fashion and commerce, not advertising," he told us. It was still just an idea, which gave us the chance to dive in early. What would be its tech edge? How would it break into the market? What was the real opportunity here?

Manish was hitting the perfect wave—social media and online shopping were booming. He framed Poshmark as "eBay meets Facebook for fashion." I had my own take: "A marketplace where women with closets full of nothing to wear sell to other women with closets full of nothing to wear."

We backed him from the start, stuck through the early struggles, and by 2018, Poshmark had topped $1 billion in revenue. Three years later, it had a blockbuster IPO. Poshmark became the biggest fashion resale platform in the US, turning everyday sellers into six-figure entrepreneurs. And it wasn't just about used clothing anymore—the social aspect made it a launchpad for influencers and businesses.

For Inventus, the impact was huge. Poshmark returned 3x our entire fund. For me, it marked another milestone on my personal journey: one more mountain climbed.

A Reckoning

In May 2008, I stood before an audience at Northwestern University's Kellogg School of Management to deliver a lecture titled "The Branding of India, Indians, and Indianness in America." There was no confusion about the message. Indian Americans had arrived, and so had India—I felt proud to witness this all in my lifetime. We had built a brand that was unmistakable—one of excellence, hard work, and success.

It was a proud moment for me because this wasn't just a global transformation; it was deeply personal. I had spent decades encouraging, promoting, and investing in this change. I knew the effort I had made over the years, the sacrifices, the adventures, and the success stories. But I don't think I had ever taken a close measure of my legacy, how I might tell my story to my children and grandchildren, until I put together this speech.

I was a numbers guy. *The numbers have to tell the story*. I suppose that's why I spent so much time thinking about the stock I didn't sell or couldn't sell or sold too early. I was looking for a neat balance sheet. I had the mentality of always wanting one more hit, something to up the score.

But the truth was, my story couldn't be told only with numbers. I had prioritized helping other people, opening doors, being a mentor to other entrepreneurs, and spreading the gospel of wealth creation, knowing that helping to improve life for a million people was of much greater value than a million dollars. This was the payoff of a lifetime of effort—and a good story.

When I first came to America in the mid-1960s, the perception of Indians was anything but flattering. We were seen as people from a backward, chaotic country—a land of snake charmers, beggars, and slums. The irony was that most of us arriving then were well-educated engineers seeking higher education and career opportunities. But the issue wasn't with us as individuals; it was with India itself. After the moral high ground of Gandhi and Nehru, India had embraced pro-Soviet economics, stagnating under what John Kenneth Galbraith famously called a "functioning anarchy."

Fast forward to the 1990s, and everything had changed. Indian Americans had proven themselves in the US, earning a reputation as hard-working, family-oriented achievers. Organizations like TiE provided a roadmap for entrepreneurial success, and we steadily climbed the ranks—transforming from entry-level workers to managers, entrepreneurs, and thought leaders.

Back in India, economic liberalization had dismantled the old Soviet-style policies, unleashing rapid growth, a thriving IT sector, and globally competitive companies like Infosys, TCS, and Wipro.

The parallel transformations of India and Indian Americans were nothing short of miraculous. Both embraced economic prosperity through values that resonated with the American ethos: hard work, education, and ambition. By 2018, India was a magnet for foreign investment, with global giants like Microsoft, IBM, and Intel pouring billions into the country. Indian Americans, meanwhile, were at the helm of major corporations—Satya Nadella at Microsoft, Sundar Pichai at Google, Indra Nooyi at PepsiCo, and many others.

People began to ask: *Why are Indian Americans so successful? What are they doing differently?*

The answer, in my view, lies in our immigrant experience. My generation came to the US well-educated but with no safety net. We had burned the bridges behind us. Survival wasn't optional; it was mandatory. And once we figured out how to survive, the question became: *How do we thrive?*

We adapted quickly, spotting opportunities and seizing them. We became doctors, engineers, professors and, increasingly, entrepreneurs. We looked at America with fresh eyes, recognizing that its core values—family, education, hard work—mirrored our own. Education, in particular, was a shared foundation. In both cultures, it was the great equalizer, the surest path to advancement.

India's diversity also prepared us for life in America's melting pot. We were used to navigating differences and coexisting with others, so integrating into American society came naturally. There was little friction. And as my generation survived, the next generation thrived.

TiE played a crucial role here, sharing the lessons of success so the next wave of entrepreneurs wouldn't face the same struggles. But there's a deeper reason for our success, one that goes beyond mentorship or timing. Indian Americans have embraced American values better than many Americans themselves.

We brought a hunger and drive that came from having nothing to fall back on. While the American middle class had grown comfortable with cars, color TVs, and suburban life, we arrived with no such expectations. We were hungry. We looked around and asked, *Why not us?*

That hunger made all the difference. America rewards people who ask that question and are willing to work hard for their slice of the pie. In the process, everyone benefits.

Timing also played a role. Indians excel in math, science, and abstract thinking—skills that became invaluable as America transitioned from an industrial economy to a knowledge-based one. The rise of computers and the Internet played to our strengths.

People used to talk about American ingenuity. Today, much of that ingenuity belongs to Indian Americans.

This transformation is one of mutual benefit. Indian Americans brought their drive, their values, and their skills to America. In turn, America offered opportunity and a system that rewards hard work. Together, we've created something remarkable. The journey from snake charmers to Silicon Valley CEOs wasn't just a shift in perception. It was a reckoning.

CHAPTER

24

The Impact of Entrepreneurship

WALKING ACROSS THE MICHIGAN TECH campus in the late 2010s, I was struck by a memory—how US Highway 41 once cut straight through the school. Back in 1970, just a year after I had earned my master's degree, the road was rerouted to the east, bypassing the campus altogether. Life is like that. Paths shift. Roads change.

That thought stuck with me late into the day when I reflected on my relationship with Brad King, a young professor at Michigan Tech. Decades ago, I had been a young Indian engineering student here, accused of cheating on a test by my professor. Now, I was mentoring and investing in one of the university's brightest minds.

The irony wasn't lost on me—it felt like something out of a movie. A real American success story.

I met Brad in 2013 after one of my twice-yearly Q&A sessions at Michigan Tech. Brad was a local boy, born and raised in Michigan's upper peninsula. He obtained his undergraduate, masters, and PhD in aerospace technology from the University of Michigan, before landing at Michigan Tech, in his beloved Upper Peninsula hometown, as a professor in rocket science—or more specifically in space propulsion research.

He was building a satellite with his students as part of his class in advanced space propulsion technology. By this time, he was a tenured professor, and the satellite was being built within the school's "enterprise" program, in which projects like this were organized and run more like businesses than classrooms. According to the school's website, students "work to invent products, provide services, and pioneer solutions."

I had sponsored nearly a dozen enterprise projects over the years, including this effort Brad was leading to build a satellite for the Air Force. He had previously built one for NASA. Again, I felt a personal connection. I had come to the US in 1967 because of the opportunities created by the space race with the Soviet Union, the success of Sputnik and America's effort to become the first country to land a man on the moon. I had worked in the defense industry for years. It was funny how the past, present, and future connected.

Brad talked me through the satellite. It was being designed as a small low orbiting satellite and incorporated a range of technology—some from Russia and some off-the-shelf parts developed for iPhones. It also had a small, powerful steering mechanism called a plasma thruster that only a dozen or so people in the world were working on. Brad was one of them. He was convinced what they were building, though in a classroom, was on the cusp of a revolution.

"Have you thought of doing this as a real company?" I asked.

"I'm a professor," he said. "I love teaching."

"Okay, then why are you telling me all this?"

"Because somebody has to do it."

"If you feel someone ought to do something, that someone is probably you."

I left it at that. I was intrigued but had other projects to review that day. Still, Brad and I kept in touch.

Three years later, I was back on campus for an event where successful entrepreneurs met with Michigan Tech community members looking to launch businesses. Brad was among the presenters. This time, he wasn't just talking about satellites as a research project—he was pitching a company. He had a vision: manufacture low-orbit satellites with cutting-edge technology to revolutionize the satellite industry.

And just like that, the road had changed again.

Traditionally, large satellites were sent 22,000 miles into space, where, in this airless vacuum, they were put into place and they stayed there, orbiting the Earth without change forever. But these geostationary satellites were extremely expensive, costing upwards of $500 million. Brad saw the advent of low orbiting satellites that would sit only 300 miles from Earth and do the bulk of what the larger satellites did at a fraction of the cost, somewhere in the range of $5 million.

Later that night, Brad invited me to have a glass of wine and elaborate on his idea. As we talked, I told him how I had first arrived in Houghton late one chilly night on a bus back in 1967. He leaned forward with a look of disbelief on his face. "My grandfather took care of those buses at night. They turned around at his place." So there was yet another connection. This was getting good.

Brad apologized for the rudimentary nature of his slides, but said they painted a picture of his dream.

"Space is not a complete vacuum at the lower levels I'm talking about," he said. "There's small motion and some energy loss and satellites orbiting at that level need periodic adjustments to stay in their orbit. These small Hall-effect plasma thrusters I'm working on, they're more reliable, accurate, and less costly than anything available. They can help change the whole business of satellites."

What he was telling me made a lot of sense. I had seen the same revolution take place in computers. Mainframes gave way to PCs and even smaller machines. Why not satellites? Brad was thinking the same way. Unlike our conversation three years earlier, now this gentleman professor was ready to bounce from the safe haven of academia into the shark-infested waters of entrepreneurship. I said, "You're not doing this because of some paper that's been published. You're doing this because you believe the revolution is about to happen. Now you have to sell your story, sell your dream."

Entrepreneurs are dream merchants. They sell their dreams. VCs and angel investors are dream buyers. However, Inventus wasn't buying Brad's dream. They were worried about the science. I was undeterred. Not only did I put in my own money, I brought in some TiE angels and helped him raise $1.5 million in seed money. He also received backing from the Michigan Economic Development Corporation. And just like that, Orbion was launched.

Very quickly Brad and his partner in this venture, Dr Jason Sommerville, a PhD from Michigan Tech, became the leader in small satellite propulsion and specialized thrusters.

No one was more pleased or surprised than Brad. When we started talking about the company, he cited numerous reasons it wasn't a good investment. There was not significant research at the time, nothing that proved he was right, most of what he envisioned was still theoretical—and, as I told him, I wasn't going to be the one to figure out if the science worked.

"I'm going to believe it will work just like you claim," I said. "You'll figure it out. I want you to show me what happens if everything works out."

"If everything works out, the world changes," he said. "I deeply believe it's going to happen."

"That's the reason you're doing it," I said. "That's the reason I'm investing. Stop being a scientist. Stop being a professor."

"And be what?"

"Start being a knife-wielding son-of-a-bitch entrepreneur."

The Part That Never Gets Told

The timing was excellent.

In 2019, Orbion secured a pivotal research contract with the US Department of Defense. By 2020, they had raised over $20 million in new funding. *Forbes* highlighted their groundbreaking manufacturing process, which slashed costs by 75 percent and boosted thruster capacity tenfold. Then, in 2021, they landed a contract with the US Air Force to tackle the growing issue of space debris—a problem as urgent as it is overlooked.

The headlines celebrated the big wins. But what they missed was the quieter, more profound impact of Brad's work.

Brad's company wasn't just building thrusters; it was building a community. Orbion created over forty high-paying jobs, many for engineers and PhDs, in Houghton, Michigan—a small college town. These weren't just jobs; they were life-changing opportunities. People moved to Houghton, bought homes, renovated properties, enrolled their kids in schools, and became part of the local ecosystem. They supported restaurants, shops, doctors, and other professionals.

It was the model I had promoted for years when talking about the value of entrepreneurs. This wasn't just growth—it was transformation.

It reminded me of a conversation I had years ago with the president of Michigan Tech. He had invited me to join the school's advisory board. At the first meeting I attended, I asked a simple question: "Who's your customer?"

The president looked puzzled. "We're a university. We don't have customers."

"Everyone has customers," I said. "A customer is someone who defines your success. Who's yours?"

After some thought, he said, "I suppose Ford and GM. They hire our students and fund our programs."

"And what happens if they fail?" I asked.

He chuckled. "That's not likely."

"But if they do?"

"Well, that would be a disaster."

"Your real customers are your students. Your job is to prepare them to succeed—no matter what happens to Ford, GM, or anyone else. Teach them to think, innovate, and, most importantly, to create. Make them entrepreneurs."

He shook his head. "We're not Silicon Valley."

"Why not? You have the internet. You have computers. What's stopping you?"

Thirteen years later, Brad showed up. Six years after that, he was raising millions, winning government contracts, and hiring top talent. He didn't just build a company; he sparked a chain reaction—one that many others have repeated numerous times across the country. Tech jobs spread beyond Silicon Valley. High-income earners moved into a Midwest town. Schools improved. Medical services expanded. Entertainment options grew. And as the town thrived, it attracted even more people and businesses.

This isn't just me singing my own tune. The *Michigan News: University of Michigan* noted that Orbion had lured engineers from across the country with six-figure salaries and given high-paying jobs to local graduates. It also reversed Houghton's population decline. Between 2020 and 2022, the US Census ranked Keweenaw County—where Orbion is located—as "among the highest-growth counties in the nation."

This is the story politicians like Bernie Sanders often miss. They paint entrepreneurs as greedy elites or exploiters of labor. But the reality is far more nuanced—and inspiring. Entrepreneurs pull the whole train along. They create jobs, not just for dozens but for hundreds, thousands, and sometimes millions. Wealth is generated and distributed. Communities are revitalized. Innovation flourishes. Life gets better—more efficient, more convenient, and more meaningful.

And it all starts with one person who dares to dream. Someone who finds a better, cheaper, or entirely new way to solve a problem.

That's the magic of entrepreneurship. As I frequently say in one way or another, it's not just about making money—it's about making a difference.

A Brief History of Work in America

Seventy percent of today's jobs did not exist thirty years ago.

Think about that for a moment. Thirty years ago, telecom and mobile sectors were in their infancy—industries that now dominate the global economy. A 2024 MIT study observed that "the majority of US jobs are in occupations that have emerged since 1940." Change happens fast. If you are not looking ahead, thinking about where you fit into the future economy, you risk being left behind. But this is not new. It has always been this way.

Let's rewind to the Civil War–era. Back then, America was a nation of self-employed individuals. Farmers, blacksmiths, merchants—the majority of people worked for themselves. Very few people worked for someone else (I'm generalizing and not including the millions who were enslaved or signed contracts with their former owners after the war, and so by definition worked for someone else). Mass production was unheard of. Then the Industrial Revolution arrived. New methods of production, made possible by new inventions, changed everything. Factories, assembly lines, and mass manufacturing came into being. Entire industries were born—automobiles, textiles, telephones, typewriters, electric lights. It was an era of new jobs, opportunity, and transformation.

The Industrial Revolution happened before the Civil War, and many people were already working in factories or as employees in shops, farms, etc. And millions of people were enslaved, which by definition means working for someone else.

These things happen at different times, not suddenly. The Industrial Revolution, starting in the late 1700s, was mostly about textiles, while the other things you mention come after the Civil War, but not "suddenly" - typewriters become popular around 15 years later, while cars don't start to catch on for almost 40 years.

With these changes came specialization. People no longer did everything themselves; they became machinists, molders, electricians, engineers. Manufacturing jobs flourished, and the economy grew. By the 1980s, though, things began to shift again. Manufacturing moved overseas—to Japan, Korea, China—where labor was cheaper. Middle-class workers in the US, who had followed their parents and grandparents into factory jobs, found themselves squeezed out.

What happened? Technology happened.

Old jobs were automated. New jobs required specialized skills and education. The pay was better, but the middle class felt the disruption. Work evolved into two extremes: high-paying tech jobs and lower-paying service jobs. By 2022, nearly 80 percent of the US workforce was employed in the service sector. Manufacturing had been outsourced, but something else began to emerge: entrepreneurship.[1]

Today, almost 10 percent of the workforce is self-employed and 47 percent are working for small business owners. In 2023, over five million new businesses were started in the US—a record high. Sixteen percent of the workforce now identify as entrepreneurs. And here's something remarkable: more women own their own businesses than ever before, a testimony to their struggle to overcome numerous legal and societal barriers. Immigrants, too, are driving this trend. Statistically, immigrants are 80 percent more likely to start a business than native-born Americans.[2]

What's happening is a return to an older way of working. Many people are once again working for themselves, by necessity or by choice. But this time, technology and globalization have made entrepreneurship more accessible. You don't need to build a factory to start a business, like Henry Ford did. You can sell shoes without owning a shoe factory.

All you need is an idea. Freelancers can handle design, marketing, and operations. Businesses are virtual, lean, and efficient.

The movie industry illustrates this perfectly. A producer assembles a team—investors, writers, directors, actors. They create a movie, disband, and move on to the next project. This is the gig economy, and it is everywhere: design, healthcare, hospitality, technology. The workplace has changed, requiring education, re-education, and adaptability. The marketplace has also changed, driven by the entrepreneurial spirit that defines not just America, but humanity itself.

Look at our history. We have always adapted, innovated, and found ways to move forward. Human beings are clever and resilient. The catalyst for all this progress? The entrepreneur. Someone with an idea. Someone who dares to say, "Why not me?"

The future belongs to those who embrace this spirit, who see opportunity where others see disruption. The world will continue to change, and faster than ever. The question is: Will you change with it? Or better still: Will you help change it?

Entrepreneurs: A Final Word

Entrepreneurs are the pioneers, the risk-takers, the relentless agents of change. They are the ones who step into the unknown, who explore uncharted territory, and return with something transformative. "Look what I found," they say.

Sometimes it's nothing, a failed experiment or a dead end. But other times, it's the electric light bulb, the Internet, the iPhone, robotic surgery, or artificial intelligence. Entrepreneurs are the ones who see what others don't. They imagine new ways of doing things—better ways. They refuse to settle for the status quo, no matter how comfortable or established it may seem. They push the world forward.

As their ideas take shape and their companies grow, they become the engines of our economy, pulling tens of thousands—sometimes hundreds of thousands—of people along with them. These are the people who create jobs, build wealth, and transform societies.

I remember back in 2016 when I was part of the TiE Silicon Valley delegation in India. We were there to promote startups, and we had a private meeting with then President Pranab Mukherjee. The President admitted that he had been wrong about private enterprise and entrepreneurship. He spoke candidly about the energy and innovation entrepreneurs bring to solving economic problems. "Seventy-five years of socialism," he said, "has condemned India to poverty." He proposed giving special treatment to startups to unleash their potential.

Was this real? Could the government of India actually embrace entrepreneurship? I was skeptical. And, as it turned out, my skepticism was well-founded. What followed was bureaucracy at its finest. The government rolled out plans, but the definition of a "startup" alone was enough to fill a book. The policies were heavy on paperwork, light on action. Startups don't need handouts. They need risk capital—venture capital—and they need it in abundance.

Luckily, capital found its way to India anyway. Not because of the government, but because of the unstoppable force of its people—their ideas, their determination, their refusal to quit. By 2025, India was climbing the ranks of the world's most entrepreneurial countries and stood out as the world's fastest-growing large economy, moving past Japan as the fourth largest economy behind the U.S., China, and Germany. It's on track to rise to third place by 2030.[3]

It's growth isn't a government success story. It's a people success story. People with ideas. People who act. People who change the world.

Entrepreneurship is not something you are assigned; it is something you choose. You opt in, knowing full well the risks, the odds of failure, and you ignore the naysayers who will tell you it can't be done. You ignore those who ask why you can't grow up and settle down. You do it anyway because you have to. Because you look at those who took the same leap—who dared to challenge the norm, who imagined a better way, who needed to take control of their own destiny—and you ask yourself, "Why not me?"

You have to find out if you are going to succeed. Are you right? You put yourself through all sorts of hardship, sometimes lasting years, before you learn the answer. Everyone thinks you're foolish. But you've got to know, will it work?

We all owe a debt of gratitude to these people who try and an even greater appreciation of those who succeed. They improve our lives. They even save them. I know this firsthand.

In March 2019, I went to see my doctor. I had a dull chest pain and felt unusually tired. At seventy-four, I thought I was doing everything right. I exercised regularly, hiked, biked, and ate well. But tests revealed two major blockages in my arteries—75 percent and 90 percent. I needed two stents. Those stents saved my life.

And where did those stents come from? An Argentinian-born surgeon named Dr Julio Palmaz. In 1978, he had an idea for a better way of treating clogged arteries than the very invasive and risky open heart bypass surgeries of that era. He took a piece of metal from his garage floor and began tinkering. It took years for the medical community to catch up. The FDA only approved stents for coronary cases in 1994. But Dr Palmaz's invention—born from an idea, a risk, and relentless effort—saved my life.

Thank you, Dr Palmaz. Thank you, entrepreneurs.

Entrepreneurs are the heartbeat of progress. They see what's possible when others see only obstacles. They take the leap so the rest of us can live better, longer, and richer lives. The world moves forward because of them.

CHAPTER

25

The Bright Light of the Entrepreneurial Spirit

I BECAME A US CITIZEN in 1975 and voted in every election thereafter. Yet, for decades, I remained politically detached—despite my deep fascination with the chessboard of global affairs and my indirect entanglement with politics through TiE.

Entrepreneurship is at the heart of the American ethos. It levels the playing field, fuels job creation, and forms the backbone of a stable society. TiE itself became a force of unity, forging connections and bridging cultures. By blending Indian and American traditions, it shattered ceilings, broke stereotypes, and paved new pathways to success.

Preaching the gospel of wealth creation made me every bit as American as Uncle Sam. I didn't just embrace the dream—I evangelized it, with conviction and authority. No one defines you. You transcend. As an entrepreneur, you plant your flag and declare: *This is my vision. This is my journey.*

In that sense, everything I did was political.

But my first real foray into direct political engagement came in an unexpected setting—a private dinner hosted by former US Defense

Secretary Caspar Weinberger, then publisher of *Forbes* magazine. It was classic San Francisco—power players from politics, academia, and business gathered in an intimate room. Weinberger spoke with certainty about the future of global alliances, setting the stage for a conversation that would shift my perspective forever.

"China is going to be America's most important ally," he declared. "Together, we will relegate Russia's influence to the dustbin of history."

I was a nobody in a room full of somebodies, but something about his pronouncement didn't sit right with me. I raised my hand during the Q&A.

"What if China doesn't become capitalist and pro-America?" I asked. "We're giving them all this technology and access … what if it backfires?"

Weinberger chuckled dismissively. "You don't understand the Chinese. They are capitalists at heart. Communism is dead in China, and it's never coming back."

"But what if it does?" I pressed.

"That's not a risk we need to worry about," he said, moving on.

I left that dinner unconvinced but energized. I realized that the big decisions shaping the world were being made in rooms like that one, by people who were often so certain that they ignored inconvenient questions. I was no foreign policy expert, but I knew that blind confidence was dangerous.

By the early 2000s, I was already active on committees at Stanford and the RAND Corporation, helping India shape policies to grow its economy. I was a critic of India's economic socialism, which had held it back for decades. At the same time, I was a vocal advocate for India's rise to global prominence. My platform was simple: entrepreneurialism. I believed in policies that encouraged innovation and growth.

When the US–India Civil Nuclear Agreement surfaced in the early 2000s, I knew it was a game-changer. Prime Minister Vajpayee initially asked for a nuclear deal that would give India the green light to develop nuclear energy in cooperation with the US while maintaining its nuclear arsenal—a critical step toward elevating India to its rightful status as a global power. The US was receptive, but the new Congress of 2004 had little interest in tackling such an agreement.

Indian Americans knew that was unacceptable. India, despite being one of the world's largest democracies, still wasn't on the UN Security Council, thanks to staunch opposition from China, but this nuclear deal was a chance to change the narrative. It had to pass Congress—both the House and the Senate. A group of us came together and organized and mobilized politically behind the scenes to ensure the deal got the votes it needed. Our efforts were unprecedented.

Political operatives Swadesh Chatterjee, Ramesh Kapur, and several others led the effort. Though I lacked political experience, I jumped in, too. I knew how to take care of business, and once I agreed to get involved, I brought that CEO mindset to the table. We hired several political consultants to map out our strategy. The advice we got was blunt and to the point: "Money talks."

Every senator needed to be approached, and every senator's political machine needed funding. One hundred of us agreed to put up $200,000 each—$20 million in total. Each senator's fund-raising machine, donated legally through their PACs, was to get $200,000. I was assigned to Senators Joe Biden and Harry Reid. I met with both of them several times, and like everyone else in our group, I made the necessary political contributions.

The plan wasn't pretty, but it was effective. Prime Minister Manmohan Singh and President George W. Bush signed the landmark agreement in 2005.

When it came up for a vote in the Senate three years later, it passed 99 to 1. The lone dissenting vote came from Bernie Sanders, who, ironically, had no qualms about accepting the money.

That victory was a turning point. Indian Americans, once politically invisible, realized the power of collective action. The nuclear deal wasn't just about energy policy; it was about changing perceptions. It brought the US and India closer together, and it showed the world that India's rise was inevitable.

Since then, the Indian American community has only grown stronger politically. What began as a small, motivated group has become a political force. Second-generation Indian Americans began winning seats in Congress. By 2024, there were five Indian Americans in the House of Representatives and over forty serving in state legislatures. Kamala Harris broke barriers in 2016 as the first Indian American elected to the Senate. In 2020, she made history again as Vice President, and four years later, she became the first Indian American to run for President of the United States.

The New York Times called Indian Americans a "political powerhouse." From my vantage point, that transformation has been extraordinary. For a community that once stood on the sidelines, political participation has become an article of faith. It has certainly become that for me.

Looking back, I see that the US–India nuclear deal was more than a policy win. It was a wake-up call—a moment when Indian Americans realized they could shape the future, not just observe it.

In Ro's Corner

I got involved with California's Representative Ro Khanna after he lost his first election in 2004.

Bright, ambitious, and full of promise, Ro was born in Philadelphia to immigrant parents. His father, a chemical engineer and IIT graduate, went on to earn his PhD from the University of Michigan. His mother was a schoolteacher. Ro's grandfather, an acolyte of Gandhi, had participated in India's freedom movement and served in Parliament. Ro's credentials were equally impressive. He graduated from the University of Chicago and earned a law degree from Yale. He moved to the Bay Area in his mid-twenties, and by 2004, at just twenty-seven years old, he decided to take on a political giant: Tom Lantos, the Valley's longtime congressman.

It was an ambitious move—too ambitious, in my view. Lantos was no ordinary incumbent. A Holocaust survivor—the only one ever to serve in the US Congress—he was also a revered human rights advocate and environmental leader. Ro lost. And when we met, I gave him some blunt advice.

"You don't just show up and challenge the biggest man in town," I told him. "Go apologize to him. Ask for his advice."

To his credit, Ro listened. He approached Lantos, who graciously took him under his wing. It was a humbling but invaluable lesson. Two years later, Ro ran again—this time against Mike Honda, another sitting congressman. He ran a stronger campaign but still came up short. After two defeats, Ro was disheartened. He began to doubt whether politics was his path.

"If you're learning to ride a horse and you fall, do you say you're never getting back on the horse?" I asked him.

"I don't know if I have what it takes," he admitted.

"You have to run again," I said firmly. "You don't lose until you say you've lost. It's the same way in entrepreneurship. You don't lose until you give up."

Ro needed encouragement, and I gave it to him. I promised my support—financially, publicly, and organizationally. By 2016, Ro was ready to challenge Honda again. This time, Mike was an eight-term incumbent, deeply entrenched in the district. But Ro ran a smart, focused campaign. In November, after a hard-fought race, Ro notched a decisive victory. At forty years old, he entered Congress as the representative of one of the most influential districts in the country—Silicon Valley.

Even after his win, I continued to push him to refine his message. Ro was naturally drawn to issues of wealth distribution, which made him an excellent fit as co-chair of Bernie Sanders' 2020 presidential campaign. He called his economic vision "progressive capitalism," but to many, it sounded like socialism.

Messaging matters. Having the right message matters even more.

"You represent Silicon Valley," I told him. "This is the land of entrepreneurs and venture capitalists. Go meet with the head of Apple. Talk to the head of Facebook. Ask them what they need from you. You're their congressman. Start talking about technology. How can it help America? How can it change lives for the better?"

Ro took that advice to heart. He began developing a message that resonated far beyond Silicon Valley. He asked the right questions: *How can technology bring prosperity to America's heartland? How can innovation create jobs and opportunities across the country?* Ro became a champion of policies that bridged the divide between the tech sector and the rest of America.

He worked with Republicans to pass the CHIPS for America Act, which increased semiconductor production in the US. He highlighted the underrepresentation of Black Americans in tech and called for more investment to address it. He understood the value of entrepreneurs and the role of innovation in driving economic growth. This made him not just popular at home, but also a respected voice in Washington, D.C.

Watching Ro's journey has been deeply rewarding. He started as a young, ambitious idealist and grew into a pragmatic leader who understands the power of technology, innovation, and opportunity. He has developed his own voice, his own message, and his own vision for the country. I'm proud of where he is today, and I'm excited to see where he goes next.

A Seat at the Table

For a long time, I have supported any Indian American who stepped up to run for office. It was my way of encouraging our community to be part of the system.

As more candidates have emerged, I've become more discerning, but my goal remains unchanged: to see Indian Americans represented at the highest levels of power in this country.

This is what it means to normalize our presence in America: to contribute, to lead, and to add value. Indian Americans have already proven themselves as engineers, doctors, professors, and CEOs of global giants like Google and IBM. Those were important steps. But we cannot stop there. We need to be decision-makers. We need to help shape policy. We need to have a seat at the table where the future of this country is decided.

If we want to be part of society—truly part of it—we must do more than excel individually. We must participate collectively. That's how we ensure our voices are heard and our contributions recognized.

A New World Order

We are living through a seismic shift in global power dynamics. At the center of it: the United States, China, and India. This is the new power triangle. And make no mistake—India is no longer a bystander. It's the tiebreaker.

The U.S. and China are locked in a high-stakes ideological and economic competition: democracy vs. authoritarianism, capitalism vs. state control. The outcomes of this battle will define the 21st century. But here's the thing—neither can dominate without India in the mix. India isn't just relevant; it's pivotal. It is a reality that has evolved over hundreds of years.

In the 17th century, India and China were dominant economies.[1] India accounted for about 20% of the world's[2] output in 1800, before Britain took over India. The 18th and 19th centuries belonged to the British; the sun never set over the British Empire. The 20th century belonged to America. Though it tipped the balance in World War I, the US was reluctant to assume its influential role on the global stage.

However, after World War II, the US was an undisputed superpower and not only accepted its position the leader of the free world but flexed its muscle. The extraordinary productivity and innovativeness of its free-market economy produced nearly 50% of the world's output. It was also the reigning nuclear superpower whose military muscle helped define a rule-based world order.

The US was not unchallenged for very long, as the Soviet Union also emerged as a nuclear superpower with an alternate vision where the Communist Party had the monopoly on political power and state-controlled economy with central planning at its heart. It wasn't long after the war that competition between two superpowers developed into a Cold War. In response, the US set up global military alliances: NATO in Europe, CENTO in the Middle East, and SEATO in East Asia to project its power. Of these alliances, only NATO survived as an active military force that provided check on the Soviet power in Europe.

India and China emerged as free countries in 1947 and 1949 respectively. Both were very poor and chose very different models. India becoming a political democracy but adopting the Soviet model of state-controlled planned economy while China modeled itself after Soviet Union. Under these systems, India's and China's economies plodded along, hampered by crushing bureaucracies that did little to encourage the freedom of thought that fuels entrepreneurism and growth.

By the early 1980s, China was being boosted by US as a potential check on Soviet Union and started to adopt free market economic policies. The Soviet Union collapsed under its own dead weight in 1989 and split into nearly a dozen countries. India, teetering on bankruptcy by 1991, dropped its planned economy in favor of a free market economy. The 20th century ended with the US and its allies in Europe and Japan controlling roughly 70 percent of the world's economy.

But the 21st century is shaping up to be very different from the past. Assisted by the US, China's economy has grown with stunning speed. India's economy also has grown at a fast pace, yet it still pales compared to China. Europe and Japan, though still large, have stagnated somewhat. What has happened? Under the guidance of Den Xiaoping, China played the long game very well, hiding its strength while talking about a peaceful rise that lulled US into believing that China would be a friendly collaborator rather than a competitor.

All that changed in 2012 with Xi Jinping coming to power. He ripped up the script. He reasserted the Communist Party's control over Chinese politics and the economy. He dropped all pretense of being a peaceful collaborator. Aggression in the East China Sea. Militarization of the South China Sea. Treaty violations in Hong Kong. A deadly skirmish with India at the border.

China overplayed its hand. And the world noticed—especially India and the U.S. That confrontation pushed the US and India closer together. The two countries began syncing on tech—particularly critical tech—while working to block access to hostile regimes: China, Russia, Iran, North Korea, Pakistan. This is strategic containment, 21st-century style.

Did China have to go this route? They were ten years away from overtaking the U.S. peacefully. Instead, they chose provocation. And now? The mask is off. The Cold War is back—with different players, different rules, and different stakes.

But here's the key difference: India isn't the non-aligned voice it once was. It has shed its illusions about China. And the U.S. is wide awake. We may not see open war, but China will not be a friend. And India will never be an enemy. If we shift our manufacturing and supply chains to India instead of China, we kill two birds: we secure our own interests and elevate a fellow democracy.

This isn't just geopolitics. It's philosophy. Two systems are colliding: pluralistic democracy vs centralized authoritarianism. The 20th century was America's. The 21st will belong to Asia. The only question is: *Which Asia?* Will it be free, innovative, entrepreneurial—and messy? Or will it be orderly, repressive, and closed?

By 2030, though, the US, China, and India will be the three largest economies in the world. China's population of 1.4 billion will overshadow US and its allies, who collectively have about 800 million people. India will be the balancer. With a population to match China's, it can be the bulwark against Chinese power in Asia. It's up to the US to help it continue to modernize.

Many other factors are in play – from aging populations in China and Europe to the crisis of government and identity gripping the US. But one thing is certain: the world is going a full circle with India and China re-emerging as top two economies by the end of the 21st century, and it presents a choice. If Chinese values win and democratic ones fail, then America loses its moral argument. Its example collapses. But if India and the U.S. stand together—imperfect but free—we can still offer a model worth following.

This is the real fight. The outcome will define the future of the world. India and the US are natural allies in this fight. Together, they represent a beacon of hope for a world that still believes, still *should* believe, in the power of democracy.

Democracy and Free Market Capitalism

If you believe in entrepreneurship, you must root for democracy.

Free market capitalism and democracy are a matched pair. They are both about choices. In democracy, you vote between idea A and idea B, person A and person B. In free markets, you vote with your wallet, choosing between product A and product B. Politicians and voters, sellers and buyers—it's all about the freedom to create and the freedom to choose.

The cornerstone of both systems is freedom. Democracy sets the rules of the road, and entrepreneurs take to the freeway—each one a unique vehicle, heading toward its own destination. All makes, colors, and sizes are welcome. Entrepreneurs in free markets are the engines driving us forward, bringing fundamental change in their wake.

Look at Elon Musk and Starlink. He didn't just create a product; he equalized the world by making high-speed internet available everywhere, bypassing the need for fiber. That's the power of entrepreneurship—it transforms what we think is possible.

Entrepreneurs can play roles both good and bad. In my experience, most are driven by idealism. They see a better way of doing things, a different way of solving problems. The world is ripe for change, and entrepreneurs are the ones who recognize the opportunity before anyone else does.

I remember sitting in the audience at Comdex in 1990, listening to Bill Gates deliver the keynote. He spoke about a future where all information would be at our fingertips. It was visionary—something only a true entrepreneur could see so clearly, and he saw it and shared it with us. It was exciting. That kind of forward-thinking perspective has always resonated with me.

It's what I look for in others, too. I recall Brad King of Orbion pitching me his idea for small satellites. He wanted to explain the technology in detail, but I stopped him. I said, "If you're right about these satellites, tell me what happens to the world if this idea works."

Brad was surprised. As a scientist, he was used to talking about how things worked. But I wasn't interested in the mechanics. I wanted to know the meaning. What would it change? How would it impact the world? That's always been my approach—as a mentor, an investor, and, most importantly, as an entrepreneur. The question isn't just *how* to do something. It's *why* it matters.

This way of thinking is only possible in a democracy. Only in a system that values freedom can you ask such questions. Only in a democracy can you dream of changing the world—and then have the opportunity to do it.

Entrepreneurship and democracy aren't just linked; they are inseparable. Together, they create the conditions for progress, innovation, and the betterment of society.

A New Chapter

I called my daughter with a proposal in 2021. I should have thought of it sooner, but I'm not one for apologies. I prefer getting to the point.

"Do you have any plans for what you want to do besides being a mom?"

It was the kind of question that would catch most people off guard, but not Raj-Ann. She was married, mom to a five-month-old daughter, and feeling claustrophobic in her Northern Virginia home while the country was slowly emerging from the scare of Covid-19. She had spent decades in the nonprofit world. I sensed the part of her that was like me, was looking for a new challenge.

"What's on your mind?" she asked.

"I have this idea," I said.

I explained that I was frustrated by all the paperwork and red tape of investing through Inventus. I had decided that rather than step down, I would manage my existing portfolio there but decline to take on any new business so I could return to angel investing and move faster. Fewer formalities, more action. I had already asked two friends and former mentees, Raju Reddy and B.V. Jagadeesh, to join forces with me in this new venture. Raju was the founder and former CEO of the global services company Sierra Atlantic, and B.V. had been CEO at NetScaler and was a co-founder of Exodus. Both were top level investors. I invited Raj-Ann to run operations as the fourth partner.

"Remember what I did with Orbion?" I asked. "I brought all these people together to help fund their seed deal. I want to do that same thing but multiply it. We'll have a syndicate of investors we can call on."

Raj-Ann was intrigued enough to immediately say yes. She voiced her concerns about not having any experience. "This will be good for you," I told her. She would absorb invaluable lessons just by being around Raju, B.V., and me. She thought like me. She would pick it up fast. I had taught her how to ride a bike. I had quizzed her on multiplication tables after dinner every night as a kid.

"This will be more of the same," I said, laughing. "And selfishly, you and Pavan and Rumi can move closer to me and your mom."

Two weeks later, Raj-Ann was in. We formally launched Silicon Valley Quad, or SV Quad, soon after. Our focus: software startups. We estimated that we could do eight deals a year for four years—or about thirty-two deals—without having to raise money. We expected a quarter of them to work. If we hit big on eight, we would make 10x returns. Will it work? Time will tell. So far, our 2021 investments have doubled our money. One failed, seven are still progressing really well.

Every day brings a new challenge, a new chance to learn. That's the thrill of angel investing. I also get to build something with my daughter and two former mentees—now equals. The baton is being passed, the lasting, impactful message of wealth creation is being spread. At seventy-five years old, I learned that growing older is not the enemy. The real danger is growing stale.

A Lesson in Life

A few years later, at nearly seventy-eight years old, I found myself standing before a crowd of several thousand at the TiE Global Summit in Hyderabad, India. Entrepreneurs, investors, and industry leaders from across the globe had gathered, drawn by the pulse of a country on the rise. Every visit to India—home, as I still called it—was an experience unlike any other. The energy, the people, the sheer momentum of progress were palpable.

From the podium, I spoke of that very energy, the driving force behind India's rapid ascent. The economy was expanding at a remarkable 7 percent per year. The average Indian had become twenty times wealthier than their grandfather. In 2022, India had surpassed the British economy—a poetic milestone, I pointed out—but what excited and amazed me in the best way, given what I had witnessed in my lifetime, was the possibility that by 2100, nearly 300 years after British rule began, India could take over as the world's largest economy.

"My dream is to see ten million entrepreneurs in India when it celebrates 100 years of freedom in 2047. I'll only be 102."

The accolades that seem to follow me at this stage of life are nice, but I still have the fire of a groundbreaker. Following the summit, I joined Raju Reddy on a trip outside the city to Nizamabad in rural Telangana, where his ambitious initiative, the Kakatiya Sandbox, was taking shape. It was a bold experiment—bringing together experts, scientists, and innovators to tackle social challenges through entrepreneurship. Education, energy, agriculture, sustainability, health—every pressing issue was being addressed with an entrepreneurial spirit.

The principle was the same as TiE: equip people with knowledge, empower them to build, and let them transform their own communities. In the Sandbox, villagers received a free education in technology and entrepreneurship, along with room and board—much like a college. They then returned to their villages, armed with the skills to implement real-world solutions: harvesting rainwater, bringing internet access, modernizing agriculture. It was a living lab, an incubator for change.

Before I even saw it in action, I was in. I pledged money toward a building that will be called the Kanwal Rekhi Rural Entrepreneurship and Startup Center. I saw the possibilities, and as always, I was willing to bet on people—in this case, the people of India. If agrarian India could leap into the digital world, the whole country could move into the future together.

I had spent much of my life helping others create wealth, but there was something deeply humbling about sharing one's good fortune. It was a tenet of my religion, part of who I am, not just what I believe but also what gives me faith, which is the idea of serving other people. Serving others is a great equalizer, a reminder that in the end, we are all human. Wealth fades, accolades are forgotten, but people will always remember how you made them feel.

In 2024, Ann was diagnosed with a fast-spreading cancer. After a year-long fight, her disease was declared terminal and she entered hospice. I sat with her every day, physically and spiritually, until we brought her home, where she passed away peacefully, surrounded by immediate family, on March 11, 2025. "She was a fiercely devoted mom, who nudged me in all the right ways towards being the best person I could be," our daughter, Raj-Ann, wrote in tribute. "The stoicism and bravery I saw in her this last year as she battled cancer was beyond amazing."

Our son, Ben, added, "It was challenging to witness her internal struggles over the years, but her compassion, resilience, and commitment to overcoming adversities was truly inspiring." We were married for fifty-four of the fifty-eight years we knew each other, and she was the love of my life and the bedrock on which my life and success has been built. Her fighting spirit was integral to my own.

In her final days, I sat with her, overwhelmed by the many ways she had made me feel during our life together while also knowing that when she was finally gone and no longer suffering, I would forever feel loved, grateful, and lucky. She was, without a doubt, my Lady Luck.

Surf Theory

I am a hardcore engineer by training. I am an entrepreneur by nature. And I had ideas.

Ideas have a way of nudging you, pushing you out of your comfort zone. I had ideas I believed in, so I left the security of a job to chase them. It was a risk, no doubt. But I was willing to trade comfort for independence—to become the master of my own destiny. I started my own company, and in the process, I changed not just my life, but a few things around me, too.

My story began with humble roots in India. When you come from nothing, risk feels easier. What do you have to lose? At every stage, I believed I could do better. Getting into IIT was one milestone. Coming to America was another. Leaving a job to start my own company was yet another. It's clear now that I was an entrepreneur at heart. I didn't choose it—it chose me.

Entrepreneurship has been more than a profession for me; it's been a way of life. Mentoring young entrepreneurs was a natural extension of that. I never set out to be an investor but investing became part of the process. You can't just talk the talk—you have to put your money where your mouth is.

Being part of this cycle—risks, challenges, hopes, and dreams—has given my life purpose. I used to think of TiE as a new kind of religion. Our meetings were like revival gatherings. We preached the gospel of entrepreneurship: creating wealth, jobs, and opportunities. What could be more noble? When you build a successful enterprise that creates thousands of jobs, it feels like a sacred act. You are doing good for society.

Entrepreneurship makes me deeply optimistic about the future. I've seen its transformative power in my lifetime. When I was young, Indians were starving. By 1966, the country was on the brink. Today, India thrives. China has lifted 800 million people out of poverty. Their children will be better off than they were. Why would they risk such prosperity for war? Wars are often fought over scarcity—over survival. Entrepreneurs are creating abundance, and with it, the reasons for conflict diminish.

I see a profound shift in today's younger generations. Over 50 percent of Gen Z and millennials want to work for themselves.[3]

There's an idealism in this—a desire to control their destiny while contributing to the world. I see this same spirit taking root in India.

India is no longer the poverty-stricken, stuck-in-the-past nation of old stereotypes. In August 2023, its successful moon landing announced to the world that India had arrived. It is a fast-rising, technologically driven, entrepreneurial powerhouse. Over 100,000 startups exist today in India. My hope? A million by 2030 and ten million by 2047, when India celebrates 100 years of Independence.

TiE, too, has a role to play. We've expanded into Indonesia, but we must go further—to Malaysia, Sri Lanka, Bangladesh, and the African continent. Nairobi launched in 2019. Lagos, Kampala, and Johannesburg are next. TiE is a force of change through entrepreneurship. It taps into an even deeper force: people helping people. Creating jobs, building wealth, and giving purpose. That is how humanity moves forward.

These days people are concerned, even fearful that AI—artificial intelligence—will put too many people out of jobs and threaten the well-being of humanity as we know it. AI will do everything and may even take over. My take? This fear has accompanied almost every technological advance. The steam engine was going to power everything. Television was going to destroy the movies. Computers were going to replace everyone. But cars, telephones, computers—all of them made us more productive.

Work has changed. The majority of people used to be involved in manufacturing and agriculture. The economy was driven by subsistence. Now less than 2 percent of people produce food. Technology enabled fewer people to be more productive in the fields and factories. As labor is freed up, people do other things—things that weren't being done before. They invent cell phone, GPS, better pharmaceuticals, electric cars, satellites, and countless uses for the internet, from blood pressure monitors to streaming music to online banking. Quality of life things, as I call them.

I suspect the same will happen with AI. I don't think we should fear AI as much as we should what humans might do or not do with it. It's up to us. Somebody has to design the robots. Somebody has to train them. And there will be some people with the time and energy who will ask, "What else can I do? What else can be done better?" This is what entrepreneurs have always done and will continue to do.

When I reflect on my life, this is what I am most proud of—being part of this noble effort.

Are you part of this story? Do you see yourself in these pages? If you're still reading, you probably are. If not, that's okay. Entrepreneurship isn't for everyone. It's not something someone can tell you to pursue. You either feel it or you don't. And once you do, you have no choice but to see if you're right. It's like finding religion. Faith can't be seen—you live it.

Years ago, I developed my "surf theory" of entrepreneurship. Entrepreneurs are like surfers. You go to the beach, paddle out, and test the waters. It takes energy just to get started. Sometimes, the surf is flat, and you wait. Other times, the waves come crashing in. You read the water, prepare, and when the right wave builds, you paddle hard.

You feel the energy rise beneath you, lifting you to the peak. Then, you take off. Surfing a wave is hard work. It takes skill. It takes luck. You control what you can and hope for a break with what you can't.

And here's the thing: whether you ride the wave of your life or wipe out, you end up in the same place—back on the beach. You catch your breath, clear your eyes, and paddle back out.

That's entrepreneurship. It's also life. It's about riding the waves. It's about enjoying the journey, wave after wave, no matter the outcome.

Acknowledgments

A LONG CAREER AND LONGER life make it impossible to acknowledge everyone who deserves to be thanked for their friendship, advice, and support, but I will do my best.

The first person to ever believe me was my mother. Though she was barely literate, she was extremely intelligent, and by entrusting me with responsibilities at such a young age, she taught me self-reliance that lasted me a lifetime.

My father also motivated me in an entirely different way. His disregard of me fueled a lifetime of wanting to prove him wrong. I only wish he had been able to see the heights of success I had reached because of it.

I have to thank my son Ben for relentlessly pushing me to write this book, and for wrangling all the elements and people needed to pull it off. It would not have happened without him.

I'd also like to thank my daughter Raj-Ann for being as sharp as they come and for continuing to challenge me on my journey. Her feedback on every draft of this book has been invaluable.

My brother-in-law Mark has been my best friend for over fifty years. Our spirited debates and long hikes and bike rides not only shaped my worldview but also helped improve my health. My brother Upi and his wife Pinky have been a huge support in my life, through thick and thin. I'm also grateful for my other siblings, Bobby, Toni, Ruby, Paul, and Binu, and the fantastic children they have raised, my fourteen nieces and nephews, who have made me proud. A special shout out to my nephew Manu, who is one of the most energetic and hard working people I know.

I want to express gratitude to the team of people responsible for helping me produce this book at HarperCollins India: Sachin Sharma for his belief in me from the beginning; my agent in India, Kanishka Gupta, for recognizing this work and the audience it might find, and our US agent, Dan Strone. I also thank the Radius Books team, Scott Waxman and Dan Ambrosio, for their persistence in bringing this into the world, and to my wonderful editor Chris Murray.

The biggest gratitude goes to my collaborator Todd Gold, who not only helped to shape my story into something relatable, but worked diligently to ensure that my voice, perspective, and my humor (I hope), come across! I will be forever grateful he brought his talents to this journey.

In this book, I make the point of saying that one person can make a difference, which I firmly believe. So many individuals have made a difference in my life—from my current colleagues at Inventus like Raju Reddy, BV Jagadeesh, Manu, and John Dougery, Jr to the ones who built TiE together: Suhas Patil, AJ Patel, Roy Prasad and the late and great CK Prahalad. In India I have to thank my friends and collaborators Saurabh Srivastava and Harish Mehta for opening my eyes to India's tech revolution. I'd also like to thank Anne Krueger of SIEPR, who and I collaborated to do an Indian economy program in the early part of this century; Rafiq Dossani at Rand Corporation, where I served as an Advisory Board Member on CAPP and learnt a lot about the evolving geopolitics of the Asia-Pacific region. Also, Rafiq and I collaborated on the telecom policy reform in India. And of course those who helped me in the beginning, at Excelan, where everything changed for me: Duane Murray, Vish Mishra, Tim Harris, Naveen Jain, and Jim Tolonen. Especially thanks to John Bosch, with the VC firm of Bay Partners, who took the risk on Indian entrepreneurs like me in the SIlicon Valley. I also cherish the friendship and mentoring of John Dougery, Sr, and late Ed Shea that started during my Excelan days and has continued ever since. Meena Ahamed wrote about me in her book, and then set us on our journey with this one. My lifelong friends Bhopi Dhall and late Umesh Malhotra, my IIT Bombay classmates. Three of us travelled together to the US and shared a place during our Michigan Tech days. I'm grateful for Barbara Blackburn, my trainer, who has pushed me beyond my physical limits and quite literally added years to my life.

And finally, the deepest gratitude goes to my wife, Ann. They say sometimes it takes someone else to believe in you, for you to believe in yourself. Her saying "yes" to me made me the man I am today. She gave me the confidence to pursue and achieve my dreams. And though she is gone now, I will carry her with me forever. None of this would have been possible without her.

Notes

Scan this QR code to access the notes.

About the Author

Kanwal Rekhi was the first Indo-American founder and CEO to take a venture-backed company public on the NASDAQ. He has founded and built The IndUS Entrepreneurs (TiE) into the largest global network of Indian entrepreneurs, and co-founded Inventus Capital Partners, where he applies his time, energy, and attention for building the venture franchise into a catalyst for India's tech revolution. He came to the United States from India for graduate studies, advanced through the engineering ranks in a number of technology companies and then co-founded Excelan in Silicon Valley to commercialize Ethernet and TCP/IP—standards that became the basis of the internet as we know it today.

HarperCollins *Publishers* India

At HarperCollins India, we believe in telling the best stories and finding the widest readership for our books in every format possible. We started publishing in 1992; a great deal has changed since then, but what has remained constant is the passion with which our authors write their books, the love with which readers receive them, and the sheer joy and excitement that we as publishers feel in being a part of the publishing process.

Over the years, we've had the pleasure of publishing some of the finest writing from the subcontinent and around the world, including several award-winning titles and some of the biggest bestsellers in India's publishing history. But nothing has meant more to us than the fact that millions of people have read the books we published, and that somewhere, a book of ours might have made a difference.

As we look to the future, we go back to that one word—a word which has been a driving force for us all these years.

Read.

Harper Collins · 4th · HARPER FICTION · HARPER NON-FICTION · HARPER BUSINESS · HCCB HARPERCOLLINS CHILDREN'S BOOKS

HARPER DESIGN · Harper Sport · HARPER PERENNIAL · HARPER VANTAGE · हार्पर हिन्दी · BOOKTOPUS